Praise for *She Got Up Off the Couch*

". . . here it is, that excellent and strange something: [Kimmel's] winning stories, filled with perfect sentences and lovely words. And Zippy, that kind, generous soul, saw fit to share the treasure with us."

—Hannah Sampson, *The Miami Herald*

"If you took the complete works of E. B. White and put them in a blender with the essays of David Sedaris, you might end up with a delicious concoction close to the hilarious, irrepressible charm that is Haven Kimmel."

—Alison Smith, author of *Name All the Animals*

"Kimmel and her prose are as lovable as ever, her humor laugh-out-loud sharp, piercing the heart when you least expect it."

—Helene Stapinski, author of *Five-Finger Discount: A Crooked Family History*

"Haven Kimmel's memoir is not only great fun, it's full of real pathos and grace. Can I have this family?"

—Sean Wilsey, bestselling author of *Oh the Glory of It All*

"Haven Kimmel draws readers in with her easygoing manner and her ability to entertain, but surprises with a bittersweet paean to childhood naïveté."

—*Publishers Weekly*

"It is a tribute to Kimmel's light touch that this [story] remains consistently fresh and frequently hilarious."

—Erin McGraw, *The News & Observer* (Raleigh, N.C.)

"Kimmel has caught time in a bottle beautifully in this poignant memoir, and her engagingly conversational style, full of italics and upper-cased exclamations and rambling sentences, makes this a story you hear as much as read."

—Carole Goldberg, *The Hartford Courant*

"Kimmel accomplishes an unlikely and cunning balancing act: She reconstructs a fundamentally happy childhood, without papering over the sad spots."

—Margaret Quamme, *The Columbus Dispatch*

"The book speaks to each of us who regrettably abandons childhood in a flurry of situations beyond our control. . . . Kimmel is a master at re-creating events and people who are so real and identifiable that we find ourselves in the midst of their turmoil. . . . The book is well-written, well-planned and filled with the bittersweet events we so aptly call life."

—Maureen Mustard, *The Star Press* (Muncie, Ind.)

"Who would have imagined being entranced by a memoir about growing up in Indiana?"

—Robin Vidimos, *The Denver Post*

Praise for *A Girl Named Zippy*

"Almost dreamlike in some of [her] elusive storytelling, [Kimmel] pulls off a feat that's harder than it looks: write for adults from a child's perspective. . . . Zippy's parents must have done something right to produce a girl who could write such a simple, lovely book."

—*USA Today*

"While reading *A Girl Named Zippy,* I started to dog-ear each page that contained a charming anecdote, a garden-fresh metaphor . . . my copy soon came to resemble a cone. . . . I've told every friend I own to get a copy, and I find myself suddenly frantic to make new friends. *A Girl Named Zippy* seems to be about the cleverest . . . memoir ever. [Kimmel is] a born storyteller. . . . I imagine everyone in the world would be grateful for Kimmel's book."

—*The Orlando Sentinel*

"Very engaging, funny . . . [I]t could be a cheerier version of the Leechfield, Texas, Mary Karr chronicled in *The Liar's Club,* if drunks never got ugly and if fathers never took a belt to their kids."

—*The Hartford Courant*

"Delightfully wry (and sometimes laugh-out-loud funny)."

—*The Indianapolis Star*

"It's a cliché to say that a good memoir reads like a well-crafted work of fiction, but Kimmel's smooth, impeccably humorous prose evokes her childhood as vividly as any novel. . . . Dreamy and comforting, spiced with flashes of wit."

—*Publishers Weekly*

"Filled with good humor, fine storytelling, and acute observations of small-town life."

—*Library Journal*

"Nicknamed for her tendency to bolt around the house, Zippy is a spunky little girl trying to puzzle through the adult world . . . in this gentle memoir."

—*People*

"Fresh, funny, delightful, and very amusing."

—*Kirkus Reviews*

"Phenomenal. This is just perfectly written and right on target and she doesn't miss a beat."

—Kaye Gibbons, author of *Ellen Foster* and *A Virtuous Woman*

"A rarity: an original book, the freshest, most compelling child's voice since *Ellen Foster.*"

—Lee Smith, author of *Oral History* and *Family Linen*

"Sly, evocative, gentle, wry, and dead-on funny. Haven Kimmel is perfect on the details and spins graceful stories that sink in and stay with you for a good long time . . . a masterful piece of writing."

—Martin Clark, author of *The Many Aspects of Mobile Home Living*

Also by Haven Kimmel

A Girl Named Zippy

The Solace of Leaving Early

Orville: A Dog Story

Something Rising (Light and Swift)

She Got Up Off the Couch

And Other Heroic Acts from Mooreland, Indiana

❦

HAVEN KIMMEL

FREE PRESS
NEW YORK LONDON TORONTO SYDNEY

*f*P
FREE PRESS
A Division of Simon & Schuster, Inc.
1230 Avenue of the Americas
New York, NY 10020

First Free Press trade paperback edition 2007

For information about special discounts for bulk purchases,
please contact Simon & Schuster Special Sales:
1-800-456-6798 or business@simonandschuster.com.

Designed by Karolina Harris

Manufactured in the United States of America

1 3 5 7 9 10 8 6 4 2

The Library of Congress has cataloged the hardcover edition as follows:
Kimmel, Haven.
She got up off the couch : and other heroic acts from Mooreland, Indiana. / Haven Kimmel.
p. cm.
1. Kimmel, Haven—Family. 2. Kimmel, Haven—Childhood and youth.
3. Authors, American—Homes and haunts—Indiana—Mooreland.
4. Authors, American—21st century—Family relationships.
5. Authors, American—21st century—Biography. 6. Mothers and daughters—Indiana. 7. Mooreland (Ind.)—Social life and customs.
PS3611.I46 Z474 2006
813'.6—dc22 2005051964

ISBN-13: 978-0-7432-8499-8
ISBN-10: 0-7432-8499-2
ISBN-13: 978-0-7432-8500-1 (Pbk)
ISBN-10: 0-7432-8500-X (Pbk)

The author gratefully acknowledges permission to quote from The Skin of Our Teeth, *by Thornton Wilder. Copyright © 1942 The Wilder Family LLC. Reprinted with permission from Tappan Wilder and The Wilder Family LLC.*

I greatly admire the two-word
DEDICATION PAGE.
I am even moved and puzzled by those books which bear no
Dedication or Acknowledgments page at all,
As if the book were composed on a rocky knoll
By the Muse alone.
MAYBE NEXT TIME.

This book is dedicated, first and foremost, to my incomparable
mother, Delonda Hartmann.

It is also for my brother and sister, Dan Jarvis and Melinda Mullens,
And in memory of my father, Bob Jarvis, and grandmother Mom Mary.
It is for Elaine, Rick, Jenny and Jessica, Josh and Abby,
And Wayne, who got The Girl after all.

It is for Beth Dalton, brave and true friend of thirty-six years,
Whose heart has never closed to me, and who allows me
To stand and consider with her
The Molly-shaped hole in the world.

It is the only way I will ever know how to thank
Julie Newman.

It is for my beloved Amy Scheibe.

It is for Christopher Schelling, who read it on the subway
And in the dead of night and while he had a fever.
Stars are being hammered onto his crown right this second.

It is dedicated to the people of Mooreland, Indiana,

With my abiding gratitude for their support and fine sympathies.
For my mistakes, misjudgments, and glib unkindnesses,
I hope to someday be forgiven.

It is for Ben.

It is for my children, Kat and Obadiah, who are even now writing the story of their own Time and Place.

And this book is John's,
As they all have been and all will be.

Contents

Preface

A few years ago I wrote some essays about the town in which I grew up. Mooreland, Indiana, was paradise for a child—my old friend Rose and I have often said so—small, flat, entirely knowable. When I say it was small I mean the population was three hundred people. I cannot stress this enough. People approach me to say they, too, grew up in small towns and when I ask the size they say, "Oh, six thousand or so." A town of six thousand people is a wild metropolis. Once a woman told me that she'd grown up in a small town of *fifteen thousand,* and I was forced to turn my head away from her crazy geographic assessment. These people do not know small. Of course there was the elderly woman who told me she was reared in a hamlet with a population of twenty-six. I offered to be her servant for the rest of her life but she was too polite to accept.

Because the town was so knowable and the times they were

a-changin' (it was the sixties and the seventies), Mooreland was blessed with a cast of characters my family and I found interesting and so we talked about them a lot over the years. There were my parents themselves, of course, and my brother and sister, my most-loved grandmother, Mom Mary, and my aunt Donita. There was the woman who lived across the street from us, Edythe, who daily threatened to kill my cats and who, in fact, was not averse to snuffing out my own life, to hear my sister tell it. There were my best friends, Rose and red-haired Julie, and their parents, who, without a sigh or a complaint where I could hear it, kept me relatively clean and well fed. There were my next-door neighbors, the kind and lovely Hickses, and all the people of the Mooreland Friends Church. But for character nothing rivaled the town itself, the three parallel streets bordered at the north end by a cemetery and at the south by a funeral home. It was the dearest postage stamp of native soil a person could wish for.

I started writing the essays as a way to amuse my mom and sister. I'd write something, call, and read it to them. I had no ambitions for the essays and one need only read the above paragraphs to understand why. Indiana is not the state our national eye turns toward for fascinating narratives, strangely enough. Mooreland is definitely not a mecca for the literary arts, although it is rich with crafts. And *no one* cares about the reminiscences of one more child with one more set of parents and neighbors and friends. I myself have been known to wince as if stabbed with wide-bore needles when faced with yet another coming-of-age memoir.

So I wrote my essays with nothing much in mind and eventually there were so many essays about nothing they made a book and then I don't know what happened. I turned around one day and the book was taken on by a publisher and then it had a cover—and I am talking about the most unfortunate cover imaginable: me as a six-month-old baby, wearing a dress my mother made. I was a tragic little monkey child: bald, with the kind of ears that look fine on woodland creatures but in human culture tend to be corrected surgically. I was holding Mom's watch, which was dripping with drool, as I was teething. I'm sorry, I need to say this all again. *On the cover of the book was my cross-eyed monkey baby picture, holding a drool-drenched watch.* I nearly fainted the first time I saw it. I called my editor and asked if she was serious and she said yes. Thus did *A Girl Named Zippy* skitter out into the world, and thus was my self-respect laid to rest.

I didn't expect much from that little book. I was and remain surprised that some people bought it and liked it. But even though it was kindly received in some quarters, I swore I'd never write a sequel. I don't like sequels, by and large, although sometimes they are welcome. The most important reason to forgo a follow-up was that I'd already sent strangers uninvited into the town and the lives of people I love and respect and I could not imagine doing so again.

A strange thing happened, though, on the many book tours that supported the publication of *Zippy* and of my two novels. In every city I was asked what became of the people I'd drawn—according to my own lights and in keeping with my memory of them—where they were now and if they were happy. That was to be expected. But I was also *always* asked this: "What about your mom? Did she ever get up off the couch?" The first time I heard the question a little bell rang on a faraway hill, and I knew if I ever did (and I wouldn't) write a follow-up (which I absolutely *would not do*), that would be the subject and that would be the title.

Of course I gave in to the six or seven people clamoring for a sequel. In the beginning I didn't intend to write anything but a continuing portrait of my family, in particular of my mother. Toward the end of *Zippy* my father and I watched Mom pedal away on my new bicycle, riding toward points unknown; we knew something was afoot but we didn't know what. *She Got Up Off the Couch* begins at that point—it seemed an appropriate jumping-off place for a book about an individual woman in a very particular place. But when Rose read the final draft she pointed out that Mother's evolution, personal as it was, is also the story of a generation of women who stood up and rocked the foundations of life in America. They didn't know they were doing so—they were trying to save their own lives, I think—but in the process they took it on the chin for everyone who followed. I know my own mother did.

I will never do anything half so grand or important. I couldn't tell this story any way except through my own eyes, but that doesn't make me the star of the show. As *Zippy* was a bow to Mooreland, Indiana, this is a love letter, humbly conceived and even more modestly written, to my father, my brother, the sister who is my very breath of life, and most of all to the woman who stood up, brushed away the pork rind crumbs, and escaped by the skin of her teeth. It is a letter to all such women, wherever they may be.

She Got Up Off the Couch

Mr. Antrobus:

Well, how's the whole crooked family?

—Thornton Wilder,
The Skin of Our Teeth, Act I

The Test

The couch in the den was the color the crayon people called Flesh even though it resembled no human or animal flesh on Planet Earth, and the couch fabric was nubbled in a pattern of diamonds. It was best to prevent the nubbles from coming into direct contact with one's real Flesh, so there was usually a blanket or a towel or clothing spread out as a buffer. Also no one wanted to pick up the blanket, the towel, and the clothing and fold them. Or even pick them up. So it was a fine arrangement.

She had a lamp, a small end table so covered with things—layer upon layer—that the stuff at the bottom was from a different decade than the stuff in the middle. She had a cardboard box in which she kept books from the bookmobile; her favorite afghan for emergency napping; a notebook and pen. There had been years with no telephone but mostly the telephone worked and was often near Mother's head—often enough, in fact, that Dad referred to it as her Siamese twin. The television was only a few feet away, and there were always animals for company. Five steps in one direction was the kitchen; four steps in the other was the bathroom. In winter the den was the only room in the house with heat, so we all lived there. In summer it was so hot I feared spontaneous combustion, which Dr. Demento reported was happening to Canadian priests with regularity. I popped in and out of the den, I was a very busy person and my responsibilities were numerous which Mother understood. Dad came and went—he also had engagements far and wide and we had long since ceased asking what they were. A man had to protect his mysteries; it was one of the primary Liberties of Manhood in our home. There were many others. My older brother, Dan, was gone to his grown-up life; my sister, Melinda, was on her way, at seventeen.

All my life there had been certain constants, facts so steady I assumed they were like trees or mountains, things you could trust to stay where you left them because they were *mountains* and yes the Bible says faith can move one but the Bible also says a whole lot of stuff that if you tried to make it true you'd end up in the Epileptic Village. My constants were the same as everyone else's: a house with quite a few rooms and utilities that came and went. Church three times a week. Church so frequently and which I so much couldn't get out of I considered ripping off my own fingernails in protest, or better yet someone else's fingernails. My family. And no one as dependable as my mom, burrowed into the corner of that sprung sofa cushion, reading and eating crunchy foods, the television on, the telephone ringing. We'd never said a whole lot to each other, given that I was a citizen of the world and was generally on my way out the door. But she always smiled when I passed her, gave me a wave. And when I got home, there she was.

Something had been on the rise with Mom for a few months. There were many tearful meetings of her prayer cell, and at least half a dozen thrown-down fleeces (bargains made with God) and phone calls and arrangements. One of her fleeces involved a television commercial of Abraham Lincoln in a classroom. He was standing at a podium saying if I was thinking of going back to college, did I know that I could test out of some required courses by signing up for the CLEP Test, which stood for College-Level Examination Program. This was all news to me. I heard Mom talk to her women at church about that commercial, and an agreement was reached: if she saw it on the following Friday, anytime before 6:00 P.M., she would call the number on the screen.

On that Friday, although I didn't know why we were waiting for it or what it would mean if she called, I spent the whole afternoon nervously watching TV with Mom. Dad was gone, so it was just the two of us. Three o'clock came and went, and then four, and five, and Mom sank deeper and deeper into a heavy silence punctuated with heartbroken little sighs, because a fleece thrown down is an unbreakable contract. At 5:55 she got up and went into the kitchen and stood holding on to the sink, as if she might throw up. At 5:57, she bowed her head. At 5:58 she looked up; I thought she had come to a decision, or was constructing a new shelter made of resignation. At 5:59 I felt my own throat swell with empathy, and at 5:59 and 30 seconds, Abraham Lincoln walked across the classroom that would become my mother's life, and when I looked up at her, she was staring at the television screen with her eyes wide and her mouth open and I knew that what I was witnessing was no less than a miracle.

We had only one vehicle, Dad's truck, and Dad didn't plan to be home on the Saturday Mom needed to be in Muncie, thirty miles away, to register for the test. He wasn't mean about it, but he wasn't exactly *flexible,* either.

I had to be home by the time the streetlights came on in the evening, and that spring I spent more than one twilight tearing down the street toward home as if the Devil were on my case, trying to beat the specific light that shone on the corner of Charles and Broad. I had taken to spending all my time out of school away from home, because there were changes afoot that couldn't be named or even described. Walking into my house felt like hitting water belly first; it looked like one thing, but it felt like glass. My dad still sat in his chair and smoked, watching Westerns and drinking whiskey, and my mom still read and talked on the phone and would scratch my back if I asked her. But there was a strange resistance in her, some stubbornness that made her unreachable, and the way Dad kept his jaw set was a fence around him. My older sister, Melinda, Queen of the Fair and all-around pinching machine, still lived at home but barely.

So in the evenings I went to my friend Rose's house, where all manner of wonder prevailed. For one thing, they had a mint-green kitchen, and they kept Velveeta cheese in their refrigerator, along with fresh milk from actual cows and sometimes Joyce skimmed the cream off the top and let us have some. It was horrible, and an experience I had repeated many times. When Joyce baked a chicken she let me have the skin.

"You can have some of the meat, you crazy kid," she'd say.

"No thanks."

Joyce made Autumn Soup, which was some very reliable form of soup with vegetables and hamburger in it, and Rose's sister Maggie and I had to peel the potatoes, because Rose had some skin disease on her hands and peeling potatoes made them break out in a rash, which seemed like a convenient time for lunatic itching, but it worked. And Rose's little brother Patrick would sit on a box for *hours* if you told him to wait there for the bus. He'd sit there till Joyce found him, anyway, and then she'd threaten to start smacking, and maybe at that point I'd have to go home, because Joyce was not above smacking—she was a Catholic—but I was a Quaker and smacking wasn't part of our religion.

But the most interesting thing Rose had was a persimmon tree, another Catholic delicacy. It grew between her house and the house that served as a parsonage for the North Christian Church, and sometimes it was the cause of feuding. Almost invariably after the persimmons got ripe a big windstorm came up and caused them to fly through the air and splatter on the parsonage like little balloons filled with orange paint. The North Christians were against it, and sometimes threatened William and Joyce with the Law. But William and Joyce just went merrily on their way, eating steaks, drinking cocktails, and smoking cigarettes.

Just a glance at persimmons reveals them to be suspicious fruits and yet we ate them constantly. Joyce put them in jams and pies, she even made something with the word "pudding" in the title although of course it was not real pudding because it wasn't chocolate and it hadn't come from a box. I was too polite to point the truth out.

When we weren't eating persimmons we were finding other uses for them. One day that spring Rose and I were sitting under the persimmon tree just as it was blooming. Rose picked one of the blossoms off and held it on the tip of her finger. At the center was a seed and all around the edges were white petals. I looked at it.

"Do you know what you do with one of these?" Rose asked me.

I shook my head.

"You put it in your nose like this," she said, placing the seed part just inside her nostril so that the petals flared out around her nose. It was beautiful, like nostril jewelry.

"Give me one," I said, picking a little blossom off the tree.

Rose added another to her own face and then she really looked like a flower garden. I was adjusting mine when I forgot what I was doing and inhaled. Up! went the little seed. Up! went the lovely little petals.

"Jeez O Flip!" I shouted. The little seed was all the way up in my brain part.

Rose leapt to her feet. "Okay, look, we've got to get that out and don't tell my mom. Or else let's just leave it in there." She looked around, furtive as one of the dope fiends on *Dragnet*. "How does it feel, can you breathe?"

I studied her as I felt around along the side of my nose for the location of the seed. "You *shammed* me," I said. I'd always counted on Rose to be a straight-up, good-grades, book-reading kind of girl, and here she was getting frisky. The little flower had been dusty with pollen. I sneezed.

"I didn't exactly sham you," Rose said as I walked out of her yard.

I sneezed again. "Oh, yeah? Then why do I have a persimmon up my nose?" I shouted back. I sneezed again. The whole thing was becoming uncomfortable, and I could hardly get any air up my left nose hole.

On the walk home I sneezed twelve more times. I had read in the *Guinness Book of World Records,* which had become my favorite book, that a man had spent the last few years of his life sneezing and then his heart wore out. I stopped in front of the Marathon and felt my heart. I sneezed again.

When I walked in the house, Mom covered the mouthpiece of the telephone. "God bless you," she said.

"Thanks." I headed straight upstairs. I was afraid for Mom to discover the truth, because she only had three rules in the entire world, which doesn't amount to many, and thus it was improbably rude that I'd broken one in public.

1. There's no such thing as a free lunch. (This was patently untrue, since about half my elementary school was on the Free Lunch program.)

2. Don't give advice to God. (Secretly I did nothing else, but I didn't figure Mom needed to know it. I said to God: Find my house slippers. Close school tomorrow. Feed the dogs. Give my mom a car so she can go to the CLEP thing.)

3. Don't stick anything up your nose.

I tried to poke at the seed with a pencil, but it seemed I just pushed it up farther. Disaster loomed. I finally figured out what I needed to do. I fetched the vacuum cleaner out of Mom and Dad's closet, and disconnected the tube part from the big flat part. I didn't have much experience with vacuum cleaners, but I had plenty with Taking Apart. I held the tube up to my left nose hole and turned the sweeper on with my foot. There was all manner of dust and cat hair in the tube, and the combination of the dust and the noise the machine made caused me to jump backward and lose control of the hose, which jumped around on the floor. I began sneezing in earnest. No way would my heart survive this one. I gave one big final sneeze and the flower came out, just as Mom turned the corner into her bedroom. I speedy quick put my hand down and let the vacuum cleaner suck up the seed.

"What are you doing?" Mom asked, truly bewildered.

"Sweepin'," I answered, pointing to the vacuum cleaner.

"You're sitting on the floor. What are you sweeping? What's all over your nose?" She leaned over, licked her thumb, and threatened me with a spit bath. "Were you vacuuming your *face*?"

"Ha! Wouldn't that be ridiculous." I pulled my T-shirt up and scrubbed hard at my nose, destroying the evidence. "I must have just gotten dusty playing at Rose's. Whew! That's a dusty place."

Mom looked at me for a minute. "Put the sweeper away, please," she said as she turned back toward the den.

"Okay! Not a problem!"

I looked out the window. There was still an hour or so of daylight left. I left the vacuum cleaner lying in pieces on the floor and ran outside.

Mom should have been upset about missing her chance to take the CLEP test, but she wasn't, and for a while I couldn't figure out why. Then one night, weeks after we saw Abraham Lincoln, I was sitting on the couch with her and coloring in my coloring book, listening to her talk on the phone. She often tucked the phone against her shoulder while she talked, and in that way could continue knitting or reading. I'd never seen a person do so many things at once. And her voice was just a steady murmur, like a voice I sometimes heard as I was falling asleep.

She was talking to one of her women friends; I couldn't tell who. I heard her say, "I have to be there by ten this Saturday to register. No, it's okay, it's all taken care of." Then she changed the subject, and in a few minutes she hung up. The phone rang a little later and she said the same thing to that friend, and by the time I'd finished coloring Snow White in Her Glass Casket, she'd said it to four or five different people. I watched her out of the corner of my eye, her head tucked down, her knitting needles ticking together in a rhythmic, hypnotic sway. All those years I had thought she was just sitting there, but it turned out she'd been quietly amassing an army, and now they were coming to take her home.

On Saturday morning, Dad didn't go anywhere. He puttered in his toolshed; he took a little constitutional around town. He drank coffee and whistled, and in his whistle was something to be devoutly avoided. I stayed around the house. We were all waiting on something. A little after nine a car pulled up behind Dad's truck. It was Mom's friend Carol, who was one of my favorites. Carol had peachy-colored skin and wore her hair wrapped around the top of her head like a sticky bun. She had a beautiful smile, and when she had laundry to do she said she had to get to her *warshing.* Her Wiener Dog had been the first dog to ever bite me, but I didn't hold it against either of them.

"Hey, kiddo!" Carol said when she saw me. She had a big voice.

"Hi, Carol! Mom's inside!" I had a big voice, too, when Carol was around.

We walked in the front door. Mom looked at us. She stood up.

✦

They left without saying anything to Dad. He came down to the sidewalk and stood with me as we watched them drive away.

"Time was, a woman wouldn't have gotten in a man's marriage that way," Dad said.

I wasn't sure what he expected me to say. *Times change?* Or did he want me to remember one of Mom's handy mottoes, like *We must live while it is day*? I looked up at him. He wasn't really talking to me.

My brother's big green Plymouth was still sitting where he'd parked it when he left for Fort Polk, Louisiana. It hadn't started in three weeks and the windshield wipers didn't work. Dad complained once a day that he'd lost the key, and so in addition to having it towed down to the mechanic who worked at the old gas station on the south end of town, he was going to have to have a key made before Dan came home from boot camp.

The CLEP test was scheduled for a Wednesday, and on Monday afternoon as I walked home from school I saw the most amazing thing. Mom was sitting in Dan's car, trying to start it. In my entire life I'd never seen my mother sit in the driver's seat of anything. I walked up and tapped on the window. She was staring straight ahead, and appeared for a moment not to see me. I tapped again. Mom's shoulders rose and fell in a sigh as she opened the door. I watched her slip the lost key into the pocket of her housedress, then she climbed out of the car and kissed me on the top of my head and started toward the house. I closed the car door. No one ever precisely asked me to, but good Lord if I'd only had a nickel for every secret I was obliged to keep.

On Wednesday, Lindy and I stayed home from school. Rain was coming down in sheets, hard enough and fast enough that I feared for the little May flowers. Melinda asked Mom what she was going to wear, and Mom produced an enormous orange dress from the back of her closet.

"Mom Mary lent it to me," Mom said, holding it up for inspection.

Melinda swallowed. "What size is it?"

"It's a 24. That should be just about right."

Lindy and I didn't look at each other.

After we got Mom in the dress, she put on the shoes Mom Mary had given her to go with the dress. "Oh no! They're too big and I'm running out of time!"

"Okay, okay. Don't panic. Sweetheart," Melinda said, turning to me, "go get today's newspaper."

I ran in the den and grabbed the *Courier-Times.* Lindy tore the front page in half, wadded it up and stuffed it in the toes of the orange high heels. "Try this."

Mom had put her hair, which was thin and baby-fine, in a bun, and when she leaned over to put the shoes on a second time, some of it slid out of the pins and fell around her face. She walked a bit unsteadily into the bathroom and looked in the mirror.

"Dear God. I look like a drunken school bus."

When Mom picked up her purse and headed for the door, I knew she was going to try Danny's car again, and I felt Dad's voice well up in my throat: *You'll never make it. You don't know how to drive, and that car's got no windshield wipers. Would you trade your* life *for this?* But I didn't say anything and neither did Melinda. Mom kissed me on the cheek and hugged Lindy, and the two of us girls went to the picture window in the living room and watched her.

She walked down the steps and out onto the sidewalk, the rain pummeling her plastic rain hat and the old plaid coat she was wearing. She took the key out of her coat pocket and got in the car, then put her head down on the steering wheel, and as she sat that way the rain gradually began to ease, and then she sat up and tried the ignition, and the car started and the rain stopped all at the same time.

"Well, I'll be a monkey's uncle," I said, flabbergasted.

Mom turned and waved at us. Danny's car lurched into Charles Street; stopped; lurched again, and Mom figured out what she was doing and drove straight on down the street.

We watched her until she turned onto Broad Street and out of sight. Melinda straightened up. "She didn't ask for much in the past twenty-seven years."

"I guess she didn't."

"She's got eighty-six cents in her purse, nothing else. I don't know what will happen to her if the car won't start when it's time to come home."

I knew I should still be worried, but I suddenly felt that anything was possible, and that most things, though certainly not all, would turn out okay.

A few weeks later, an envelope came from Ball State. Mom opened it like it was the Academy Awards, and sat for a few minutes studying the results.

"What's it say? How'd you do? Did you get a A plus?" I asked, trying to peer over her shoulders.

"I tested out of forty hours," Mom said, flipping through a catalog that had come with the letter.

I counted. Forty hours was not quite two days. But two days out of school was better than nothing.

"Sorry about that, Mom," I said. I thought I might ride down to Rose's house and tell her Mom passed.

"That's a whole year, sweetheart," she said as I headed toward the door. I stopped.

"A whole *year*?"

Mom nodded. And then I saw on her face that she was as shocked as I was; she didn't know any better than I did what to make of the news. For a few more seconds we were just frozen, and then she shrugged her shoulders—*What can you do?*—and reached over and picked up the phone.

I Knew Glen Before He Was a Superstar

Dad called me inside when it started to get dark. He told me that if I'd come in and take a bath without fighting him I could watch the Glen Campbell show. I acted bored with Glen Campbell, but in fact, I thought he was the best singer in the world besides Barry Gibb. Plus his little cap of blond hair always lay on his head as still and soft as a sleeping cat.

I had an album of his that had on it maybe the best song of the decade, "Where's the Playground Susie," which is essentially about a good-looking blond man asking for directions. Dad sometimes called my sister Susie, for vague historical reasons, and Melinda and Glen would have made a very handsome couple, so I was glad they had never met. It was bad enough that my sister had the attentions of Joe Overton who lived down the street and was a friend of my brother. He had, strictly speaking, been my first love, and I was only beginning to recover from him.

❦

Once I got in the tub I usually had quite a good time. I played an ongoing game that was essentially a bathtub version of Evil Queen, my favorite game to play with Rose and Maggie, reduced to just one player. In this game I was forced to slave away at an Evil Laundromat. Before getting in the tub I collected all the washrags I could find. My job was to wash them in front of me, then swirl them around in the rinse water on my right side, pass them behind me for drying, and fold them on my left side. At a good Laundromat that would have been the end of the game, but because it was Evil, as soon as I got them folded I had to start all over again. The washrags never got clean enough.

I hated personal hygiene, and yet once I got in the tub it was hard to get me out. Dad used to become convinced that I'd drowned, because I played so quietly. I worried him to no end. The bathroom was connected to our den, where we did all our living, and so Dad kept time on his watch from his favorite chair in front of the television. Every seven minutes he would call out, "Zip? You all right?" and I would yell back, "Playing!"

I finally got out of the tub only a few minutes before Glen Campbell was supposed to begin. I was hot and thirsty from sitting in the water so long. We had our own well, which had the coldest, most sharply metallic water in town. All other water tasted like soap to me. Rose's water, for instance, passed through a softener and an aerator as it came out the tap, so it was foul-tasting *and* full of holes. On the bathroom sink was a plastic coffee cup Blue Bonnet margarine came in. We had a million of them. I stood naked in front of the sink, drinking cup after cup of cold water. I probably drank eight cups before I felt better. Once I put the cup down I realized that my belly was sticking out like an orphan's and that I couldn't very easily bend down to pick up my pajamas. I took a step toward the bathtub and heard water sloshing around in my stomach as if in a jar. I stopped. I took a step. Water was most definitely making a noise in my stomach.

I threw open the bathroom door and ran stark naked into the den. My dad turned and looked at me without any discernible surprise. Mom looked up from her corner of the couch, where she was knitting.

"Listen, listen! No, wait—turn down the TV!"

Dad stood up and turned down the sound. My parents gathered close to me, and I swung my suddenly fat little belly back and forth, and there it was, the sound of the sea.

"Well, listen to that," Dad said, wide-eyed.

"Now, what do you suppose is in there?" Mom asked, looking at my dad.

"It's water! I drank about a hundred cups of water and it's all sloshing around!" Before they could express any more wonder at my trick, the Glen Campbell show started.

"Okay, that's enough, everybody sit down for the show," I said, directing them to their standard locations.

"Aren't you going to get dressed?" Dad asked, turning up the volume on the TV, by which time I was already curled up on the couch next to Mom.

"She can sit here like this for a little while, Bob. Let her get dressed during a commercial."

"Yeah," I said. "Let her get dressed during a commercial."

Mom pulled the end of the afghan she was knitting over my legs. It was soft and warm, even though it had so many holes in it. Dad handed me my best coloring book, "Sleeping Beauty," and my crayons. I had to have my own because I pressed down so hard that Mom and Melinda refused to share with me anymore. And all through Glen Campbell no one reminded me that I had to get dressed, and so I got to spend the rest of the evening happily working on my coloring book, naked.

The Rules of Evil Queen

Object of the Game: Evil Queen has no objective other than complaining and the avoidance of beheading.

The Players: Rose, Maggie, and Zippy. Patrick plays only by contributing his cloth diapers. (Note: Always use clean diapers. The game can take a disastrous turn if the diapers have been used even a little.)

The Rules: Player One stands at the baby washtub and washes the stack of cloth diapers by hand. She then hands them to Player Two, who is stationed at the canopy bed. Player Two removes the canopy pegs and hangs up the just-washed diapers, holding them in place with the canopy pegs. They dry immediately. Player Two hands the diapers to Player Three, who is stationed at the miniature ironing board, which Zippy secretly covets for its smallness.

Player Three irons the diapers and hands them back to Player One, who washes them and hands them to Player Two, etc.

Restrictions: Players may not, at any time, discuss anything but their own downtroddenness and the shocking fertility of the Evil Queen, who has 137 children. Players may occasionally note the suffering of the other serfs, such as those working in the Evil Bread Shoppe and the Evil Forge, wherein are made the Evil Breads and Evil Horseshoes, but Players must endlessly remind one another that no one works harder or under worse conditions than the Evil Diaper Service. (Note: Restrictions apply to all variations of the game, including Evil Laundromat—washcloths—and Evil Shoeshine.)

Conclusion of Play: Often corresponds to dinnertime or the sudden, uncontrollable sleepiness of Player Three.

Vacuum Cleaner

The following is a transcript of an actual tape made on my blue tape recorder. The setting is my Mom Mary's house on Shoppe Avenue, in New Castle.

DAD: Donita, look at this.

DONITA, MY DAD'S SISTER: (Shouts) Mother, what are you doing in the closet?

MOM MARY, MY GRANDMA: (Inaudible, from the closet)

DAD: Donita.

DONITA: (Shouts) I know you're tearing something up in there.

GRANDMA: (Still inaudible)

DAD: Donita, look at this.

MY MOM: What's she doing?

DONITA: God knows. It sounds like she's taking down all the winter coats.

DAD: It's a tape recorder.

DONITA: I see that. It's very nice.

DAD: I got it for taping Lindy's speeches. You just push this silver knob around: up for Play, left for Rewind, right for Fast Forward. To record, you press this red button and talk into the microphone.

DONITA: For taping Melinda's speeches, you say?

DAD: Yeah. This way she can hear what she sounds like. She can time them, too.

MY MOM: Look, she made it out of the closet. Lord, she's got her vacuum cleaner with her. Is she going to start sweeping?

DONITA: Mom, just turn around and put that vacuum cleaner away—

GRANDMA: (Coming into the room talking, she becomes audible in something like the opposite of the Doppler Effect) . . . show Bobby my new—

DONITA: —because we've got company and you're not going to start—

GRANDMA: —vacuum cleaner.

DONITA: —sweeping again. This house is as clean as it's gonna get.

DAD: It's got pretty good sound. Lindy says she doesn't sound like herself on tape, but she does. There's probably a lot we could—

GRANDMA: Bobby?

DAD: —do with it. Record a lot of things.

GRANDMA: Bobby, I want you to look at this.

DONITA: That's real nice.

MY MOM: Bob, your mother's trying to show you something.

DAD: I saw it at Grant's, and I thought, well, I could get that to help Lindy with her speeches. You know she's going to the state finals in St. Louis in May.

MY MOM: I'll look at it, Mom.

GRANDMA: Kenneth bought it for me. It's got this long hose and the cord doesn't tangle. On my old one the cord was forever getting tangled.

MY MOM: That was very nice of Kenneth.

GRANDMA: I'll miss that old one—

DONITA: Where *is* Melinda?

MY MOM: She's helping Danny look for an apartment.

GRANDMA: —though. I had it for nearly twenty years.

MY MOM: He's decided to move to New Castle since he's working at Anchor Hocking.

DAD: The microphone came with it, I didn't have to pay extra. I told him he should stay home with us, but no, no, he can't just listen to his old dad.

GRANDMA: Bobby?

DAD: There's plenty of room in our house and there's no need to just rush off—

MY MOM: Danny gets his mind set on something—

DAD: —this way, but you can't talk to the boy.

MY MOM: —it's difficult to talk to him.

GRANDMA: Bobby?

DAD: Yep. (Stretching) We're all going to St. Louis in May. We're staying in a hotel. I figure Lindy can practice her speech all the way there.

DONITA: You say you're all going? (Turning to me) You're awful quiet.

DAD: She's always quiet. She's my girl. Whose girl are you? Tell it into the tape recorder.

ME: Daddy's.

DAD: Whew! She's still my girl! I was worried you might have changed your mind.

GRANDMA: Bobby? I want you to see something.

MY MOM: Here's your poor old mother sitting right here and you show no compunction about saying you're Daddy's girl. Who nursed you for eighteen months? Who carried you on her hip till you were three?

DAD: (Inhaling his cigarette) St. Louis is a rough place. But we're all going.

GRANDMA: Did you eat any of this cake, Dee? Have some.

MY MOM: I had a big piece. It was good. No—that's okay, I don't want any more.

GRANDMA: Well, give it to that child. She don't eat enough to keep a bird alive. I never saw a child so skinny.

MY MOM: I don't think she can eat any more either. She had a big bowl of chicken and noodles, too. You want any more, honey? She can't eat any more, Mom.

GRANDMA: It's an applesauce cake.

MY MOM: It's good.

GRANDMA: You should have some more.

MY MOM: I can't. See if Bob will have some more. It sure was good, though. Moist.

GRANDMA: That's the applesauce. Bobby? You want some more cake?

DAD: I had enough cake. You're always trying to overfeed me.

DONITA: I hope it stops raining soon. I need to mow.

DAD: You mow too much.

MY MOM: Bob doesn't believe in cutting the grass until little children begin disappearing in it.

GRANDMA: Bobby?

(There are many flurries of noise. Enter Danny and Melinda. Melinda enters talking.)

MELINDA: You could too have turned on A Avenue.

DANNY: (Silence)

MY MOM: Hey, kids. Did you find something?

GRANDMA: Sit down and have some cake. You both look like you don't eat enough.

DAD: She's going to try to kill you with cake. For God's sake, sit down and have a piece so she'll shut up.

DONITA: Did you find an apartment?

MELINDA: Well, we found something, but it wasn't big enough for him. Tell them about it. He said it was too small, which was a bunch of crap, because how much room does he need? Enough for his sleeping bag and his fossil collection. That's about eight square feet. And he needs a kitchen for storing his five-gallon drum of peanut butter. Tell them about the second one. He said it was too expensive, which was also a bunch of crap, because he doesn't spend his money on anything.

GRANDMA: Did you get you some cake, honey?

MELINDA: Thanks, Mom. I don't know what he wants. He's impossible.

DAD: Did you see I've got your tape recorder out here?

MELINDA: I see that.

DAD: I was just telling Donita how you can tape your speeches on it.

MELINDA: Yep, that's what he bought it for.

DONITA: He says you're going to St. Louis.

MELINDA: In May.

DONITA: He says you're all going.

MELINDA: That's what he tells me.

GRANDMA: Danny, son, do you want some milk with that cake?

DANNY: (Silence)

MY MOM: I'll get it, Mom.

GRANDMA: Lord, honey, I'm already up. (She leaves for the kitchen.)

DONITA: If I don't mow soon, the neighbors will start complaining.

DAD: You mow too much. That grass is barely peeking out of the ground. Give it a chance.

GRANDMA: (Setting down Danny's milk) Bobby?

MY MOM: Bob?

MELINDA: Dad? Your mother is trying to talk to you.

DAD: We need to hit the road. I've got stuff I've got to do.

MY MOM and MELINDA (in unison): Places to go, people to see.

DAD: That's right.

MELINDA: What important stuff do you have to do?

DAD: It's private. This little one here has to get to her feeding. There's some starving animals at home.

MY MOM: Bob, we've only been gone an hour.

GRANDMA: Bobby?

DAD: Mother, whuu-uu-uut?!

(Brief silence)

GRANDMA: I want you to see my new vacuum cleaner.

DAD: Is that it? That all? It's real nice.

GRANDMA: Kenneth got it for me.

DAD: (Lighting a cigarette) So I hear. Bully for him.

GRANDMA: The cord doesn't tangle. I'd had my old one for twenty years. This here's a Kenmore. I should have it a long time, too.

DAD: Well, that's real nice, Mom. I'm so glad that Kenneth could buy you a new vacuum cleaner, since he never comes to visit.

GRANDMA: Oh, Bobby, now. He's just busy with his car lot.

DAD: Hmmmph. You always did love him best.

GRANDMA: I did not! The grief *you've* caused me, I hardly had time to love anybody else.

DAD: I'm an angel on this earth.

(This causes a generalized uproar of laughter.)

DAD: (Smacks the table) We've got to go. Zip, where are your shoes? Did you even wear—

(The recorder is abruptly shut off, and begins in the middle of a speech:)

MELINDA: —do about American apathy towards crime? We can begin by—

(Interrupted by much crackly handling of the microphone, and then Glen Campbell singing "Wichita Lineman" on television. In the background a dog barks.)

Cowboys

Every couple of weeks Julie and I rode our bikes down to the junkyard half a mile from the Newmans' farm to scour it for treasures. We called it a junkyard, but really it was just a stretch of woods of questionable ownership, where people stopped by the side of the road and threw their trash in.

These things never changed: a wringer washer slowly sinking and two old tractor tires. For a while there was a metal kitchen chair with a yellow plastic seat. Sometimes we sat on it. Eventually Julie got the idea to move it to our tree house, which just left four holes where the legs used to be. We had long ago pulled all the pop bottles out of the dirt and cashed them in at the drugstore, leaving a little minefield of half-buried aluminum cans, their jagged, toothy tops propped open in a parody of dinner. Sometimes live things fell in the cans between our visits. We squatted down to inspect.

"Now, be careful not to touch those can lids, Julie Ann," I said, ever alert to her tendency to court bad diseases. "My dad says you can get lockjaw from rusty metal."

"Hmmm," Julie answered, through her nose.

"If you get lockjaw they just have to straightaway kill you, because there's no hope of you ever eating again."

This got her attention. "How do they kill you?"

"They just whomp you in the forehead with a big hammer. I hear it makes your eyes pop out to here," I said, holding my hand out a foot from my face.

Julie didn't answer, but just very gently reached down and ran the tip of her finger along one of the rusty lids, causing my heart to skate past a beat. I knew better than to acknowledge my fear, however, because she would just take it as a dare. Once while playing hide-and-seek, Julie had skittered halfway up a giant pine tree. When I saw her red hair through the branches I made one little innocent squeal, causing her to climb all the way to the top. By the time she reached the uppermost branches, the tree was swaying back and forth as if in a windstorm.

I stood up casually, pretending that Julie's blood was no issue with me, and gave the junkyard an appraising squint. There was a cat hunkered down at the edge of the tree line, watching us.

"Hey, Dumpcat. C'mere, Dumpcat," I called, holding out my arms and heading toward it at the same time. The cat moved nothing but its eyes, watching me get closer and closer.

I could see that he was junkyard-colored, probably a gray tabby under all the layers of grime, and one of his ears was a hopeless jigsaw. Every cat I'd ever owned had, during some brawl, lost a hunk of ear. It was a standard cat condition. The Dumpcat's left eye drooped, too, and he appeared to have lost all his whiskers. This stopped me in my tracks, because I knew from my dad that cats used their whiskers to help them see. Dad told me a cat won't stick his head anywhere his body can't fit through, and his whiskers tell him how wide his body is. *Good Lord,* I thought, *this cat is headed for disaster.*

As I got closer, he made a little rumble sound deep in his chest and darted away. This kind of cat was a test: one could either lose one's temper and dive at him or be a good Quaker and keep going at him with gentleness. I pursued him nicely, in a way that would have made my sister proud, with the vague idea that I might catch him and put him in the treehouse with the chair and the dirty magazine we'd found in the barn and couldn't hardly stand to look at.

During my friendly pursuit, Julie had wandered over silently, like a redheaded Indian, and suddenly she was right at my side, causing me to jump. The cat sat still. Julie leaned over and headed toward him, moving her fingers like she was asking for money. She got closer and closer, and before I could even work up an indignation she was scratching the back of his head and he was all raising up bumping into her hand and making a ratchety purr, like a tractor that hadn't been started all winter.

"Now, you can just look at that cat and *know* he smells," I said, seemingly involuntarily. "You be careful, Julie Ann, about ringworm. It gets out of their butts and is perfectly round. If you get it on you, they have to cut off that part of your skin, because nothing can kill a ringworm."

"How do they cut it off?" she asked, scratching the cat's chin. I could see fleas jumping ship by the dozen.

"With scissors. It hurts like the dickens. And after they cut off the ringworm they pour iodine straight in the open hole. You can beg all you want for Mercurochrome, but forget it. It's iodine or gangrene, and you don't want to know about that."

"I know about gangrene," she said quietly. The cat had flipped onto his back, and was twisting up like a question mark under Julie's fingertips.

It was a pretty long sentence for Julie, so I assumed she was drunk with cat love. I had seen her get that way at home, with her calico cat, Tiger. Tiger was square and heavy as a brick, and once those two got going there was cat hair all over the place, and claw marks, dander, you name it. Tiger lost a baby tooth once loving Julie's shoe too hard.

I turned and headed toward the baby swing, where we used to swing our baby dolls a long time ago. Actually, I swung my baby dolls in it and Julie swung her Lone Ranger doll. She had two outfits for him: a tan one that looked like real leather, and the other a light, light blue with fringe on the sleeves. Julie called it his dress-up suit. The Lone Ranger and Tonto and their many, many horses and their many, many saddles sat on a shelf Julie's dad had made for her; we didn't play with them anymore. I didn't have anything to put in the baby swing.

"Hey!" I said, having a great junkyard idea. "Do you think Rebecca would let us bring her baby down here and swing him? He'd about fit in this thing."

"Nope," Julie said. She was not the least bit interested in babies.

I was thinking about trying to fit the Dumpcat in the swing when I saw it: a child's rocking horse, the big plastic kind on a metal stand with thick springs, completely buried in the dirt. Just its side and head were visible.

"The *Lord,*" I whispered, and motioned for Julie to come.

The horse's head was thrown back, as if someone had pulled too hard on his reins, and his mouth was open, filled with dirt. He was *biting* at the dirt. I could see the rivet that held the plastic reins, but the reins themselves were gone. All of the horse's colors had faded into one pinky-gold color, and in the black dirt and the shade of the trees it appeared that he was casting out light. His one eye was wild. Both of us stood motionless a moment in the presence of a horse in the dirt, and then Julie knelt down and started to brush at it.

"Be careful; that's a fossil," I told her. "You can go to jail for disturbing a fossil. My brother told me all about it."

In fact, my brother had quite a large fossil collection, many, many pounds of stolen rock. The collection completely surrounded his bed when he lived with us. It seemed that no one in my family had thought it odd that he kept the pointy stones there, even given his propensity to roll out of bed a few times a week. It used to wake us all up, the thump, the moan, the granite scraping across the floor as he made his way back up into his sleeping bag. He'd also set up traps in the doorway to his room, some big enough for a badger, so I don't know what we would have done if he'd ever gotten really injured falling on a rock. My mom had concluded that his whole bedroom situation had something to do with how hard he'd gotten Jesus. Just *remembering* Jesus out here in the junkyard made me want to spit.

I spat. Julie spat. Her hand lingered near the chest of the horse. The Dumpcat watched us silently from deep in the trees. I looked at the horse and just knew he was never coming out of the ground: *What's done is done* was the principle in operation. As I stood up I noticed five or six sticker burrs caught in Julie's blue knit cap, and one actually in her red hair, gathering a tangle up around it like a nest.

"Julie," I said, standing up. "We better get home and get that sticker burr out before every hair on your head gets caught up in it and we have to whack it all off right down to your scalp. I once heard of a woman who about lost her scalp to a sticker burr. I think peanut butter is the trick for getting them out."

As we walked toward our bicycles, Julie reached up silently and pulled the burr out of her hair; dozens of flame-colored strands came with it. She tossed the whole mess down in the junkyard, where, for just a moment, it blazed up, and was consumed.

The Love Bug

A woman named Bonnie moved into a house on Jefferson Street, and never in my life have I been more tempted to be rude. The very first time I mentioned her to Mom I almost said, "Have you seen that Big Fat Bonnie woman?" And once when I was riding my bike and passed her getting into her car (a totally surprising dark blue VW Beetle, about half the car necessary for such a person), I just about shouted, "Hey, Big Fat Bonnie!" It wasn't as if I didn't have experience with plump women, some of it in my own home. But there was something about Bonnie that was *essentially* large. I didn't know what it was until she and Mom became friends.

I came home from school one day and there she was, sitting in our living room. She was wearing a pink polyester top that zipped up the front, and white polyester pants. The outfit, along with her piled-up blond hair, made her look like an enormous ice cream sundae, with strawberries.

"Well, I'll be &*@! if I can't teach you how to drive, and I will, too, you can bet your &*@!" Bonnie was saying. "No man would keep ME from driving a car, forget it! What is this, a Turkish prison? What do you do all day, just sit around watching the %*#^ TV?!"

Mom blushed, but also looked a bit sheepish, then noticed me. "Bonnie, this is my daughter."

I just continued to stand frozen in the doorway. I wanted to raise my hand and wave, but I was afraid I'd break the spell and miss a whole stream of good swears.

"Yeah, I know who you are, you little monkey," she said, fishing a pack of cigarettes out of her shirt pocket and screwing up her mouth like a truck driver. She was pretty, in a truck driver way. "You don't ever do your homework, do you?"

This caught me off guard. I shook my head no.

"Of course you don't! You're too &*#@ busy riding around town on that bicycle."

"Bonnie," Mom said, quietly. I suddenly realized how very demure and ladylike she could be. "This is actually a Christian household, and we try not to use such language."

Bonnie tipped her head back and roared with laughter. "Yeah, I hear that." She wiped her eyes. "I'll bet your husband is a %*$# Christian, too, isn't he? And that's why he keeps you locked up in this little (#%)hole of a town, right?"

"You'd best go outside and play, sweetheart." Mom only glanced at me. She was embarrassed, but she was smiling.

I turned around and headed back outside. "Dad ain't a Christian, actually," I said as I turned the doorknob.

Bonnie blew smoke out through her nose. "I knew that. When you come home look up the definition of sarcasm, you little Ne'er-Do-Well. Now scoot, shoo, out the door with you."

Just as I stepped outside I heard her say to Mom, "So what about those +&^$ driving lessons? You want 'em, or not?"

I guessed Mom had gotten a taste for the open road, and decided she needed a driver's license.

When Dad left the next Saturday morning to go wherever he went and do whatever he did, Mom called Bonnie and said she was ready. I went out to wait on the front porch, and from the swing I could hear Bonnie's blue car start two blocks away. I heard her drive down the alley that ran behind Edythe's house, and then there she was. She pulled up in front of our house and honked her horn, even though I was sitting right in front of her. The horn sounded like a cat vomiting. Mom walked out and waved at Bonnie, and Bonnie kept honking. Mom opened the passenger door and turned to tell me something, and Bonnie honked again.

"For heaven's sake," Mom said, looking in the car.

"Well, speed it up," Bonnie said. "We haven't got all day."

"We do have all day, actually."

"Act like we don't." Bonnie revved the car's little engine.

Mom waved at me and said she'd be home soon. I walked down and stood in the yard; I couldn't wait to see the two of them in that one single car. After Mom climbed in, that Volkswagen was literally *stuffed* with women. How they found the gearshift I'll never know.

I was just leaving the post office parking lot on my bicycle when Mom drove past me in the Bug, its engine making a little *tuck-a-tuck-a-tuck-a-tuck-a* sound. She was driving about a mile an hour. The car died at the four-way stop sign, so I beat her home by about five minutes. But when she stepped out I would have sworn she'd won the Kentucky Derby: her cheeks were pink, her hair was flying, and she and Bonnie were laughing to beat the band. Bonnie climbed out of the car and gave a hoot that sent a flock of starlings flying for cover.

"How'd it go?" I asked when I reached Mom.

"We killed a chicken!" Mom said, with the same tone she might have used to say, *We scaled the north face of Everest!*

I peeked under the car and sure enough, there were some feathers stuck to the undercarriage. I whistled through my teeth.

"What's Dad gonna say about this?" I asked, scratching my head.

"Aw, #*$& him if he can't take a joke," Bonnie said, wrapping her big arm around Mom. And the two of them lumbered up the sidewalk and into our Christian household.

Treasure

I couldn't for the life of me figure out how long a person had to live, or how good she had to be, to get her hands on some treasure. My mom, for instance, spent all her time sitting on the couch eating pork rinds and reading books from the bookmobile, and yet she had some valuables that tempted me sorely, things so fabulous I wanted to steal them and then destroy them so I wouldn't have to think about them anymore. She had a trick box, for instance, that had belonged to her dead daddy. It was a normal box shape, except it was formed out of thin strips of wood, and no way would the lid open. It couldn't be pried or prayed open. The trick was to press two of the strips of wood at the same time, which caused the *end* to slide out like a drawer. Oh, it vexed me. Mom refused to teach me how to open it, and with good cause. But she did let me see what was inside: a token from the 1929 World's Fair. A little naked plastic baby doll. A driver's license issued to her father, Edward A. Bartuska, of Whiting, Indiana. Long deceased. A beautiful watch that didn't run. A picture of my mom as a little girl, with the expression she always wore as a child: comical and worried. (It turned out she'd needed glasses.) A Masonic lodge pin, in the center of which was a fabulous and genuine red stone. Mom would let me paw through the box maybe once a year, taking every single thing out and asking her what it was and where it came from, and then I had to put it all back nicely and she would put the box away.

My father! My father had a whole jar of teeth. They once belonged inside the mouths of strange and exotic animals. He had a shark's tooth, the incisor of a grizzly bear, a little molar from a coon dog, the two yellowed front teeth of a horse. He had a watch on a steel band that was quite odd-looking, and it was the only watch he could wear. He shut off all other watches when he got near them. When I asked him why he said it was because his body was magnetized, and after that I was afraid of him getting stuck to the refrigerator. He had a bottle of liquid mercury. I didn't ask. Once, he let me pour a drop of it out on a tray; he said, "Don't touch it!" and I didn't touch it, but I wanted to put my whole finger in it. The mercury remained a perfect, crazy globe, and rolled around on the tray like a marble.

My sister had a long, long chain made out of gum wrappers, which were precisely folded into little triangles. It was one of the most beautiful things I'd ever seen, and smelled like nothing but good news. Juicy Fruit and Teaberry. She also had three statues of a little naked boy and girl (who didn't have any parts); each statue described a different rule about love. My favorite was Love Is . . . Never Having to Say You're Sorry. This was, the good Lord knew, a dream of mine. But every time I refused to apologize for something, Love seemed to just fly out the window. I stole the little statue for two whole days and took it with me everywhere I went. I was going to flash it like a badge if I got in trouble. But

Lindy found me out and gave me a hard pinch, and then I said sorry and she didn't.

My brother had, and this hardly seems possible, an actual bow-and-arrow set. He took them deer hunting. There were some parts of the bow that attracted me, like the very shiny wooden grip, and the knots at the end of the bowstring. It was a delicate operation on the whole, and yet very powerful and strong. But what I really wanted were the arrows, especially the little hairy parts on the end. The arrow tips were sharp as a razor and just cold steel, and then right down on the other end of the shaft were some colored parts that looked like the head of a woodpecker, and you could only rub them one way; if pushed the wrong way they would have been ruined, and so would I. Danny hung the bow and the bag of arrows off a hook at the end of Dad's gun rack, and sometimes in the evening I would stand on the back of the couch and rub my fingers over the colored parts until I was nearly hypnotized, and then my dad would notice what I was doing and thunder, *Zip!* Which meant Did I think for a moment it was all right to play with a deadly arrow, and I'd get down, but my fingertips would feel smooth as silk, like I'd rubbed my own fingerprints off.

I myself owned nothing good and could not imagine the day I ever would. When I complained to my mom about it, she pointed out that I had not one but two stuffed things I loved, both of which she had made for me: my baby doll, Suzy Sleepyhead, and a little brown velveteen bear with crossed eyes named, naturally, Gladly (the Cross-Eyed Bear). Yeah, yeah, I'd say. What the heck good were those? I wanted something so excellent and strange that when I showed it to my friends their bellies would start to ache with covetousness, the way mine ached a whole bunch of the time, almost every time I took a look at the world and saw how little of it belonged to me.

⁂

Another great thing my mom owned and took for granted was a collection of rain hats that came folded up inside their own little suitcases. The suitcases were plastic, in various pastel colors, smaller than an egg. Some of them had their own little handles, and on the top of each lid was a bunch of plastic flowers, and I'm not talking about painted-on flowers, these were flowers sitting in a little bouquet right on top of a little suitcase, and inside was an actual rain hat. The rain hats were folded like the most complicated map in the world, forward/back, forward/back, maybe 7,000 times, until the whole thing was skinnier than a ruler, and then the length of it was folded over and over into a one-inch square. I can't think of a greater moment than the one in which Mom popped open the lid, took out the folded-up square, and shook out the clear plastic hat, which would tie under her chin. I wanted to find all the little suitcases in the world and open them all at once, and take out all the rain hats and shake them like the stars coming out. After that I was unclear what would happen, because no one in the free world could figure out how to get the hats back into a square.

Sometimes Mom would let me wear a rain hat if I'd been particularly good. They were too big for me, and often slipped down over my eyes.

"Ah! I'm suffocating! Keep away from children!"

"Sweetheart, just scoot it back on your head."

"Oh."

Dad was late coming home from work at Delco Remy, which was entirely usual. I was sitting on the floor coloring in my Disney Princesses coloring book when I heard his truck pull up outside. My rain hat was down over my eyes, and I could see through it just enough to know which page I was on, but not enough to know where the lines were, so I was just coloring randomly.

The front door opened and I could hear Dad talking to someone. No one ever came to visit us. I stared at the doorway to the den. My dad appeared, rainy-shaped, and beside him was a rain-shaped stranger. I dropped my crayon and looked at Mom. She was a blur. I pushed up the hat.

In earlier years I had been terribly shy, but I was coming out of it. I jumped up and ran over to Dad and whoever was with him in the doorway.

"Dad! Hey! Who's this guy with you?" And then, to the stranger, "Who are you? Whatcha doin' here? What's your name?"

"Zip! Slow down, sit down." Dad turned to Mom, who was looking at him in an interested way. There, in fact, was the same face as in the magic box: funny. A bit alarmed. "Dee, this is George Christy. He's going to be staying with us a few days."

George could see immediately that some charm was in order, so he crossed the den in a single stride, stepping over my coloring book, a stack of Mom's library books, a pair of Dad's shoes, my empty lemon phosphate cup, a bowl of popcorn seeds, a sleeping cat, a basket full of unfolded laundry, and a disassembled 12-gauge shotgun on an opened newspaper, which Dad was in the process of cleaning.

"I'm pleased to meet you, Dee," George said.

I studied him pretty hard. He was wearing a blue work shirt that appeared to have been around a long time, with the sleeves rolled up; a pair of khaki walking shorts; a wide leather belt; woolly socks that most people would have worn in winter—and it was June—and hiking boots. He was tall and broad and muscular, like my dad, only younger. He had very dark hair and eyes and a big bushy mustache. I gave a little astonished whistle.

Mom shook his hand. "Nice to meet you, George. How did . . . where did . . ."

Dad cleared his throat and picked up a pile of blankets at the end of the couch, so George could sit down. "Actually, I just met George a few minutes ago. He was sitting at the side of the road in front of the Shively Homeplace, and I stopped and asked him if he needed a ride."

Mom swallowed. "So you're a hitchhiker, George?"

"Hey!" I said, bombarded with information. "Wait a second. You were sittin' at the side of the road? Across from the Mount Summit *cemetery*? What was you doin' there? What's a hitchhiker? Where's your car? Where's your house?"

"Sweetheart, that's enough," Mom said.

"No, ma'am, I'm not precisely a hitchhiker," George began.

"What's a hitchhiker?"

"I'm actually walking across the United States," he said to Mom. "I just graduated from college, and I started out in California at the beginning of May. I've walked twenty-four hundred miles so far. Your husband here"—George smiled at Dad—"offered me a place to camp for a couple days, since I didn't actually need a ride. If that's okay with you, that is. Because I can just head on, if you'd like."

"No!" I shouted. "It's okay with her, it's just fine. We have hitchhikers all the time. She loves them."

"Bob, can I talk to you just a minute?" Mom asked.

I took George out to the porch swing. Something huge and orange was propped up against the house. "What the heck?"

"That's my pack. I carry it on my back by these straps, and this bar unfolds so it can stand up on its own, see? Do you want to try to lift it?"

I slid my arms inside the straps. I had an old Army backpack that was big enough for a canteen, a pocket knife, some beef jerky, and a comic book, so I thought I'd do fine. But George's pack weighed about 482 pounds, and was as tall as my shoulders, and when I tried to lift it my legs started wobbling and my face turned purple, and he laughed and said, "Whoa, there. Don't blow a gasket."

"Are you really a hitchhiker, and what's a hitchhiker?"

"No—hey, is your head screwed on tight? Because didn't I just say I'm not a hitchhiker? Do you ever stop talking? A hitchhiker's a person who stands at the side of the road with his thumb out like this. You try. Excellent. You were born to hitchhike. And he tries to get strangers to give him rides. It's a way of traveling."

"But you don't do that? You just sit at the side of the road with your thumbs tucked in?"

George threw his head back and laughed. We sat down on the swing.

"What all's in that bag? You think maybe you could show me tomorrow?"

"Sure. There's a sleeping bag, and a tent, and some rain gear."

"I've got this rain hat."

"Yes, I see."

"What else?"

"There's food and some dishes, a can opener, a couple of books, my journal. Postcards and stamps. Clean clothes."

I was so flabbergasted I could hardly speak. George Christy owned more stuff than I did, *and* he carried it around in a huge orange bag on his back.

"I'll tell you what I don't have, though," he said, studying me. "I don't have a shirt with a big fish on the front."

I looked down. "Yeah. I've got the only one."

Dad walked out and joined us on the porch. He smoked a little, flipped his cigarette toward the sidewalk.

"Nice night," he said.

"It's beautiful," George answered.

"Dee says you're welcome to stay, as long as you camp in the yard. She says it wouldn't be appropriate for you to stay in the house, since we've got these two girls, Zip here and our older daughter, Melinda." Dad seemed more than a little miserable to be making such a speech.

"Oh, of course, I wouldn't have . . . I don't really stay in houses. It's against my rules."

Dad took a deep breath. "You're a lucky man."

George smiled. He smelled like pine needles.

❦

George went back in the house to have some popcorn with us before bedtime. He sat on the couch with Mom and I sat on the floor.

"Hey! Do you know any jokes?" I asked him.

He pondered a minute. "I do know a pretty good joke. Okay: Why do ducks have flat feet, Zippy?"

"Why?"

"To stamp out forest fires."

I gasped, then nearly fell over laughing. It was the funniest joke I'd *ever* heard, and I'd been collecting jokes for a while.

"No, wait! There's more. Why do elephants have flat feet?"

I couldn't speak, so Mom asked why.

"To stamp out burning ducks."

I just collapsed face-first onto my coloring book. I rolled around in a little ball until tears were running down my face.

George made a sound like a fire truck. "Emergency! We've got a burning duck down over here!"

Even Dad had to laugh. "George, you're gonna kill her."

I finally stretched out on my back and begged for mercy. Hitchhikers. Good Lord.

I slept in my clothes all summer, so I could just hop up in the morning and go. I was working on simplifying my life, which I had discovered could be done very easily if I ceased to do the following: wash my face, brush my hair, brush my teeth, wear shoes. The morning after George arrived I got up with the first light and tiptoed down the stairs. Mom was still asleep, but the living room and den smelled like coffee, and I could hear Dad in the bathroom, shaving. I slipped out the front door, careful to catch the screen before it slammed.

And there it was, sitting right in the middle of our backyard. A yellow tent with a man in it. I crept across the dewy grass, silent as an Injun. I studied the tent from every angle. It seemed to be made out of canvas, and had seen better days. I didn't have much experience with tents, but God knows I wanted some. When we went camping we always stayed in a trailer. I'd had one brief tent experience with the Brownies, before I'd gotten kicked out for streaking. But this one was entirely professional. I was standing in front of the zippered flaps, imagining how I could live all the rest of my life in a tent, when a deep voice said, "Is that a BAR sneaking around my cabin door? Because I believe I hear a BAR outside."

I jumped backward probably three feet, slipped on the wet grass, and fell straight down. "No! Hitchhiker Man, don't shoot! It's just me!"

George quick unzipped the tent and stuck his head out. "Oh, hello."

"Hello."

"I don't have a gun, actually."

This was puzzling. "You better get one. There's danger everywhere."

George shook his head. "Listen, you're by far the most dangerous person I've met on this trip."

"Psshht. You should meet my sister." Lindy had spent the night at her friend Cheryl's and had not yet received the news of the hitchhiker.

George parted the flaps, then climbed out of his tent and stretched. He, too, had slept in his clothes. He even still had his *boots* on. If someone had spoken the words "soul mate" to me right then, I would not have considered it out of the question. There was no doubt in my mind that George Christy was living my real life.

"And this is where Rose and Maggie live," I said, on our walking tour of Mooreland. "Rose is left-handed and has a canopy bed with a white canopy and matching white dressers, plus a little brother, a box collection, and a miniature ironing board and iron. Oh, and a little record player of her very own with a record that has these songs on it: 'Itsy Bitsy Teenie Weenie Yellow Polka Dot Bikini'; 'Little Nash Rambler'; the 'Monster Mash'; and one that says, 'Makin' love under shady apple trees.' Rose wants to know what 'makin' love' means."

"Hmmm," George said.

"Do you know?"

"No," he said, shaking his head.

"Yeah, it's a mystery."

We walked past Dana's house. "This is where Dana lives. She's at camp right now. She has a Ping-Pong table and a very fancy pair of roller skates, and yellow curtains in her bedroom made out of sheets. Her picture got taken for the Mooreland Fair Princess contest and she's dead serious in it."

Back at our house, George asked what sorts of things I had. I only had two things I could show him. One was my little office in the corner of the living room. I'd been building it for weeks. The office had a table in it and a stool, and I had taken a big cardboard box and cut off one side of it, so it formed walls around the table.

I kept all my work in a cigar box. "I write up the bills like this right here, then I scoot them over to this side of the table and stamp them with this stamper. Then fold 'em. Then they go underneath the desk to get mailed, and when I pick them up on the other side they're all finished and go in this box."

"I see," said George. "What are they bills for?"

"Well, this one is for six hamburgers. This is for a tractor and disc. This one is for 'services rendered,' I don't know what that means. Mom told me to write it. This one's for a statue my sister stole out of my rightful possession. I'm charging her $4.72 for it. That's with tax."

"She'll never pay it," George said, shaking his head.

"Darn tootin' she'll pay it, or I'll contact the Law!"

"Did you hear that in a movie?"

"I guess so."

"What's this hanging on the walls of your office?" George asked, pointing to my messages. They were hung up with Scotch tape I stole from Mom.

"I wrote those out myself. That's my handwriting, there. My sister says it's shameful. That one is the birth-of-Jesus story that starts, 'For lo unto you this day a child is born in Bethlehem.' This here's a part of a Trixie Belden book, *The Red Trailer Mystery.* I'll read it to you:

> The girls ate hungrily and drank several tall glasses of the delicious spiced juice. They were so busy eating and listening to Mrs. Smith ramble on and on that they didn't notice how dark it had suddenly become as storm clouds scudded across the sky. "And to think," Mrs. Smith was saying, "I might have called in the police. Oh, dearie me, heaven be praised that I didn't. Nat would never have forgiven me. But he'll shoot that crow this very night or my name's not Mary Smith."

"What do you like so much about that?" George asked.

"Oh," I said. "There's plenty to like in there."

I went upstairs to get the only other interesting thing I owned. I had to fish it out from under my sister's bed, where I had hidden it. It was a puzzle in a can. My parents had gotten it for me in a fit of complete madness. I'll never know what they were thinking. The puzzle showed a dark street in a very old and exotic city, like London. The moon was high in the sky, and tearing down the street, running right toward me, was Dracula, and he was in a state. His cape was flying out behind him, he was furious about something, and there was blood running down his chin.

I held the puzzle can out in front of me so I couldn't see Dracula. George took it and shuddered.

"That's horrible," he said.

"I think so, too," I said, pushing it under the couch, "but it's about all I've got in the way of treasure. I've dug around in the backyard some, but I can't find anything. Dad let me use his metal detector out there, but all I found were bottle caps. I reckon my life is never gonna get any better."

"Hmmm," George said, thinking. "Looks to me like you've got it made. If you closed up your office, everything you owned you could carry on your back. I think that's the only way to live."

I studied him a minute. What he'd said sounded suspiciously like something my dad might have said. There was a lesson aspect to it I didn't like one bit.

"Yeah, well. If I had an orange backpack to put it in, maybe."

On George's last night with us we had my favorite meal: corn bread, tomatoes, and hot dogs, all cooked up together in the oven in a cast-iron skillet. Melinda came home and she and George got along fine. He told her a couple jokes that almost made my heart stop.

The next morning we all gathered on the porch to say goodbye to him. He shook my dad's hand and declared him a Good Man. He hugged Mom and made her a little teary. They had apparently had some conversations about the nature of College, which she would be starting in the fall, if, as she said, the Good Lord was willing and the creek didn't rise. Then he took my hand and asked if I'd walk him to the corner.

"Zip, it was a pleasure."

"Thanks," I said, scuffling my foot.

"I'm heading that direction. What's over there?"

I looked. "The cemetery. The highway."

"And then what? What's way past all that?"

What a vexer. "I don't know," I said, shrugging.

"Well, that's what you need to ask yourself."

I looked up at him. His clothes still looked clean, and his black hair was shining in the early sun the way Rose's did. That big mustache was something to see. He hitched up his pack and fastened a belt around his waist, then messed up my hair with his open palm, as if my hair needed more trouble.

"I thought of something you have no one else does," he said, walking backward away from me.

"What's that?" I yelled, even though he was still close.

"Your own hitchhiker," George said, then turned around and walked away.

A Member of the Wedding

I never could get what was the big deal about being pretty, it all seemed like a bunch of hokum to me. Who had time to think about such things, and who would bother? I knew girls who even had those life-sized decapitated Barbie heads, and they would very concentratedly paint Barbie's eyelids a shade of blue not seen on a human face since Mooreland's too brief acquaintance with a town slut (or as my mother called her, man-dependent). And Barbie's lips would get painted a cheap crayony pink, with lumps and streaks, and it was not many hours after Christmas morning that my toiletry-leaning friends discovered that no matter what one did with Barbie's hair it turned out creepy and couldn't be undone. Then there she sat, gathering dust on her cheerful, ruined face and chopped-up vinyl hair and I don't know why my friends didn't just get themselves a talking evil clown doll and be done with it.

But my sister was a different story. Rose said Lindy was the prettiest girl she'd ever seen, the prettiest of all their babysitters. I would have liked to say the same but I'd never had a babysitter in my life except Melinda herself, and generally our time together involved pinching (her) and being spun around in the rocking chair (me) until my eyes shook back and forth and I stumbled around the living room like a little drunk.

"Someday," my brother commented, after seeing me walk directly into a doorframe, "we're going to shake something permanently loose in there."

"That's the hope," Melinda replied.

Melinda was pretty without meaning to be and without trying. She just couldn't help it. Her hair was blue-black and her eyes were gray-green with long black lashes and she had the sweetest smile in the world. Never mind that she was made of pure Satan and that our family never had the money for clothes or makeup or Barbie skulls on which to practice. Melinda just was what she was, and the same went for me. (Actually, Melinda was what she was and I was not what I used to be, before she and my brother figured out that if they spun the rocker hard and fast enough, I *couldn't* get out because of centrifugal force. But I was making the best of what was left of me, which wasn't much.)

Both Dan and Melinda were in the marching band with the director who they called Mr. M. Mr. M. was in all ways the model of a band director, and by that I mean he could have led an assault on an innocent nation, enslaved its peoples, and had them marching in pinwheels, all in the course of one profoundly hot afternoon. Dan was a drummer—he marched with a snare, but could also play a kit—and Melinda played the clarinet. Dan had a genetic sense of rhythm (so did Dad, so did I) and marched in time as if his feet were machines. In this way the family was divided, as Mom could not keep time if there were a pistol held to the head of one of her beloveds, and Melinda was little better. Lindy couldn't play the clarinet and march at the same time at all, so she had to choose. Mr. M. helped her choose by smacking the backs of her thighs with his baton when she fell out of step, which meant that for the four years she was in marching band, she fingered the notes and pursed her lips and never made a sound. And still sometimes she got smacked. I tried to feel sorry for her but mostly I just wanted to steal her clarinet case. I didn't care about the instrument, but the purple velvet inside the case made me crazed with longing, as did the tiny music stand she could clip onto the clarinet. And also that yellow cleaning cloth, which was so soft I didn't understand why everything wasn't made of it. Mr. M. smacked Lindy for losing hers and later she smacked me.

In the fiefdom of Mr. M. there were many crimes. One could talk in class. One could fail to memorize a piece, forget new reeds, raise or lower one's music stand too quickly or too slowly. M. himself could play every instrument with such grace he might well have been Paul McCartney and shucked the rest of the Beatles. He was eight feet tall, incredibly handsome, charismatic, and unyielding. During the basketball season the band assembled in the bleachers in a tight rectangle, and no game was complete without its flawless rendition of the Vikings fight song and the various works Mr. M. used to somehow make Indiana high school basketball *even more exciting than it already was,* which was nearly unbearable.

During the summer marching season, Mr. M. stood atop a wooden platform some fifteen feet in the air at the end of the practice field, wearing aviator sunglasses and white shorts and shirts so bright he seemed a rogue planet, or an eclipse that threatened blindness. He blasted his whistle three times for the band to begin and begin they did, on time, in step, so mathematically perfect the lines of each section could have been connected by invisible electric threads. If he saw something that didn't satisfy him from the platform, he'd come down the scaffold twitching his conductor's baton, very often at my sister, who was marching along in the punishing heat, not making a sound with her clarinet.

"Did he LEAVE?" Melinda shouted, coming inside, the screen door slamming behind her.

I was lying on the couch in the dim den, watching *The Beverly Hillbillies.* One of my favorite games was to try to anticipate the dialogue and change it very subtly, so if Miss Hathaway said of her boss, Mr. Drysdale, "I don't know; he was here just a moment ago," I'd second-guess her and say, "I don't know; he was root beer just a moment ago."

"Did who leave?" I asked, not looking at her.

"YOUR FATHER. Did he leave without me?"

"I guess. He was root beer just a moment ago."

"I'm going to KILL HIM. He does this on purpose. Where's Mom?"

I shrugged.

"Oh God oh God oh God," Melinda said, pacing. "How am I gonna get there?"

"Where's Wayne?"

Lindy stopped; let her hands drop to her sides. "I don't want to talk about it."

I missed her boyfriend, Wayne Mullens, who had been around for a while. I missed him even though he called me Nuisance and sometimes Pesty. I wasn't sure he even knew my actual name. While Melinda and Wayne were dating, Dad used to make me sit on the porch swing between them so they couldn't hold hands. Dad also made me go on their dates. During the times I wasn't being forced to accompany them, I accompanied them because I wanted to.

All I knew was that one day Melinda had Wayne's class jacket and his gigantic ring and the next day items had been thrown, shouts shouted, and Wayne was gone to another city to do a temporary carpentry job. I didn't know for sure, but it seemed the shouts had concerned another girl, or rumors of another girl. Only one thing was for certain, which was you didn't want to get my sister that angry or else a class jacket would go airborne.

"I'm running down to Cheryl's to see if she'll take me," Melinda said, grabbing her clarinet case and her purse and flying out the door.

On television Granny said, "I've made some possum stew," which I frankly couldn't improve. Beverly Hills, wherever that was, looked like the grimmest, most unhappy place in the universe. I would have rather been in *Land of the Lost*.

Lindy ran to Cheryl's but Cheryl was gone, so she headed for the bank to see if anyone was in the parking lot and no one was. Just about that time a young man, someone not from Mooreland, walked out of the drugstore and headed for his car, a green Camaro with a spider painted on the hood. He looked a little seedy, Melinda would report later, or as if he were wearing *a seedy-person costume,* but was in fact as pure as a lamb.

"Hey, whoa!" Melinda said, running up to his car and opening the passenger door. "Where are you going?"

The boy froze. "To work."

"Great," Melinda said, climbing in the car. "I need a ride to Blue River right this very second and don't try any funny stuff; I've got at least two inches and forty pounds on you."

Rick, his name was. He just did as she told him, got in and drove her to band practice. Within a couple weeks he'd given up his nickname, Spider, and stopped hanging with borderline hoodlums, and the next thing I knew he was around our house all the time, quiet, hardworking, gum-chewing, as dependable as the sunrise. He didn't call me names or tease me in any way, and the fact that I accompanied him and my sister on every date seemed just fine with him. He was willing to take me everywhere, anywhere Melinda said, whatever Melinda wanted. Rick only had one facial expression and I believe if there were a recipe for it you'd mix undying devotion with fortitude and shock. My sister had been the biggest surprise of his life. He was shocked every time he saw her. I was very fond of him, but I still wondered where Wayne had gone.

Suddenly there was to be a wedding. I took this news as if someone had reported that vegetable pods had overcome the whole of humanity and I was the only thinking person left standing. My sister was to be *married*? She was seventeen years old. She was just a senior in high school, still getting stung by a band director's baton, still getting caught rolling a stolen wheely chair down one of Blue River's long, waxed hallways. We had just accompanied her to St. Louis, where she *walloped* all the other speakers because she was that good, and she would get better. That was *her* room at the top of the stairs and to the right, painted light blue, and even though I coveted it I hadn't meant to steal it. That was her corkboard, her long chain made of origami gum wrappers, her little statues of hugging naked people that declared "Love Is . . ." Those were her records, her bell-bottoms, her stuffed animals won at the Mooreland Fair by boys who could never get near her.

It all happened so fast: the creamy invitations with an embossed peace cross that read "Our Joy Will Be More Complete If" on the inside. Rose's mother, Joyce, who was the most frightfully talented woman since . . . well, ever, had offered to make Melinda's wedding dress and veil. Joyce was going to *make* them. She might as well have said she was going to make *gravity.*

Melinda asked if I would stand up with her. Her friend Cindy would be her maid of honor and I would be her bridesmaid. I nodded, of course, of course, I had no idea what it meant, what I was being asked to do, but Mom was making my dress: pink satin with a wine-velvet sash around the waist. I'd never wanted to be a maidenhead but for Melinda I'd even wear something pink and scratchy.

There was an announcement of the engagement in the *Courier-Times.* There were fittings at Joyce's house where we could see the lace and beads she'd sewn on by hand, the intricate cuffs of the sleeves. There were photographs taken in the dress ahead of the event by Jimmy Carnes, our local photography genius, and in all of them you can see Melinda's sweet smile, tears in her eyes.

At night I lay in my bed, clutching my Suzy Sleepyhead doll and sobbing. I wouldn't let Melinda know. I was terrified to let her know that if she left, if she really got married and moved out of the house, I would have nothing, I would have no one, I might as well be tossed in a river tied up in a sack, like a bag of kittens.

On the day of the wedding, June 23, Melinda just barely graduated from high school, I went limp as a rag doll and allowed myself to be manipulated. I was bathed, my hair was rolled up in curlers, I did as I was told. I moved and felt like a zombie, only without the flesh-eating joy that seems to drive zombies around neighborhoods like Jehovah's Witnesses. I kept passing Lindy's little alligator-green night case sitting on a chair by the front door; it made me feel like I was going to throw up. At one point I carried it outside and tried to hide it, as if that would stop the whole mess, but I knew the bag wasn't the issue so I brought it back inside.

We walked down to the church and got ready in the private place brides go, and Melinda was very shaky. "I don't want to do this," she kept saying, and no one would listen. It was nerves, Mom said, and Cindy told her all brides feel this way. But I could feel my heart beating in my face—I couldn't get near her enough to say "Then *don't,* you don't have to."

Charlie Kurz, a spirited friend of the family, was playing the organ for the ceremony. He'd also driven Melinda in his convertible MG when she was Mooreland Fair Queen, and had dressed in a Styrofoam hat with a red, white, and blue band for the parade. He had an impressive mustache and was not against a drink in the middle of the day. It was, perhaps, the case that he had tipped the bottle a bit before this particular event. We heard him play the songs Melinda had requested (*Is this the little girl I carried? Is this the little boy at play?*) and then something none of us recognized. It turned out to be a slow, waltzing version of "Hot Time in the Old Town Tonight." When Mom recognized it and stuck her head out, Charlie moved his mustache up and down and gave Mom the wink.

It was time, long before I was ready, to follow Cindy down the red aisle, each pew decorated with a pink bow. Everyone kept reminding me to walk slow, walk to the beat, until I felt like just going on a wild slapping spree—*I* was the one with rhythm, I wasn't going to speed up what already felt like death. And then just before I took my first step I heard Melinda meet Dad in the vestibule. She hooked her arm through his, that handsome, well-dressed Johnny Cash of a father and the young, gray-eyed girl, the prize of the county, if anyone was really paying attention (Rick was). It should have been a photograph for the ages. There should have been monuments built to the scene. But what I heard her say was "I don't want to do this, please, please don't make me do this," in a voice so shaky I nearly stumbled on the runner. Dad responded, "We've paid for this wedding; get moving."

Someone took a photograph of me just as I'd begun the descent, and it's clear I'm crying those brand-new tears, my face completely solemn and unmoving, just tear after tear streaming down my face. I, who had sat so stoically at the screening of *Bambi* my sister believed me to be a frog spawn of Hell. In the next picture: Melinda and Dad, Lindy still wearing that photographic smile, and it occurred to me later, looking at the album, that really she was smiling at Jimmy Carnes whom she loved dearly, trying to be as brave as possible for him. Not for Dad, who is so dignified as to seem presidential. Maybe he'd had a few with Charlie Kurz out in the parking lot. Drunk men always walk with greater care than the sober.

Beloved Pastor Eddy Cline asked, "Who gives this woman in marriage?" and my dad answered, his deep voice more glorious than the Mooreland Friends Meeting was accustomed to, "Her mother and I." He lifted Melinda's veil and kissed her tenderly, handing her over to Rick, this sweet stranger. I stood at the altar just behind Cindy, each of us clutching our single red rose. I stood frozen, listening to the sermon, the exchange of vows, the catch in Melinda's throat, and might have stood that way forever except that when Rick and Melinda went behind the altar to light the Unity Candle, Melinda turned her head too quickly and her veil caught fire. There is nothing quite like a bride aflame—it really puts a capper on an otherwise ordinary day. Rick, who had, as the sacrament would suggest, already become a husband, put the fire out with his bare hand, and it was only those of us up close who saw the near disaster and stood helpless to prevent it.

The reception in the Fellowship Room, which was really just indoor-outdoor carpeting and sliding plastic doors, was the usual fare. Folding chairs, long tables covered with white paper, streamers. There was the white cake with Crisco roses; the bowls of mixed nuts; the mints made of butter, sugar, and mint flavoring. My aunt Donna made them, and I loved those little leaf-shaped wonders. I had once eaten them until my gallbladder seized. There was no drinking at the reception, no dancing, no music, just the paper plates and people milling around, and then Rick and Melinda opened their wedding gifts and everyone oohed and aahed over the dish towels and crocheted pot holders. I sat in a folding chair in a most unladylike fashion, thinking only of the alligator overnight bag waiting by the front door at home. I felt like Trixie Belden or Nancy Drew, someone trapped in a mine shaft or about to be hit by a saw blade . . . what to do, what to do? How to prevent this honeymoon in Kentucky? How to prevent her from leaving? How to somehow iron out the spiky thing grown up between her and my father that was making her marry someone in the first place? And then it occurred to me: I would just *say no.* I would just say she could not leave, I wouldn't allow it, I was her sister and I had my rights.

It was dark by the time we got the church cleaned up, the coffee urn washed and put away, the floors swept, and the sliding plastic doors slid closed. Rick and Melinda stayed to the very end, stacking the folding chairs and placing them on the cart; this is what one did at a wedding at the Mooreland Friends Meeting. The night was gorgeous and fair on the short walk back to our house, and I held Melinda's hand all the way there. It wasn't until we were in the door that I said, "You can't go, you can't leave me, I can't let you go without me," and the look on her face must have been identical to my own, because she turned to Rick—her husband—and said, "I think we ought to take her with us." And he, whatever he had dreamed of or most fervently wished or even expected, just nodded and said, "Sure, Melinda, whatever you want." So I ran to the dirty clothes pile in my parents' bedroom and grabbed what I thought I would need and jumped in Rick's car and off we went, married now, to Kentucky.

Brother

When you have a brother so far away, you will take what you can get; you will steal memories, you will eavesdrop and sneak pictures out of boxes if that's what you have to do to get near him. I barely knew him. He was the great physical thing in the world, a wonder like Niagara Falls if Niagara Falls was your brother. So tall he ducked in doorways and sat slouched in cars; one of his ears had a bold horizontal scar from the time Doc Austerman wrecked his truck when Dan was working as a veterinary assistant. His arms were muscular, enormous; his hands were my father's made even more refined. He had one gold tooth, a cap, right in the front on the bottom, and it was the flaw that made him too handsome to take in—a pirate flash in a man of unqualified honor. Before basketball practice he ate cereal out of a giant mixing bowl, and peanut butter from a five-gallon bucket that came, somehow, from the government. On the court he was grace and rage personified; he shot free throws as if in prayer, and we attended every game. There was something between him and my father that flared up black as the fairy tale you don't repeat or record, but in the gymnasium Dad never took his eyes off his son and he cheered him with an openness we never saw anyplace else. There is even a photograph that appeared in Dan's senior yearbook: Dad is leaning forward, clapping, the look on his face one of joyous pride, and I am leaning over on Dad's leg, yawning. The caption was "Excitement for Dad Is Boring for Sister." My hair looks like it had been purchased at a rummage sale after all the real hair was gone.

Here are the things I remember, and they are mine: one Halloween as Melinda and I were walking home from trick-or-treating with Lindy's friend Cheryl, Danny came running down a dark alley toward us in a Dracula cape and we couldn't see his face until he was right up on us under a streetlight dimmed for the occasion, and all three of us, the grown girls and me, nearly died from heart attacks. It was, perhaps, the most frightened I have ever been, and yet as soon as I knew it was my brother he swept me up off the ground and carried me home on his shoulders. That night I lay in bed, stuffed with Reese's cups and surrounded by candy wrappers and I couldn't forget it; it had become a moment not of terror but of beauty so sharply honed it hurt me instead of scaring me. I wanted to see it again and again—his great silent stride, the cape flying out behind him, the split second when the three of us, stunned, recognized him and clutched our hearts and were grateful.

Girls called our house for him and Mother took messages because Danny wouldn't talk to them, he wouldn't date, he would not trifle. A beautiful blond girl pursued him for months, a girl who could have had anyone, and he stood his ground miles away from her because he was waiting for someone else and he hadn't met her yet.

He loved fossils; he loved fishing and hunting. He could shoot a bow and arrow and hit a running rabbit. His vision was flawless, he never let his hair touch his collar, he belonged to the Fellowship of Christian Athletes and he sang in a Christian group called the New Beginning. His voice was so fine he even made a record, a Christmas song about a giant tree that didn't want to be cut down but ended up in front of the White House.

His room was next to mine and it was gray and fossily and above his bed there hung an old framed picture of a wolf standing on a winter hill, howling. There is a valley below, and lights on in the small houses, smoke coming from the chimneys, but the wolf is alone. He slept in his bed, in a sleeping bag and under many blankets, all through the winter, no matter that there was no heat upstairs; the rest of us camped in the den around the coal stove but Dan stayed in his room.

At night I used to lie with my ear pressed against the wall so I could hear him sing. One night he put on a record and sang along with it; he played it many times until he understood how to sing it better than the recording. I slipped out of bed and lay down on the floor in front his door, my ear in the gap, holding my breath so he wouldn't know I was listening. On my little blue tape recorder I had captured hours of useless conversation and even hours of television, but if there were only thing I could go back and preserve it would be that night and his voice and that song.

He ran cross-country; he played practical jokes with his friends. One time my father hit him so hard Danny was knocked halfway across our street, and when he got up he didn't say anything or do anything, although by that time he was such a specimen of a man he could have killed Bob Jarvis. That moment was the measure of him, and he did not fail, depending on your point of view.

He referred to the crazy old woman across the street as "Ede," which drove her off her remaining three inches of cliff. He sometimes asked her on dates. Edythe *shook,* he made her so angry;

clearly he did not understand the rules, which were that he was to be afraid of her as I was afraid of her, and he was to keep a distance which she dictated and she owned. Danny didn't see things Edythe's way, and so he was forced one night to write on the street outside her house, in soap, *Ede! Will You Marry Me??* And then we got to sit on the front porch and watch her pour boiling water on his proposal and scrub at it with the broom she had probably just climbed off of after a trip to the bank.

Like my father, he was a natural driver of anything, any vehicle, and like Dad he was not averse to driving angry. He flexed his jaw muscles almost all the time and could not be made to converse if he chose not to, but with his friends he loved to tell a story and he laughed and laughed. There was never a time he didn't love Jesus; there was never a period in his life when he was faithless, and as he grew up he became more and more devout, and more hurried in his desire to leave home, which he did.

He joined the National Guard and there was boot camp at Fort Polk, Louisiana. He wrote letters home and included a picture of himself on his bunk in a white T-shirt, a sweet smile on his face we rarely saw, and then he came home. He had become a man meant to wear a uniform. Uniforms were only concepts until the first time Dan Jarvis wore one and then the universe stepped back and said *Ah, so that's who they were for.*

He found a girl so pure she could have been made from Ivory Soap. When I first met her she seemed only barely older than I, she was so petite and shy, and she had the delicate facial features of a cat: blue, almond-slanted eyes, high cheekbones, a small nose, long black hair. My sister said she was a size "aught," and maybe her dresses were even in the negatives. Elaine. I met her and thought she must have been floating around in a purity bubble all seventeen of her years, nothing mean or crude touching her, but it turned out she was stubborn in her goodness and that's how she had kept it. She was so tender to me and her hands were so small;

when Dan gave her his letter jacket she looked like a child adrift in giant's clothes. Where Elaine was concerned, quiet as she was amid our family of scalawags and jesters, there was nothing not to love, and Dan married her as fast as he could. The high school girls, the lovely blondes with money and lake houses, disappeared like dandelion fluff.

He and Elaine gave us our first new baby, Jenny, and she too was breathtaking, and all of us had to acknowledge that there had been a certain amount of beauty, a pool available to our family, and Danny got nearly all of it, then gave it to his daughters, including Jessica, who came two years later. And none of us resented it, because you can't resent the sublime when you are lucky enough to see it, and it's pointless to resent a man you cannot reach or touch. He took his wife and little girls and moved away.

Here are memories I stole. He had a terrible temper and Mom asked Dr. Heilman the best way to deal with it. Dr. Heilman said, "If he throws a tantrum tell him you're going to take away his favorite thing until he calms down. Then give it back to him." Dan's favorite thing was his Davy Crockett coonskin cap, and one afternoon when he lost his temper Mom said, "Danny, I'm taking your cap away until you can behave yourself. When you're done acting this way, you can have it back." He looked her dead in the eye. He was three years old. He said, "I don't *ever* want it back." And she knew right then that she had snapped a little something in him entirely by accident, a part of him that must have been born fearing the way love unzips us and leaves us vulnerable to assault. He zipped that part up. Mom never took anything away from him again, but it wouldn't have mattered if she did.

She could not prevent him from sneaking outside and peeing on the street. When she asked him why he insisted on doing so, he said he didn't want to miss anything; he wanted to watch the cars go by.

He had a little red wagon in which he pulled around a tombstone. The tombstone remains a mystery, but he loved it. Then in winter he would silently leave the house in the morning, pull the wagon down to the elevator, and pick up scraps of coal to help us heat the house. Our father didn't help him, didn't stop him, didn't acknowledge it, and Dan performed this task without a word.

Later he did many things to save my father from shame, and even though those things might have made Dan feel ashamed himself, they too were done in silence. He was just a boy. My sister used to hide under her pillow and weep about the wagon and the disgrace; she couldn't bear it. Those are her memories but she has lent them to me.

They were one family and I was another, so late, an Afterthought. They had one set of parents and I had another; they had a decade already shot past and I missed it. But I loved him, loved him, a little girl is helpless against her love for a brother. I climbed on him, harassed him, begged him to carry me, take me with him wherever he was going. From a distance he seemed both cold and receding, a man whose most familiar feature was his back as he walked away as fast as he could. But there are pictures of him, many of them, holding me as a baby, standing with me as a little girl, and the eye of the camera sees what nearly everyone but Elaine missed: a tenderness so wounded it had grown ferocious and fixed as the evening star. Really, I barely knew him. When our family's darkest days arrived he could not be reached, he demanded to be left alone, he wanted no part of it, and for years I believed he hated us. I thought he had simply wandered into the wrong family in the first place, like a toddler at a strange picnic who grew into the handsomest of princes but remained bound by name and history to the peasants who had lured him with potato salad and a tricycle.

In truth, if there could be said to be one truth about my

brother, it is that he carried both a tombstone and scraps of coal in a little red wagon, and what that did to him and what it meant to him is written in a closed book in a library guarded by dragons. He sang like an angel, he was faithful to God and he waited honorably for the wife he believed God chose for him. He made two daughters who shone like mirrors in the direct sun; he blazed his path with a scythe and his broad shoulders, and he was who he *chose* to be, which is the hardest and bravest thing a man can do. He looked at us, his parents, his sisters, his whole crooked family, and he flexed his jaw muscles, packed up his truck, and drove away.

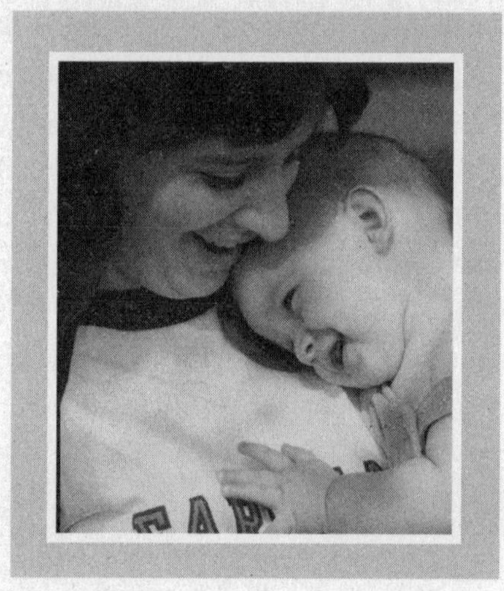

Church Camp

When Melinda found out she was pregnant she told me in the library of my elementary school, where she'd come to pick me up after school. I still remember what she was wearing: it was early March and she had on a pair of pale blue and black plaid pants with a pale blue mock turtleneck. Her hair was in a ponytail and she was wearing gray eye shadow. Lindy was friends with our school librarian, Mrs. M., who was married to the very handsome, tyrannical band director, Mr. M. Melinda had even bought a puppy from them, a parti-colored cocker spaniel named Callie. Calliopia. She was one of those precious cockers with eyes like a Walt Disney dog, not the other kind that bite children in the face for kicks.

Lindy told me, and she told Mrs. M. at the same time. Mrs. M. was a tall, gorgeous, elegant blond woman with perfectly straight hair and a perfectly straight nose and teeth; she had come from another planet, obviously, and had an aunt she called DaDa. Mrs. M. exclaimed, "That's so wonderful! Congratulations!" and touched Melinda's belly in a proprietary way. She asked the stream of questions that was bound to follow, "When are you due, do you want a boy or a girl, what did Rick do when you told him?" I just stood there in Juvenile Fiction, trying to get out of reading another book by local author Dorothy Hamilton. She was wonderful and I was very very happy we had an author in Indiana (they weren't thick on the ground in the Hoosier State), and I'd already read about a hundred of her novels. What I really wanted was something by Judy Blume, something not about freckles. I was aiming for the scoliosis book and praying Mrs. M. didn't see me sneak it off the shelf. Judy Blume was the personal savior of every girl in the Mooreland Elementary School and I swear if not for her none of us would have known the first thing about the first thing.

I had my hand on the book but I wasn't moving, because Mrs. M. and Lindy were chattering away and Melinda was pregnant. It wasn't as if it should have surprised me; she'd wanted a baby ever since she got married. She'd made a nursery in her little house right away, painting a big smiling yellow sun on the wall so it would be the first thing the baby saw in the morning. She had sewn white eyelet curtains, and even set up a crib. She had made a room so irresistible no baby floating in the heavens could resist it. And one had seen her, and flown down.

I was happy for her and slightly sick at the same time. There was the pregnancy situation, which was mysterious and a tad ghastly, and there was A New Thing where there had only been my sister and me before. She called us War Buddies. She said we shared the same memories of the Trenches. I had exactly one sister and so did she, a mathematical situation that seemed to suit us both fine. Yes, I was a Nuisance and Pesty but the preschooler Jesus knew I could keep a secret. Not without a price, but I could hold on to information anyway. There had been the time she was babysitting me and we decided to walk over to the trailer where Rick was living at the edge of the park (this is when they were dating), an entirely forbidden thing to do, and Melinda told me if I'd wait outside on the rickety wire steps and not tell Mom and Dad she'd buy me a new jump rope. I was a great jump-roper. I forced her to toss in a little doll I'd seen and we sealed the deal and not one word was uttered by me. I got the whole package, even though she wasn't in there but a couple minutes.

We left from school together and Melinda seemed very happy. "So," she said, "do you want a boy or a girl? A nephew or a niece?"

I shrugged, slipped the Judy Blume novel out from under my shirt where I'd stolen it. "I don't care."

"You're such a gigantic turd," Melinda said, looking away from me.

"*You* are."

Melinda was one of those pregnant women who don't complain and don't get weird and don't suffer the sort of psychosis that makes some mothers want to slice out their babies to save them from their own baby evil. She was relaxed and philosophical, and as time passed I became quite fixated on watching for the baby to turn or kick or hiccup, anything to suggest there was a person in there. It was gross, for sure, but also quite interesting.

Rick called us when Lindy went into labor and we drove to the hospital in New Castle without singing; everyone was nervous. All of Mom and Dad's children had been born in the same hospital. It was early December and bitterly cold; Dad drove with care on the snowy roads. In the waiting room my dad paced and smoked as if this were a Cary Grant film, and Mom worked on a sweater and made friends with other people passing through. I stared at the clock. Everything seemed really festive, like we'd all found ourselves in the middle of a natural disaster—trapped in a cabin in a blizzard, or riding out a tornado in a shelter.

If I had been asked, before Melinda had a baby, if I knew what love was, I would have said sure. I would have said I loved *The Beverly Hillbillies* and Glen Campbell. I loved Mountain Dew. I really really loved my bicycle and Julie's horse Angel, and other things involving transportation, like riding in the back of Dad's truck, or lifting up my shirt on a steaming hot day in my sister's new green Impala, then letting my back stick to the vinyl seat. Then peeeeel my skin off the seat and let the wind blow it. Then lean back and get sweaty again. Then peeeeeel.

There was even evidence I loved my parents, and I sure felt something for my sister, although sometimes it was a palm itching to hit her. Then the double doors leading to the delivery room opened, and Rick walked out with my nephew Josh in a blue blanket, and it turned out I'd been right about disaster, because that's what happened to me as soon as I looked at the baby's face. There's no other way to describe that sort of love. Even if I'd been warned, I'd have gotten it wrong, I wouldn't have understood. My passion for him was like a cartoon anvil falling on my cartoon head.

Mom and I were walking to church. I was thinking about Josh, about whether Melinda had dressed him warmly enough and whether he had taken up any new habits since I'd seen him the night before. Mom was saying, "And a special offering was taken up just to send you. The Meeting is paying for you to go."

"I'm sorry. Are you talking?"

"Yes. Church camp. The Meeting is paying for you to go."

"I don't care," I said, kicking a big rock and hurting my toe. "They can just get their money back, because I ain't going."

"Don't say ain't. Yes, you are going."

My mom had made me do some entirely objectionable things

in the past, things that made me spitting mad. I'd been forced to wear dresses, and take one bite of spinach, and wash my hair. But she'd never insisted on anything that scared me, until now.

We stopped on the corner of Charles and Jefferson, right at Reed and Mary Ball's house, and looked both ways. Nothing was coming.

"I cannot possibly go to church camp, and I won't go to church camp, and if you try to force me I'll go down to the woods at the edge of the park where you say there might be bad men and I will hop a freight train with them."

She took my hand as we crossed the street, out of habit. I pulled it away. "You'll love camp. There's a beautiful lake there, and cabins, and you can play games and sleep in the woods. You love all that stuff."

I stopped with my hand on the door to the Mooreland Friends Church. "No, I certainly do not. Not anymore. I can't abide any of those things you just named."

We walked inside quietly, and my eyes automatically scanned the pews for Melinda and her little family. Not so long ago I only wanted to sit with Andy Hicks and Laurie Lee. But everything had changed. I stepped over Onis Hatcher, a very fat old woman with a bright pink scalp, as if she wasn't there. Melinda was holding Josh against her shoulder. She dressed him like every day was picture day, and on this Sunday he was wearing a knitted white jumpsuit with a hood that made him look like a lamb. The hood even had ears. I felt something in my stomach, something like joy mixed up with blind panic. "Give him to me," I whispered, and Lindy handed him over. His neck smelled like baby lotion and his suit smelled like Dreft. He was so perfect he could have been a baby in a painting, or on the face of money. No way was Mother going to make me go spend a week (seven days!) with a bunch of strange Christians I didn't know and didn't in my whole life ever want to know. No way was she going to make me leave a helpless baby. Melinda was a great mom and all, she really understood the whole lamb-suit concept, but I felt, deep in my heart, that the only thing that stood between Josh and tragedy was my constant attention. He was five months old. He gurgled, blew a spit bubble, raised a little fist, and hit me in the collarbone. He loved me best; it was perfectly clear.

Not only did I have to go to church camp, I'd ended up getting placed in the teenager week, because my own age group was full. I wasn't sure the news could get worse. Maybe if Mom had said, "And oh, by the way, crazy Edythe from across the street will be there whistling and banging on an out-of-tune piano. And you'll be eating rabid boar and hominy," maybe then I would have been more scared. I'd seen some teenagers in my day, and it hadn't been pretty. The only person there I would know was an older Hicks boy, Robin, who was nice just like all the Hickses, and very nice to me, but I feared he might hold a secret grudge, because once when we were playing Hot Potato in the backyard I threw the Hot Potato with maybe just slightly too much enthusiasm and broke one of his front teeth in half. I'm talking about one of his big, front, permanent teeth. Broke it right in two. And neither he nor any of the other Hickses had ever acted like they were mad at me about it. It seemed to be just another accident.

The rules at church camp were simple enough. Girls had to wear a T-shirt over their bathing suits while swimming in the lake, even if the suit was a one-piece. Everyone had to bring a Bible. Days were devoted to activities; afternoons were Bible study; after dinner was chapel. Every night. Church every night. The boys' camp was divided from the girls' by a wide trail, called the Mason-Dixon Line, and by the counselors' cabins. Campers committing serious infractions would be asked to scrub the pier with a toothbrush, which didn't sound so pacifist to me and which Melinda had been forced to do when she herself was a camper. My family already had a *history* on that pier.

Three weeks later, early on a Saturday morning, I sat on the floor of the living room, packing and repacking my few belongings in my Army backpack. My sister had lent me her number one favorite T-shirt for modest swimming. It was white and had Mickey Mouse on the front (the older, skinny Mickey Mouse who still looked something like a rodent). I had my little pink New Testament, which I had no intention of opening. I had my nose plugs; a bottle of Chigarid; a bottle of Campho-Phenique; a small can of Off!; my cowboy pajamas; a couple changes of clothes; and a towel. Mom was going to make me take a toothbrush, even though there was no point. I thought I might burst into tears at any moment. I knew that just down the street Josh was waking up, smearing breakfast everywhere and making his new "oooooo" sound, wondering where his auntie was. He probably believed I'd taken up with some other, lesser child.

Mom came in and saw me sitting on the floor, bereft.

"I've got some things for you to take with you," she said, holding a stack of clothes and a thin white bag.

"What are those?" I asked, pointing to the clothes. They looked suspicious and degrading.

"Well, you have to wear a skirt to chapel every night, and—"

"WHAT?"

"And panty hose. It's a rule."

I fell straight back on the floor, bonking my head so hard I saw stars. "You hate me."

"Sit up. You know I don't hate you, I love you. Now. I borrowed these skirts and blouses, some of them might be a little big . . ."

I tried to make my heart speed up and kill me, the way rabbits could.

". . . so I've sent some safety pins. Just gather up the extra."

Down the street Melinda was saying, "Who's a good boy? Who's a perfect cereal eater?" And Josh was smacking his hands up and down on his high-chair tray, slinging squashy rice and bananas everywhere, gleefully.

"And *panty hose*?" I said, now very close to tears. "Have I done something?" I quickly corrected myself. "Something new, I mean?"

"The panty hose are also not going to fit, unfortunately," Mom said, tucking them in my backpack. "Just pull them all the way up and roll the tops down as best you can. And you'll need to take your saddle oxfords for church, not just your sandals. Oh"—Mom held out the white paper bag—"and here's the other thing."

"What is it," I asked, not even as a question.

"It's stationery. There are stamps on the envelopes already, so all you have to do is write to us and mail it. Do you know our address?"

I sighed. For heaven's sake, she acted as if I'd been in a terrible car accident. "Yes, jeez. Are you really going to make me do this?"

"Make you write letters?"

"No, make me go far away to this bad place! Are you really going to make me go?"

"Sweetheart," Mom began, sitting down on the edge of the couch. "This experience will be like lots of other things in life: you'll be reluctant at first, and then you'll discover you're having a wonderful time, and as the years go by you'll look back on it with great fondness."

"Does that mean you *are* going to make me go?"

Mom pulled out her big gun, as mottoes went, and she had a million. She generally saved it to the end. "Happiness is a decision. You decide how happy or unhappy you're going to be."

I stood up and grabbed my backpack by the strap. I marched out to the truck where Dad was sitting waiting for us. He had his arm out the window and a cup of coffee in his hands, as if he were already on the way. I climbed up on my box next to him.

"Ready to go, Zip?" he asked, starting the truck.

"Yes, but I've decided to be unhappy about it."

"Ah. Been talking to your mom, I guess."

Mom came out and got in the truck with us. "Okay, let's go!" she said, cheerfully. "Shall we sing on this trip?"

There were five girls in my cabin besides me, all of them between fifteen and seventeen. At first they thought I might make an excellent mascot. One said she had a little sister at home, and she'd be happy to teach me how to apply makeup. I made a vomit face, politely. Within about seven minutes, all the girls had realized I was not going to be the sort of little sister any of them had ever wanted, and took to ignoring me.

I lay on my upper bunk while the girls arrived one by one. There was nothing to do until lunchtime. I'd already looked at the allegedly beautiful lake (it was a lake; I'd seen plenty), and the pier I was undoubtedly going to have to scrub with a toothbrush (intimidating), the dining hall (institutional), the chapel (rustic, the end of the world). Lunchtime. Melinda would feed baby Josh and put him down for a nap in his little yellow nursery room with the sunny face painted on the wall. My stomach started to ache. What if she put him too close to his stuffed bear? What if she forgot to wind his mobile? *What if she set the house on fire again?*

I sat up on my bunk and put my head between my knees and took deep breaths. The girls were chattering with one another. It seemed they all had very dramatic problems that they took dead seriously. None of them mentioned babies or burning houses. Rich Girl's parents hadn't accompanied her to camp, they'd had her *flown* to some rinky-dink airport in she didn't even *know* what town and then driven here by a stranger who *smelled*. One girl had a boyfriend who hadn't called her since he'd gotten to his grandparents' house in Nevada, *and* she'd had to have surgery on her knees because she'd already worn them out with sports. This girl had taken to using something called dry shampoo while she was recovering in the hospital, and now she used it all the time. It came in a can like hair spray. Sports Girl bent over so her head was upside-down and demonstrated. Her long straight blond hair fell nearly to the floor. She sprayed her scalp with the aerosol, which looked a little powdery, then flipped her hair up and brushed it with the same sort of black-bristle brush my sister used. My sister, Melinda. It was summer, I reminded myself. She wouldn't be using the Franklin stove when the temperature was 88 degrees. The third girl felt herself to be under an inhuman amount of strain, because she played on her school's volleyball team, but was also in 4-H, and would probably be the valedictorian of her class. Valedictorian made vague reference to a boyfriend who pressured her. The other girls all nodded in agreement. The fourth girl was, even by my modest standards, so physically tragic she couldn't possibly know what boyfriend pressure felt like. She wasn't allowed to wear makeup, she said, and even I could see she desperately needed it. In fact, she probably needed surgery. She had almost no eyebrows and no eyelashes, so she appeared startled and desperate. Her hair was brown and frizzy; she had terrible acne, and her teeth were yellow. I watched the girls very subtly shift away from Ugly, acting at first as if she were one of them, as if they were interested in her, and then as if she were invisible.

And then the last girl entered, late and out of breath, all apologies. "Hi, I'm Claire," she said, but from the expressions of the other campers, Cher might as well have introduced herself. "I just got here, which bunk is left, oh—good, I'll just take that one. What a drive, I thought I'd never make it, I hate getting up in the morning. Hi, who are you?"

The girls presented themselves one by one, reminding Claire that they'd been at camp with her for the past three years.

"And who are you?" she asked, popping her head up over the top of my bunk and giving me what by all accounts was a winning smile.

"You can call me Zippy," I said, studying her. Her dark brown hair was shiny and like liquid, chin-length, and was pulled off her face with a rolled-up red bandanna. The effect made her look casual, even woodsy, and efficient. Her skin was flawless and tanned, and her eyes were the warmest chocolate color I'd ever seen. She had narrow, fine eyebrows; full lips; and teeth so straight they could have come from a Chrissy doll. The little red shirt and white shorts she wore made everything about Claire clear: she was fully baked.

"Well, hello, Zippy. I guess we're bunkmates."

"I reckon so."

Claire looked at the other campers, pointed back at me with her thumb. "She *reckons.*" They all laughed, not wholly at my expense.

Claire moved her suitcases over beside her bunk and flopped down dramatically. "Jesus H. Lord!" she said. "I've got cramps something *awful.*"

I leaned over my bunk to see what was wrong with her. Sometimes after riding my bike all day I got charley horses in my legs that made me light-headed.

The other girls in the cabin all fluttered around Claire like hens. "Poor you!"

"Do you need some aspirin?"

"Did you bring a heating pad?"

"Would you like me to bring your lunch back to you?"

Claire looked at Ugly with a wide-eyed vulnerability. "Would you? How sweet you all are! Lunch would be great, and aspirin if you've got it. Oh, and if they serve Coke with lunch bring me one but if it's milk forget it. Unless it's chocolate milk."

Ugly dashed over to her suitcase and ripped a page out of a diary with an orange sherbet-colored cover (which bore the title *All About Me*) and began writing with a little pencil. She took Claire's order as if we were all at Bill's diner in New Castle on fried chicken night. I watched the proceedings with a raised eyebrow.

"Oh," Claire said, remembering one more thing. "There'll be a boy at lunch named Scott, you can't miss him. He's got brown hair and he's tan and thin. And tall. He'll be wearing a jersey from Tri-High cross-country with the number 17 on the back. Just tell him I'm here."

After the other girls had left the cabin (whispering about Scott, whoever he was), I jumped down off my bunk and headed for the door.

"Hey, Zippy," Claire said. She was raised up on one elbow holding a book called *They'll Never Make a Movie Starring Me.*

"Yeah?"

"Remember me in your prayers at lunchtime," she said, smiling.

I looked at her bandanna; at the pink toenail polish. I noticed for the first time that she was wearing a little silver chain around her ankle. "Sure thing," I said. I didn't bother telling her that I wasn't much for praying, and even if I had been, I wouldn't have wasted my time on somebody who already had everything.

Lunch was soup and grilled cheese sandwiches and there was certainly no Coke to be had, which Claire would have known if she'd been any sort of Quaker. But I was beginning to understand that there was a world of difference between Quaker A (the Philadelphia sort, who spent the whole hour in silence and for whom no one was in charge) and Quaker B (our kind, who had ministers and Sunday school and loved to sing songs). This experience was potentially going to be Quaker C (more like the Pentecostals, where people actually got the Fruits of the Spirit and fell down slain). I sensed weeping and salvation in the air, two of my least favorite things. Before lunch we had prayed for a looooong time, longer than was respectable and something certainly prohibited by Paul's Letter to the Hebrews, where he says prayer should be private and silent. But who asked me.

I ate alone. I walked back to my cabin alone. The woods

around Quaker Haven were dense and hearing people talking but not being able to see them was festive, and I would have given anything not to be there. In the hours following lunch we were to read our Bibles (oh fattest of chances) and then meditate on what we'd read there. Instead I got out my stationery and wrote my first letter:

> Dear Mom listen. Josh likes to have TOO pugs not just one, he likes to keep the blue pug in one corner of his mouth and the pink one in the other corner this is his favrite way. It looks silly and funny and I think that's why he does it. Now I know it is warm in the days but the nights can still be chilly so tell Melinda to make sure she puts on his BLUE fuzzy jacket with the HOOD and to put the hood UP and TIE IT. Also she should attach BOTH pugs to the Donald Duck thingy because he is forever spitting them out. She will remember that time in kmart when we searched high and low for the blue pug and when we got home it was INSIDE the blue fuzzy jacket. Make sure she does not cook with grease with the flame to high and remind her it is flour not water that puts those fires out as she probably can recall anyway. I hate this place and want to come home it is mean that you made me come. How's Dad and all the animals? How are you, I miss you even though you did this very mean thing. Love. Xoxo

I was flat worn out from writing that letter and it sure seemed I would never write another. For good measure, and because some of the other girls were in the cabin, I flipped through my little pink New Testament, read some of my stolen Judy Blume book, then lay down and took a nap.

We did all the counselors had threatened: we canoed, we swam, we played tetherball. All was done with prayer and with the fervent hope Jesus would be present. Perhaps some built dams, I don't know. I did everything alone. Then it was time for chapel, and we went back to our cabins to change. This was apparently a very important moment in the lives of Rich Girl, Sport Girl, Valedictorian, Ugly, and Claire, because it meant they got to see one another relatively undressed as if there were a contest, which anyone just walking in the room for the very first time would see was no contest at all because Claire had won before she arrived. She put on a little blue skirt, the requisite panty hose, and a white sweater with her initials embroidered above one breast. She had showered after swimming and now her dark hair fell perfectly straight to her chin.

The blouse my mother sent had perhaps belonged to one of her friends at church, because the shoulders kept slipping off me. I knew safety-pinning was critical but where? How to safety-pin something to your shoulder? Then there was the plain brown skirt, so big I had to double the waist, and every time I put the pin in and fastened it, it just popped back open and stabbed me. I found that if I pinned it to the minimum amount of fabric it would stay closed, so I took my chances.

Then there were the panty hose. Claire's were so sheer and nudely they were just called Nude. Mine were a cross between a Band-Aid and Silly Putty, and Mom had been correct, they were queen size. I wrangled them on, rolled the top down, rolled it down again. It was never going to work, so I ended up putting my underwear on OVER the panty hose to keep them up, something an old woman in church used to do when her dementia really got up and going. I stuffed the oversize panty hose feet in my saddle oxfords and followed my cabin mates down the path to the chapel.

The minister was an emotional man who was deeply concerned about the temptations facing us as teenagers. I had not yet met a single temptation that hadn't worked to my advantage, so mostly I stared at him. We had to sing a lot of old-timey emotional songs about the blood of Jesus and the power of the Cross, and sure enough the minister got teary-eyed, and his wife, a woman who looked like a giant canary, was flat distraught. I could feel it—I could feel something building like a high-pressure system, and I did not like it.

"Margie," Minister Bob said to his bird wife, "play 'I Come' for us, slow and quiet, while I invite these boys and girls to join me at the altar for prayer and healing. This is what you've come here for, my friends, to invite the Lord Jesus into your heart permanently. I'm going to stand here with my eyes closed and let the power of the Lord work its way down through my body, and you just come on down to the altar and let the Lord fill you. If you're not ready, just kneel down and close your eyes and pray along with your brothers and sisters."

Kneel down? I looked at the floor of the chapel; it was rough boards with gaps between them wide enough to hold—and this was just in my line of sight—a bobby pin and two pennies. I was a Quaker, not a Kneeler. Rose knelt at St. Anne's but Catholics were prepared for this sort of thing and thoughtfully provided a little padded rail for the occasion.

"Just go ahead and get on your knees and ask the Lord what He would have you do," Minister Bob said, reading my mind. All around me obedient campers were struggling down to the floor, and Margie Canary was playing the same bits of the slow hymn over and over, trying to hypnotize us. I gave up and knelt, joined the people around me, cursing Minister Bob and my mother and indeed the whole of Christendom. I watched with the stink-eye as a number of people went to the altar and got hands laid on them. There was much weeping followed by joy, and I hated everyone there, and when I stood up, the knees had torn in my queen-size panty hose.

❦

We were supposed to learn to sail on the perfectly flat, windless lake, so I volunteered to clean the kitchen instead. During the Nature Walk I offered to straighten our cabin and take Claire's turn at latrine duty. I had no experience cleaning anything and I *volunteered*—such was the depth of my despondency. Every day I wrote home to Mom, letters more and more bitter and frantic, certain that Josh had forgotten me or that Melinda had shoved his little head through the bars of his crib by forgetting to tie down the bumper pad. "The bumper pad must be TIED SECURLY," I wrote, "even if it looks like it's on their fine TIE IT AGAIN." Josh was blond, blue-eyed, a perfect perfect American angel specimen of rightness. "You know he's got that little white hat that looks some like Gilligans, a sort of baby fishing hat. Now you should make sure Lindy puts that on him before going out in the sun or else the strawberry mark on his head will get even brighter and maybe sunburn, I very much hope you are not just throwing these letters away but giving them to Melinda who as you know HAS BEEN KNOW TO SET THE HOUSE A FIRE."

On the second night of chapel I wore the torn panty hose and believed it might shame me forever. All the other girls had brought more than one pair. I did not accept the altar call, and Mrs. Canary began to give me both the bird-eye and the beak. Claire developed such bad cramps from being religious that on the walk back to the cabin, Scott, who bore an unhealthy resemblance to Shawn Cassidy, was allowed to support her, even though it meant breaching the boy camper/girl camper line. Claire was crying and limping a little, and I noticed a small gold cross on a delicate gold chain against her throat. Scott held her tenderly, and back in the cabin all the other girls ministered to her and she was grateful. A Coke even appeared, as if Jesus himself had sent her a gift.

⁂

On the third day I asked to use the office telephone, explaining that my family was prone to emergency appendectomies (true) and I believed it was my time. Mom answered the phone and I said, "Well, now I've gone and gotten really sick and it's time for my appendix to come out."

"Is that right," she said. I heard her turn the page of a book.

"Yes. I don't believe I need to remind you that Danny's *burst* on the *operating table* and had to be removed with a *spoon,* and if you'd waited too long you'd be sonless."

"Tell me what your symptoms are," Mom asked, without inflection. My mother could not abide a sick person in any form, not fevers, burns, protruding bones, heaving, headaches, diabetes, or amputations. She had once been a Christian Scientist and it had gotten in her like a virus and even though she had been a Quaker since long before I was born, she still believed the Seven Beautiful Daughters of the Seven Beautiful Kings were Perfectly Healthy Within Us.

"I've got an ache in my side." That's what I remembered from when Julie had it.

"Where in your side." Again, this was not a question.

"Over, you know, between my ribs and the rest of me."

"Which side?"

Blast the woman! Blast her eyeballs! I only had a 50–50 chance and those were not good odds as any daughter of Bob Jarvis would know. I did the only thing I could: I guessed. "The left."

"I'll see you at the end of the week, sweetheart," she said, hanging up.

I would not sing Kum-Bye-Ya around the campfire. I would roast marshmallows but I would not sing. I would not play games of tag in the dark, where the boys and girls were allowed to hunt for one another, and find each other, in ways that made my veins run cold. The air was desperate, scented with blood. I snuck back into the mess hall and washed all the tables with bleach.

During the days we swam. Scott was a lifeguard and wore practically nothing, just trunks, sunglasses, and a whistle around his neck. He looked like he was preparing for a life as an anemic Erik Estrada. The T-shirt Claire wore over her string bikini somehow managed to be more revealing than the suit itself. Every day she would swim languidly out to the dock where Scott was sitting. She'd pull herself up slowly, water streaming off her as if she were a seal, then sit in the chair next to Scott where it was perfectly obvious no one else was allowed to sit. They would talk, and then something frisky would happen and wrestling would commence, and Claire would get thrown in the water, and the whole thing would begin again. I lay on an inner tube not far from the shore, floating around in circles in Melinda's Mickey Mouse T-shirt, watching.

I did not accept Jesus as my personal savior on Tuesday night, or Wednesday, or Thursday, or Friday. My panty hose were now in shreds. It was Friday night that Claire decided to go, having waited for most everyone else to take their moment up front with Minister Bob. It turned out that when Claire did open her heart it was a wide, wide avenue, because she sobbed and vowed to change all her secret ways, and Bob was so moved he kept his hands on her a long time, and Mrs. Canary bobbed her head so steadily it appeared she might go all the way down and take a drink of water. Nearly everyone wept that night. I stayed on my bruised, abraded knees and imagined the light in Josh's nursery first thing in the morning, the way he woke up babbling a happy baby language. Claire was so saved, as a matter of fact, that Scott had to walk her back to the cabin, only halfway there they took a turn and disappeared into the woods and I was the only one to see them go.

❦

At breakfast on Saturday morning, which would be our last full day and night at church camp, Mrs. Canary told me that I was the only camper who had not taken the walk to the altar. She had tears in her eyes as she said this, and told me that it was a great pain to Minister Bob and to all the staff but most especially to Jesus himself. Couldn't I just? she asked me. Couldn't I just put whatever was stopping me aside and accept eternal salvation? And if I couldn't, did I realize I wouldn't be able to attend the going-away sock hop that night? Because I could be an influence, she said, still on the verge of crying. I could be a dark influence on all the beautiful souls who had already said yes.

At chapel Saturday night the moment for the altar call came and I could not move. Because it was the last night, like the last night of a fair, everybody streamed past me, making my stubbornness even more apparent and perverse. There was loud praying and shouting; Claire, I think, came close to fainting, and there I stayed, on my knees. The safety pin in my skirt had come undone and was performing the appendectomy I didn't yet need. The old bird at the piano watched me with her one black eye, and I watched her back, and when we left the chapel that night everyone else headed to the dining hall for the sock hop and I headed back to the cabin.

I sat on the front stoop in my cutoff shorts, barefoot. My T-shirt and bathing suit and towel were hanging on the line in the moonlight, drying, and for some reason I found the sight very reassuring. No one was around; the crickets were noisy, and I could hear the music from the dance coming up the hill very clearly, but it wasn't for me and I didn't want it. I heard footsteps and feared an assault by a ministerial brigade, but it turned out just to be Robin Hicks, my neighbor. He said, "Hey, you."

I said, "Hey, Robin."

He smiled at me and there was that broken tooth—I had done that and he still liked me just fine. He was seventeen, and I was eleven. "I came up here to see if you'd like to dance."

The song that began was "If," by Bread, a song I already found so painfully beautiful I couldn't add it to my record collection at home. *If a face could launch a thousand ships, then where am I to go?* I stood up in the leaves and pine twigs, and took a step toward Robin. He very gently put one hand on my waist and one on my right shoulder, and we swayed so slowly I bet to the stars it looked like we weren't moving at all. When the song was over he kissed the top of my head and walked back down to the dance, and I went inside the cabin to pack. To go home.

Hairless Tails

Our three faces had seen better days. Rose was sitting in her backyard studiously avoiding bees or any reference to bees, because she had become convinced that she was allergic to them. She no longer walked barefoot because of the premeditated way bees hung about in the grass exactly where her foot might land. Her sting-allergy fear was unrelated (except perhaps at some very deep level) to the fact that the whole left side of her face was swollen and bruised, the result of a dog bite by a Saint Bernard at a family reunion. The dog, a grown male who had been unprovoked, had gone for her eye—her good eye, the one that didn't wander—and had missed by about a quarter of an inch. She was full-out traumatized, and I feared by the dejected way she was sitting that she might become afraid of anything with teeth, anything with stingers, and eventually, anything with seeds, like a woman in our church who was constantly pointing out the seeds in certain vegetables and fruits.

Three days earlier, Maggie, in an act of derring-do, had twisted the rings on the swing set until they were only about two inches long, then hung on them as they righted themselves. By the end she had looked like a little tornado. Her feet got out of control, and the momentum moved up her body, ending with her head, which smacked against the swing set at about the speed of sound. Remarkably, the soft part of her temple connected exactly with one of the swing set bolts, which entered her head as if it had been made of butter. She had required stitches, and now the side of her head was all a greeny-yellow bruise, and she refused to leave her bandage on, so the stitches were crawling across her temple like a black bug.

After bragging to great excess, and for many years, that I was immune to poison ivy, I had contracted a deadly case of poison sumac while camping the previous weekend. It was, apparently, a rare form of creeping rash, because it had begun in the bend of my elbow, had crawled all the way up my arm, my shoulder, and my neck, and was currently inflaming the left side of my face. I told all the white trash kids in town it was leprosy, which made them run inside to their fat mamas.

Rose was so deeply worried by her dog bite and Maggie's head injury that I didn't know what to suggest we do. My boredom and her quietness were both so acute that I started to feel spooked. Maggie was sitting on the swing, not really swinging, because her head insides were still wobbly.

Rose's house was bordered at the back and on one side by alleys; across the side alley sat an abandoned house. It was a good-looking house, as far as I was concerned, although it had occurred to me that I coveted nearly every house in town, and spent a fair amount of time imagining living in them. This one was large, wooden, and had a variety of shapes, like a house a witch would live in. At the back was an enclosed sitting porch that had floor-to-ceiling windows with so many small panes that they had probably been cleaned once in the past century, and then by someone conscripted, as atonement for acts of public indecency. The sitting porch was the only part of the house I had explored—the rest was too frightful even for someone as intrepid and with such low standards as myself. What stopped me in the living room, in addition to the general metric ton of detritus, was a pair of men's overalls, lying spread out in the doorway as if their occupant had simply vanished while crawling into the house. Something had eaten a hole clear through the bottom and into the crotch, and I was deeply afraid, not of the hole or the crotch but of the Something. The sitting porch, however, was about as civilized as some parts of my own house. There were some metal chairs still arranged, by accident, as if to accommodate a long conversation over lemonade. The floor was covered with broken Ball jars. Walking on them created a noise that was akin to a whole, dreadful lifetime of tooth grinding. I enjoyed it. There were some intact jars in there too, blue ones and green ones that had bubbles right in the glass, and old whiskey bottles. I considered telling my dad about them, but it was a private place, as far as such things went.

Sitting in Rose's yard that day, I could see her cat Snowball coming and going from the house, sometimes languorous and sometimes agitated. He went in through a broken basement window and came out through a hole in the back door. He sat on the porch licking one paw and rubbing his eyes with it like a sleepy baby; looked up at the sky as if he had just remembered the single most important event in his life, then turned his attention to his butt. I lost track of him for a few moments while looking at Rose, and then heard a scuffle coming from the basement. Snowball made furious hissing and screaming noises, followed by what sounded like a football being thrown against the door of a clothes dryer. Rose and Maggie and I ran out the gate and into the alley as quickly as our plagues and punctures and sutures would allow, just as Snowball emerged from the basement carrying in his mouth the broken body of a yellowish-white rat fully half his size.

The three of us skidded to a stop a few feet from the cat. Snowball was making a low moaning sound in his throat that was half pleasure and half revulsion. The rat hung upside down as if its bones had all just given up hope. Taking a few more steps toward us, Snowball dropped the rat in the gravel, inviting us to inspect it. We all squatted down around it, our hands tucked protectively against our legs.

I guessed it to be a male rat, by its general fierce hideousness. He was so menacing he could have been the leader of some outlaw rat posse. His front two teeth were yellowed and long and protruded down over his bottom lip like something prehistoric, and his claws were still engaged in a fighting position. I picked up a stick and turned him over on his belly, so that he was looking at us. Even in death, his eyes were grotesquely intelligent, and they continued to emit a kind of brightness that made my stomach clench. His long tail, a pink cable, lay stretched out behind him, the end of it curved in an imitation of grace.

I stood up, light-headed. Snowball had gone back to grooming himself. He was, obviously, a solid white cat, and very clean. I guessed he kept himself so beautiful in order to compensate for his deafness. Rose and Maggie continued to poke at the rat as I started home. The afternoon sun was blinding, and I felt like I either needed to eat or had gotten too full. There was no place I was fully safe. My whole life was infested.

I am sure the mice were always there and I wasn't aware of them, but as I grew older there were more and more, until finally my life was punctuated by encounters with them.

For instance, one afternoon I was walking through my parents' bedroom, on my way upstairs, and as I passed their bed I stepped on something, and the way the stepping on it felt made me lift my leg up slowly, without looking down, and remove my sock, and turn around and walk out of the bedroom as if I was sidling up to a trance state, and go call my sister on the phone.

"I've stepped on something," I said, clearing my throat to get all the words out.

"Good for you," Melinda said. I could hear her stirring her husband's lunch.

"I don't know what it was."

She stopped stirring. "Are you hurt?"

"I think you better send Rick over here."

It was my favorite pair of socks, too, white tube socks with a blue stripe between two bright yellow stripes. I considered them my dressy socks, and often wore them to church. They had grown very soft with wearing. I feared, rightly, that I would never see them again.

When Rick and Melinda arrived, I was sitting on the couch staring straight ahead, my hand still resting on the phone. I pointed to the scene of the disaster, and Rick went straight in and squatted down and lifted up my sock. Melinda was standing a few feet outside the doorway, close enough to gossip with but far enough away not to see.

"What is it?" she asked, leaning just slightly toward the mess.

"I don't know," Rick said slowly, "but it had an eyeball."

Melinda had a way of stifling a hoot that involved quick putting her hand over her mouth and letting it just come out of her nose like a sneeze. It made her eyes get really big like maybe her whole head was going to explode. Her method of unlaughing was actually worse than if she'd just let it come out.

I pulled my legs up and put my head down on my knees.

"Lindy, you'd better get me some kind of a bag," Rick said, "and a spoon."

I moaned out loud and Melinda had to turn her back to me to keep me from seeing the devilish transformations of glee her face was undergoing.

When she came out of the kitchen with a trash bag and a tablespoon, Lindy asked if I wanted to go sit on the porch, but I just stayed where I was. It couldn't possibly get any worse. I would carry with me forever the feeling of my weight coming down on my heel, and the something underneath it giving way, and the sound it made.

"What do you want me to do with this sock?" Rick called.

"Just, Rick, just"—Melinda waved her hands at him—"just put it in the bag."

She walked over to me and knelt down. "Let's take this other one off, sweetie," she said, peeling it off and tossing it in toward Rick.

"Those were my best socks," I said, from between my knees.

"Well, honey, they were there when you needed them."

We kept a fifty-pound bag of dog food on the back porch, and one evening my dad reached in with the dog's pan, and a rat ran up his arm. Dad threw the pan so hard it broke the light fixture above the door, and in trying to shake the rat off, spun himself around in a circle and smacked his face against the door frame. There wasn't just one rat, either, there were three, which I believe qualifies as a pod of rats, and the two who had not assaulted my dad became agitated and began to eat their way frantically through the waxy paper of the dog food bag. Dad took off running in the wrong direction, and ended up sprawled over the old wringer washer. All of this happened in just a few terrible seconds, and then he was back in the house, battered and wild-eyed.

The method of extermination my dad chose was to put out so much poison in the basement, where the dogs and cats couldn't get to it, that my mom feared it would seep into the ground and kill everyone in Mooreland. He had, apparently, discovered quite a nest down there, and he was having trouble sleeping at night for fear the rats would come up the basement stairs, use a credit card and unhook the latch on the basement door, creep into the den past the dogs and the cats, and climb into our beds and eat off our noses.

"A rat will eat off your *nose*?" I asked, horrified.

"They're especially fond of noses, as I understand it," he said, mixing some toxic rat cocktail that was filling up the whole downstairs with mustard gas.

"What is that you're mixing?"

"I don't know. I found it down at the hardware store. Roscoe said it's so deadly it was banned about thirty years ago. He had a case of it in the back room."

I picked up the papery gray box the powder had come in. Thirty years ago packaging was not so sophisticated, and the distributors had chosen as their brand name Poison. Under the name was a convincing skull and crossbones, and a warning label that stated the contents included arsenic, and that a potential ingestor stood absolutely no chance of survival.

"This ought to do the trick," I said, putting the box down and wiping my hands on my jeans.

The rat carcasses began piling up. At first we just put them in the barrel where we burned our trash, but on the first Wednesday we attempted a rat pyre, a bird flew too close to the smoke and died. We had to find an alternative plan. We couldn't really bury them, because of what it would have done to the grass. Mom was growing weary of the whole mess, and told Dad she didn't care where they ended up as long as their wretched bloatedness was out of the house and she didn't have to smell them anymore. We all had headaches, and my dad had developed a nervous jerk of the shoulders.

The only option left to us was the county dump, and Dad started driving them there. One day, however, he left for work without the day's allotment, and when I went outside for the first time I saw two plastic bags sitting on the front steps, the handles tied up tight. I knew if I left them there I would be deviled by them all day, the shapes in the bottom that were just barely discernible, and the fumes rising up out of them like heat off a highway. I was so reluctant to pick them up that my mouth began to water, as if I had to spit, but I grasped the knotted handles and headed for my bike. Just as I was climbing on, my sister pulled up in front of the house and said she was heading for Grant's department store, in New Castle, and wanted to know if I'd like to ride along. Grant's meant one thing and one thing only—a frozen cherry Coke, for which I would have compromised any principle—but I had my rats to worry about.

"I was just gonna ride these rats over and toss them in the gravel pit," I said, raising the bags enough that she could see them.

"Oh, for God's sake," she said. "Why didn't Dad take them?"

"He forgot, I reckon. Anyway, I can't just leave them sitting there all day."

"Well, come on. I'll go past the dump on the way."

I opened the passenger door of her big green Impala and started to get in.

"Don't even think you're bringing those rats inside the car with us," she said, shooing me back out.

"What . . . didn't you just tell me you'd drive me to the dump?"

"Yes, but you're not putting them up here."

"Well, unlock the trunk for me, then, and I'll put them back there."

She opened her door and started to get out, then thought better of it. "No. I don't want them in the trunk, either. I don't want them anywhere inside the car."

I thought maybe she was a little sensitive, because one time she and her friend Terri had set off on a big adventure to Muncie and halfway there the engine started to smoke, and when Melinda pulled over and opened the hood, the source of the smoke was Terri's cat, Poot, who was permanently affixed to the motor and a couple other hot places onto which he'd leaked.

I threw up my hands. "I give up. How do you suggest we all get to the dump, then?"

In the end we tied the two bags to the door handles, one on her side, one on mine. As we pulled away from my house I noticed Melinda was driving rather gingerly, but after a few miles she sped up, and by the time we got to the dump the bags were flying out beside the car like ears, sometimes twisting around and thumping against the doors.

The man who attended to the dump waved us over as we pulled in.

"Hey, Larry," Melinda said.

"Hey, Melinda. Got some rats there?"

She nodded.

"Your dad's been throwing them right over there. You can see there's a pretty big pile already."

I got out and untied the bags. Melinda sat motionless during the whole operation. I walked over to the edge of the big pit and looked around. The sights in the county dump could take my breath away. There were refrigerators and tires and broken toys, an old pie safe missing its doors, a kitchen chair, all manner of paper and debris. It looked like a shadow house, turned inside out, a life being lived invisibly. I arced my arm backward as if I were pitching a baseball, and threw the first bag of rats in, and as it was sailing, I threw in the second. They were bottom-heavy. They didn't go far, even though I'd thrown them as hard as I could.

Another thing every grown-up in my family was obsessed with was conserving heat, a very boring topic, quite clearly. Our house wasn't insulated, and so my parents were always scheming to keep heat in a room, or move heat around a room, or get heat from one room to another. It was a hopeless task.

Built, apparently, during the period of American history when human height often exceeded ten feet, and no one, ever, cared about conserving heat, our ceilings were twelve feet high. As soon as the trend arrived, in the seventies, of lowering ceilings with a flimsy metal frame and papery sheets of pressed fiberglass, my dad was all over it; he started in the den, where all of our heat began and ended.

When he was finished we were astonished to discover that finally, one single thing in our house looked normal, like the houses of other people. We had a uniform, white ceiling. My mom was so moved by it that she threw caution to the wind and invited her prayer cell over to our house for coffee one afternoon. I don't think any of the church women had been inside our house before.

By the time they arrived, the house was as respectable as we could make it. Rather than sitting in the living room, which was large and airy and managed to belie what was actually happening in the rest of the house, Mom chose to have everyone sit in the den, under the new, pristine ceiling. My job was to hover, offering more coffee or more sugar cubes.

Even straightened up, the den was shocking. There was almost no light; the furniture was old, unmatched, and beaten to a pulp; cats and dogs lay about coughing and scratching and attacking their dander. Most of the room was taken up with the black enamel coal stove. Beside it, in a strange alcove, stood a tall metal medicine cabinet that wouldn't fit in our one, tiny bathroom. The doors to the medicine cabinet had long since ceased to close, so from anyplace in the room one could see the stack of thin towels, boxes of sanitary napkins, and various sundries that took up the top shelf. The church women were kind and fond of my mother, but the situation was clearly worse than they had expected. One woman, Betty Hardaway, seemed especially disconcerted by the omnipresence of weapons: above one of the couches my dad's gun rack loomed, the rifles and shotguns polished to a deadly shine, boxes of ammunition stacked up on the bottom shelf. Hanging next to the gun rack was the bow and quiver of arrows Danny had left. Fishing rods and tackle boxes rested against the wall behind the television, and on Dad's little table next to his chair, where he kept his brown radio, his ashtray, and his glass for whiskey, was his jar of animal teeth.

At what probably would have been the midway point of the ordeal, the ceiling began to emit a strange sound. I froze, desperately trying to pinpoint the source of it, but my mom continued to talk as though she heard nothing unusual.

It was mice, and from the sound of it, about fifty of them. They were apparently being disgorged from one of the holes in the original ceiling that Dad hadn't bothered to patch when he hung the new one. It sounded as if they were all getting off a big mouse bus, happy and friendly and looking forward to their vacation. They skittered and dug around a moment in one corner of the room, and then took off running as a herd, right over our heads. When they reached the opposite corner, they turned and ran back. All of our cats leapt up on the backs of the furniture in agitation, staring at the ceiling and making growls deep in their throats. The dogs watched the cats, interested.

The sound of the little mouse claws running over the hollow ceiling was deafening. I looked at Mom, my mouth open in horror, and saw that the prayer cell women were all biting their lips and staring at their coffee cups. Mom continued to speak, seemingly unfazed, about her plans to lead a local boycott against the Nestlé corporation.

Soon enough, one of the women with leadership potential announced that the prayer cell was of one mind on the Nestlé issue, and that they ought to be going. My mom saw them to the door, and then came back in and began picking up the coffee cups and plates.

"Have you *ever*?!" I said, my arms raised in surrender.

"It sounded like they were playing football," Mom said, carrying dishes into the kitchen.

I flopped down on the couch, sending up a cloud of dust. "Do you think the church ladies will ever come back?"

"Oh, I don't think so."

I looked up at the ceiling where, it suddenly became clear to me, all of the heat in the room would go. The mice had come to a sauna, and there was no doubt in my mind that, as the months grew colder, they would tell every other mouse in the world. The whole flimsy structure trembled under their collective weight.

I grew phobic of mice, just as there were more and more of them to fear. My cat, PeeDink, who my father swore was retarded simply because of a combination of unfortunate physical characteristics, was a terrific mouser, and because of the crazy and abiding love we shared, he naturally wanted to give all of his dead mice to me. My parents walked in on many scenes of PeeDink chasing me around the house, me screaming and waving my arms in the air, the poor captured mouse kicking its hind legs, trying to free itself from PeeDink's jaws. Like most cats, he wasn't interested in flat-out killing vermin; he wanted to kill them just a little bit and then play some really fun games which involved the mice trying to get away while he killed them a little bit more. Once when my dad came home from work I was up on the back of the couch and PeeDink had left three dead mice on the floor for me. He had grown so fat on mice that he no longer showed any interest in eating them.

One summer night, after I had moved back upstairs to my bedroom, I awoke from a deep sleep and discovered that the absolute worst thing had happened. Mom was asleep in the bedroom at the bottom of the stairs, and without moving a muscle I began to call for her. She heard me, even over the deafening racket made by the fans running between every room.

When she reached my bed, after tripping and kicking her way through the wreckage on my bedroom floor, she asked me what was wrong, and I told her that there were twenty-seven dead mice on my bed. They were completely surrounding me, so that I couldn't move any part of my body without touching one. She stood up straight and looked me in the eye. I appeared wide awake and lucid, but was not.

"What should I do?" she asked.

"You need to pick them up and throw them away."

She looked around the room until she spotted my trash can. It was overflowing, so she just dumped it on the floor, then walked over to me and began picking up the mice.

"Count them, so I know you get every one."

"Here's one," she began. "I'm going to get these ones around your head first, so you can turn it. Here's two and three."

And in this way she removed all twenty-seven, picking them up by their phantom tails, the part of a mouse that unnerved me the most. When she was done she bent over and kissed me on the head and told me to go back to sleep.

"What are you going to do with them?" I asked, trying not to look right at the trash can.

"What do you want me to do with them?"

"I want you to make them gone."

She nodded. When I got up in the morning, they were gone.

By the following Christmas, Rose's face had healed perfectly from her encounter with the rogue and murderous Saint Bernard, and Maggie just had a little zigzaggy scar across her temple. I had completely forgotten about poison sumac, which left no trace of its devastation on my body.

I spent Christmas night with Rose and Maggie, and around midnight we were awakened by a crash and a strange glow. We ran over to the window and saw that right across the alley, directly across from where we stood, the abandoned house was on fire, and in a serious way. It was a beautiful fire, raging but not spreading, and the three of us stood there a long time in our nightgowns, not even thinking about getting Rose's parents or calling the volunteer fire department. It burned and burned. I knew that there had probably been many rats and mice living in that house, given how cold it was outside. I remembered a time when the death of them would have caused me pain, when I would have considered their suffering, but I couldn't feel it anymore. All I felt was that warm shot of relief, the kind that comes with breathing when you've held your breath too long, as the windows of the kitchen blew out and, somewhere in the distance, a siren began to wail.

A Short List of Records My Father Threatened to Break Over My Head If I Played Them One More Time

1. **"50 Ways to Leave Your Lover,"** by Paul Simon. You need only listen to this song once to realize it is the greatest work of genius since **"Beep Beep (The Little Nash Rambler),"** by the Playmates. Also, it provides a person with the bonus of rewriting the chorus 700 times a day. For instance, a girl might say, "I'm ridin' my bike, Mike," or "I'm goin' to my sister's, mister." She could also string together many such sentences, as in, "I'm feelin' sad, Dad. Maybe you could get me some candy, Randy. Don't be such a slob, Bob, just listen to me." If the Dad ever actually held the record in his hands in a threatening way, he could be told that the emergency backup Paul Simon song was **"Me and Julio Down by the Schoolyard,"** which for some reason was even more objectionable.

2. **"Beep Beep (The Little Nash Rambler),"** by the Playmates. A morality tale about a little car, a Cadillac, and a transmission problem. This song brilliantly gains momentum, and is sung faster and faster right up to the hysterical ending. Could be sung in the truck so frantically the father in question would sometimes have to stick his head out his open window while praying aloud.

3. **"Someone Saved My Life Tonight,"** by Elton John. I understood only one line of this song: "And butterflies are free to fly, fly away." The rest was completely lost on me. I assumed the British did not speak English, which was a puzzle as they were sometimes referred to as the English. Not understanding the lyrics required me to listen to the song hundreds, perhaps thousands of times, filling in with nonsense words, which my sister said made me look oxygen deprived and sad.

4. **"Somewhere They Can't Find Me,"** by Simon & Garfunkel. In addition to **"50 Ways to Leave Your Lover,"** this was probably my most obvious theme song. It could have been written for me. The singer has done something terrible and now his only option is to sneak away: "Before they come to get me I'll be gone, somewhere they can't find me." Oh indeed. How very very true.

5. **"He Ain't Heavy, He's My Brother,"** by the Osmonds, featuring Donny Osmond. A lie, as anyone who knew my brother could attest. But if it was sung by Donny Osmond I could try to believe. I wanted to believe. This was a favorite to play not at top volume in my bedroom, but downstairs on the stereo that was shaped, improbably, like a Colonial desk. I liked to sing along with Donny (we had the same voice) while simultaneously pretending to draft a version of the Bill of Rights, using a fake quill pen. (In truth, a turkey feather.) This was a combination of activities my father found interesting, blasphemous, and wrong.

6. **"Along Comes Mary,"** by the Association. A wordy song. A wordy, psychedelic song, the meaning of which has never been determined by humans. Tailor-made for me. From the beginning, the song is just one long puzzle. "Every time I think that I'm the only one who's lonely someone calls on me." Who? (Mary, my sister would explain, through clenched teeth. Yes, but Mary who?) What follows is so unusual it doesn't bear repeating, although I most assuredly could.

7. **"I Started a Joke,"** by the Bee Gees. Again, a world-class head-scratcher. He started a joke, and it started the whole world crying. I sensed astonishing depth in the Bee Gees' lyrics, and also were they all boys? Including the one with the Bugs Bunny teeth? Was she truly never funny and that's why the world wept? I knew people like that. Later in the song one of them, a Bee or a Gee, begins to cry and that gets the whole world laughing, so everything turns out fine in the end. (An additional work of genius is "The Lights Went Out in Massachusetts." Massachusetts: A state? A prison? Dad was silent on the issue.)

8. **"Swamp Girl,"** by Frankie Laine. One of the great pieces of poetry in the civilized world, and flat-out terrifying. Frankie Laine is sick, or tired, or both, and a bad woman (the kind with narrow eyes, I'm guessing) is calling him from the yuck of a swamp where she lives. "Where the water's black as the Devil's track—that's where my Swamp Girl dwells." How simple it was to secretly change the lyric to "where the water's black as the Devil's crack," never ever letting anyone hear me do it because this is a dead serious song and also one doesn't rhyme lightly about the Devil. Particularly where there's a Swamp Girl involved, her hair floating on the water. Frankie Laine was famous for other songs about rawhide or jerky or wagon trains, something like that, and all along his masterpiece was known only to me and my family. A shame.

9. **"The Night the Lights Went Out in Georgia,"** by Vicki Lawrence. Woe to the person who believed Vicki Lawrence was merely Carol Burnett's separated-at-birth twin and game sidekick! No! She also performed this stunner, a song about . . . wait. Bad things in a bad place. The night "they" hung an innocent man, and not trusting your soul to some hmmm hmmm something lawyer. Wherever all this happened, someplace in Georgia, was about as ugly as it gets. People had blood all over them and essentially no one was to be trusted, which made for a chorus I could sing *for days.*

10. ***The Best of Ed Ames,*** by Ed Ames. A member of the Ames brothers, Ed also played Daniel Boone's faithful Indian companion on television. This was because, I was quite certain, he was a real live Indian. My mother insisted he was Lebanese, whatever that meant, as if a Lebanese would look that good in Indian clothes and as if his name wasn't Ames, as in "aims a bow and arrow like a real live Indian." In truth, Ed Ames was more shockingly handsome than any man I'd loved before him, including Glen Campbell and my brother's friend Joe Overton. Ed was in a different category of attractive, I was discovering. He also had a voice that defied description; it was big and deep and pure, all those things, but it was also sad in some songs—heartbroken—and angry in others. He sang the way men would talk about things if they ever talked about things. ***The Best of*** was primarily show tunes and new songs that were flat philosophical, like "Windmills of Your Mind" and "Who Will Answer? (Aleluya No. 1)." What was this about? Who put a "No." in a song title? It was the unmatched wonder of Ed Ames to combine such groundbreaking effects with songs that moved my mother to tears, and made me imagine life on the frontier, where buckskin stayed so *clean.* I was willing to share the record with my mom, as a matter of fact, right up until she heard me re-

peating a phrase from "Who Will Answer"—"in our stars or in ourselves"—and she needlessly told me that Shakespeare wrote those words. I waved her off and from that point on Ed stayed in my bedroom where he belonged.

A Short List of Records That Vanished from My Collection

❦

"50 Ways to Leave Your Lover," by Paul Simon

"Me and Julio Down by the Schoolyard," ditto

"Beep Beep (The Little Nash Rambler)," by the Playmates

"Someone Saved My Life Tonight," by Elton John, also "Don't Let the Sun Go Down on Me," probably for good measure

All Simon & Garfunkel records

The Association's Greatest Hits, but it just went to my sister's house because I'd stolen it from her earlier and she'd stolen it back

Ditto with all the Bee Gees records

"The Night the Lights Went Out in Georgia," by Vicki Lawrence, met a particularly ghastly fate in our trash barrel. I eventually found only the charred label.

I was left with Frankie Laine and Ed Ames, who were hidden in my closet. Life might have taken a vicious turn here, but my brother-in-law Rick gave me his old eight-track tape player, along with two John Denver tapes. John Denver became the only good-hearted naturalist my father ever threatened with a lynching.

Bull

I didn't know why everyone was always going on so about shoes shoes shoes—what was the point when we had been given perfectly adequate feet for getting around on? Same with hairbrushes and toothbrushes and washcloths. Absolutely no use. But I reached the conclusion that I'd lost a fight and was going to keep on losing it, so I might as well decide on what kind of meanness was going to get put on my feet. I chose the dignified saddle oxford, white and black with the liver-colored sole. I don't know the reason for this choice, particularly as the soles were slick as snot and I could often be found sailing down the highly waxed stairs of my elementary school, clinging to the handrail and hoping for something other than another head injury upon landing.

I have no memory of shopping for the saddle oxfords; they simply appeared year after year, and never new. They had come from some other person's feet, the soles worn down to a glassy smoothness. My mom would hand them over and I'd utter minor addresses to the infant Jesus who as far as I could tell had done nothing so far but forsake me, and then I'd put the blasted things on.

They were supposed to be saved for school and generally I did that, because if I wasn't in school and I wasn't in church I had no need for footwear anyway, but on one great Saturday late in the summer Debbie Newman was leaving the Marathon station and she said grab some shoes and hop in and come on home with me and those were the shoes I grabbed. I also pulled a pair of white bobby socks out of the laundry pile in my parents' bedroom, a pile in a shape I later recognized in *Close Encounters of the Third Kind*. If aliens had come to Mooreland they would have landed on that laundry mountain, and what a shock for them. The socks didn't match and they weren't the same shade of "white," but they were generally shaped the same and who cared anyway.

The Newmans always had a nice car, a big boaty silver car with maroon interior, and even though their cars were nice and newer than anything we drove they still smelled flat like the barnyard and sometimes bits of straw waggled in the air vents. In fact, corn dust and fertilizer and manure covered the dashboard and the windows, and once in a while there'd be a trace of anhydrous that I found pleasing. Not as delicious as leaded gasoline, but close. I wasn't singing on the ride out to the Newmans', or even making any sound, as my talking drove Debbie to distraction and she would often have to tell me so in ways that were directly to the point. Julie was in the backseat beside me in her jeans and cowboy boots and a white T-shirt with a big red Viking head on it. That was the thing about Julie; she always looked exactly right for whatever she was doing, whereas I always looked like I'd walked through the wrong door into a story that had nothing to do with me. I believe I was wearing shorts with my unmatched bobby socks and used saddle oxfords, and some inappropriate upper-wear, like a discarded short-sleeved dress shirt belonging to my father.

"What are we gonna do today?" I asked Julie.

She shrugged. That could mean a lot of things. It could mean she had 62,000 chores and I was going to help with every one. It could mean we were going to ride horses or else take her new moped out around the countryside. It could mean her bedroom needed painting and if I didn't work fast enough she'd give the raised middle-finger punch on the upper arm that left a bruise for days. Or her shrug could mean nothing. It could mean she didn't know and since we were only going to the best place on the Earth, where every single minute of every day was different and filled with promise, what the heck difference did it make what we were gonna do.

We looked at some kittens that got born in the pole barn. They were way little and their eyes were still glued shut. The mama cat hovered around hissing at us—she was feral and would never tame. We shot a little pool on the bumper pool table in the dining room and Julie beat me so hard so many times I put my stick down and told her she was cheating. She ignored this. Julie never cheated. We went out to ride the good horse, Angel, but she had a cut on her foreleg and Big Dave said no. We thought about sneaking off on Mingo, the horse in league with the Devil, but decided against it. Pretty soon we were climbing over the barbed-wire fence and out into the rolling land across the road that wasn't farmable, wasn't quite grazable except up by the road. It wasn't worth much but beauty. There was a steep walk down to a stream, and on horseback the horses would have to walk with small, careful steps as we leaned completely back, almost lying down to accommodate the angle. There was maybe thirty acres over there—the grazing land for some cows, the valley and stream, and the rise up to a stretch of woods where a few times we'd seen a great horned owl.

We rode that land all summer, me behind Julie on Angel's wide back. We rode without speaking. I often got thwacked by branches that missed Julie altogether. Julie could set Angel up to a canter that seemed to work fine for Julie but shook all my internal organs loose until I was googly-eyed and begging for mercy, but not very loudly as my lungs had collapsed. Only a month before our current stroll we'd taken Angel around on a slow walk, leading her to the old pump at the edge of the field. We meant to pump water for her, but instead we found a dead cat there. She was a black and gray tabby cat, as pretty as could be, lying on her side with her one green eye staring at the sky. Angel stopped. Julie and I froze. I said, "Is this one of our cats?" Julie said, "Nope. But she could have been." And Angel wouldn't drink from the pump so we rode on.

Today we were just on our own feet and it was hot outside. We passed the cows, stopped to look at some calves, then headed down toward the creek. We knelt at the edge, looking for crawdaddies or snakes or anything really, but it was hot enough outside that all living creatures had departed for shadier places. We crossed the creek on rocks, a leap to the left, the left, the right, the opposite bank, and climbed the hill up toward the stretch of forest. We weren't saying much, weren't heading anywhere directly, when both of us heard the same noise and froze.

"What was that?" I said, looking around.

"Shhhh."

The sound came again and it turned out to be two sounds—a small, lowing cry from one direction, and a deep, bass-note exhalation through what sounded like bovine nostrils. On one side of us, Julie figured out, was a calf, maybe only a day or two old, and on the other was the mama. Sure enough, here came the mama cow pawing at the ground and moving with a swift assurance that cows are typically not permitted.

"Get up that tree!" Julie said, not quite yelling as that wasn't her way.

I ran behind her to a gnarled old something, I never bothered finding out the names of trees as what difference did it make, and watched her take the trunk in a single gesture. I don't know how she did such things; it wasn't as if she had tentacles or suction cups, she was just a red-haired human girl but nothing had any *force* over her. She was up the tree and out on a fat horizontal branch while I was still holding on to two little branches, my butt out in the air where the cow could eat it, my saddle oxfords sliding down the trunk like they'd been dipped in baby oil.

"Ummm," I said, pulling myself up, slipping down.

"Good Lord," Julie said, laying herself flat down on the branch and reaching for my hands. She somehow managed to pull me up beside her just as the cow, which I could now see was the size of a mobile home, hit the tree trunk with her flank—she was that mad. Plus her eyes were rolling around in the way that gave rise to the term "Wild-eyed Cow," a look my dad sometimes got.

"That is a *bull,*" I said.

"Psshh."

"I'm telling you that is no cow, Julie Newman." Whatever it was continued to stare at us and snort out great blasts of fury through its nose, while the baby continued bleating away somewhere beyond the tree line.

"You saw the bull behind the fence with your own eyes, Dumb." Julie scanned the area behind us, looking for the baby.

"A fine thing, letting a bull just run around loose like this, fixing to kill some children."

"Hush up."

Hours passed. Oh, hours and hours. The bull stared at us and chuffed and pawed at the ground and made a terrible sad sound about his baby, but wouldn't move. Then the baby would cry out and the whole thing was nearly tragic.

"My butt is about broke, and I've got bark all up in my shorts," I said, throwing a piece of twig down onto the bull's back.

"Hush up, I said."

The baby crashed around in the woods and the cow stopped giving us the murderous hairy eyeball for just a minute.

"Do you see it?" I whispered.

"I might see it if you ever stopped talking."

The baby came a little closer, making a sound that was so like "ma ma" it made a person wonder about how nature was really organized. The cow pawed at the ground and ran toward an old stretch of fence, only about six feet long and mostly lying flat. Calves aren't very bright, as it turns out, because this one had thought itself trapped behind the broken fence the entire eighteen hours Julie and I had been stuck in the tree.

Mother/father and baby were reunited with great licks of their gigantic tongues. "I'm gonna jump," Julie whispered, "and you follow me. Then we're gonna have to run, Jarvis, you hear me?"

"We can't jump! We're like a hundred feet in the air! Our ankles would turn to sausage!"

"Hush up," Julie said, leaping to the ground, her red hair fanning out behind her like a cape. And just like that, the bull decided the Girl Threat was still imminent, and came charging, so Julie just reversed course and was back up beside me before I'd ever seen her land.

"Oh! Oh, this is rich!" I said, waving at the beautiful weather, the stream fifty yards away, the clouds of mosquitoes all around us. "When do you reckon they'll find us up here, huh? When it's time to *slaughter* that calf? After it's made the rounds at the 4-H Fair?"

Julie gave me the look, so I turned my back to her.

"Plus I am starved out of my mind."

"You're out of your mind, all right."

"AND I have wasted a whole day I could have been doing something else."

Julie said nothing.

"I could have been, I don't even know what."

Silence.

"Your mom made me put on *shoes* for this and I am covered, I am outright covered I tell you with mosquito bites and I don't know what-all. This horsefly has landed on me twenty times now and horseflies have *teeth,* Julie Ann."

The big cow and the little cow were now happily resting under our tree, the baby nursing, the mama grazing and periodically looking off across the pasture as if in appreciation of its beauty, just before she looked back at us as if she had rabies.

"And what happens when . . ."

Julie punched me in the arm. "You stop talking."

Now I knew I was doomed. Julie had no ideas and the sun was going down. I'd gotten the knuckle-punch and my thighs were rubbed near bloody from the rough bark of whatever tree it was we were in. We could have yelled and yelled and no one would have heard us; there was too much land and too many animals between us and the Newmans' house. There wasn't just the cow lot near the road, there were pigs, and two secrets about pigs is that they never stop wagging their tails and they never, ever shut up. There's some noise coming out of those things around the clock. I was trying to imagine one, even one single option when Julie said, "There's David Lee."

Now if this whole event had happened at my house and my sister had eventually come looking for me, it would have gone like this: she would have stopped about fifty yards away and yelled, "What are you doing up there, big stupid?" And I'd have had to yell back, "I'm trapped up here in this tree by a bull down below! A bull and its baby! It's the biggest thing I've ever seen and mean as hell!" And Melinda would have said, "I'm telling Mom you said 'hell.'" Then maybe she would have saved my life or maybe she'd have let me stew for a little while longer. But at the Newmans', this was the course of action: David Lee came up the hill from the stream. He saw the cow and the calf. He saw Julie's white shirt and red hair up in the big branch. He took off his seed cap and his own white T-shirt and waved it in the air, yelling, "Whoo! Whoo-ee Mama!" which caused the bull to turn and look at him for about a split second before deciding David Lee needed killing. The instant the bull ran, Julie not only jumped, she pulled me down with her and I landed in such a way that both my ankles felt like someone had rammed lit sparklers in my shoes.

David Lee ran, zigging and zagging down the hill, yelling, and the bull followed him. Julie and I ran straight down, right through the creek, up the hill. Twice the cow decided it hated us more than David Lee and changed direction, and then David would have to wave his shirt even harder and yell even louder. We ran past the old pump, and rather than toward the cow lot, we went toward the pigs, which were surrounded by a wood fence, no barbed wire.

"Jump that fence," Julie said, not even winded.

"Oh Lord," I said, my lungs aflame. But I jumped it, and landed in two feet of mucky goo, Indiana's quicksand. Julie pulled her cowboy boots up and out with a squelching sound I wouldn't soon forget, and kept going. There was no way she was going to leave her brother out in the hinterlands with Babe the Ox chasing him. She climbed the fence at the road's edge and I did the same. We landed in the grass and something felt funny. I looked down and I had neither shoe nor sock on either foot.

"Huh," I said, looking back. And there they were, stuck like bones in a tar pit, sinking. A pig walked over and picked up one of the socks, carried it away like a to-go order.

We ran to the mudroom door, where Debbie was hoisting a saddle onto a sawhorse. "Where have you been?" she yelled. "Where's your doggone brother? You wash those feet off, Jarvis, before you come in my house, and then Julie Ann there are potatoes that don't know how to peel themselves."

David Lee ran up behind us, his shirt back on, his cap back on his head.

"Aren't you supposed to be helping your dad?" Debbie said. "Get on, you buncha lazies."

That night Julie and I practiced doing backward somersaults while watching cowboy movies, and when our necks started to hurt we ate a half-gallon of vanilla ice cream right out of its box. While we were sleeping David Lee walked into Julie's bedroom with a blanket wrapped around him, his hair standing straight up as if he'd just pulled his hat off, his eyes unfocused. Julie said, "You're sleepwalking, go back to bed," and he turned around and disappeared.

In the morning we were called for breakfast and it was beef brains. "I'm not eating this," I always said, every time Debbie fixed it, and she would answer, "You'll eat it or you'll go hungry," so I'd pile my plate high because in truth I thought it was delicious. Scrambled beef brains. They tasted like wild mushrooms, like something strange and dangerous you could only find by accident.

August 8, 1974

She knew me before I was born. Her hands would trace the span of my mother's stomach and Olive saw me whole but wouldn't tell what she knew, only that I had decisions yet to make. When I was born I became so ill I nearly died from a staph infection in my inner ear, and Olive told Mom to let go of me, that I belonged to God and I wasn't at all certain whether I should stay on this earth. So Mother rocked me that day, falling asleep as she did so, and as she slept she let me go. The infection burst and my heart turned outward, or so Olive said, and some part of me came to believe I could survive the world.

If Quakers had saints, then Olive Overton would have been one. She had narrow eyes that in a mean woman would have been threatening but in her were like a laugh happening no one else could hear. Her lips were thin and she had moles everywhere—sometimes I sat behind her in church and counted them but it was like counting rows of corn and I always gave up. She kept her gray-and-black hair cut short and springy with little curls she made with bobby pins, and she always wore a dress and sensible shoes and often an apron. She understood the old ways, where you had your two sons and then you were a matron with a round belly and hands bright red from bleach water. I don't believe a puff of powder or a trace of lipstick ever touched her face, nor so much as an earring, because life was about everything but adornments. Life was about really hot Constant Comment tea in chipped mugs, it was about Chinese checkers and doing right at all times. It was about keeping your ironing done and your flowers planted, and your little curls springy from their pins. If I named a thousand perfect things about her, one would have to be her son, Joe, whom I loved so much I wrote letters to him in crayon when he was at the Vietnam situation. I hated writing letters and it was a flat waste of crayon, but he was handsome like a movie star and Olive was his mother. Joe and my brother ran together and sometimes they would come home in their dark blue hooded sweatshirts and even for one such as I, whose heart belonged to Telly Savalas and Glen Campbell, those two were a sight that started a clock keeping time.

Olive lived with a man named Orville, an old bachelor with suspiciously good taste in furniture. He owned a house that didn't belong in Mooreland, with a glassed-in sitting porch and rattan furniture. Inside was a museum of dark velvets and curved legs, breakfronts sitting on the backs of gargoyles, Oriental rugs he'd acquired on journeys to places the rest of Mooreland would never hear of; even if a spinning globe stopped dead on that country and someone asked, "What does that say?" the answer would be "I don't know." Olive "lived in" with Orville, which was about as weird as life could get if you asked me, living with an old man who kept to himself and had an unnatural affection for antiques.

She had her own bedroom and bathroom and they were plain in the Quaker way, with just two photographs on her dresser, one of her late husband and one of her sons, Charlie and Joe. All through the rest of the house was flocked wallpaper and Turkish runners, glass-front cabinets filled with porcelain. There were so many doilies it was best just to not even look, but when you stepped into Olive's bedroom there was nothing and that was much more intimidating. I closed my mouth good when I entered Olive's bedroom and I didn't touch anything, either, or even rest my fingers on her closet door the way I *might have* at someone else's house. Because Olive knew me, and that is both a good thing and a bad thing, depending on the moment.

On a particular day in August, I was invited to spend the afternoon and night at Orville's as I sometimes was, and staying with Olive got inside me and saved those parts of my life that were still maybe fence-sitting on the whole staying alive business. I didn't have to tell her anything; no one did. She was my mother's best friend and I don't have one memory of them talking out loud. Olive understood that I was born an outcast in an ancient and subtle way; I was conceived out of some grief or darkness and would be made to pay a price for it. Once she took my hand in church and pressed into it a sleeping doll she knew how to make out of a handkerchief, and I held the doll but saw myself that small. Not sick—I wasn't sick in what I saw, I had been *left* to die. I stroked the little cotton hanky-head. Olive was on one side of me, my mother on the other. In the next row up was my evil sister. I don't know what I thought, I don't know how I saw it, but I knew that world, the world where I had been abandoned in a forest or on a hill, had been one possibility and it had passed away, and instead I had arrived where these women were: my gentle mother, who let me go and so I lived; Olive, who smelled of cough drops and mothballs and was a maid to a man none of us would ever know; and Melinda, who if I'd dared try to take my leave of this life would have jerked a knot in my tail, then pinched me in that soft place under my arm.

On my way to Orville's I crossed the street so as not to run into Edythe, who was pacing the sidewalk with her hands behind her back, whistling. I took a peek in Saffer's store, long since abandoned, and gave myself a jungle case of shivers thinking of the hundreds of pairs of shoes still stored in the upstairs, lined up like soldiers, some of them the kind that required a buttonhook. At night those shoes marched, I knew for absolutely certain, but during the day they kept their peace and for that I was grateful. I skipped down Broad Street past houses where I knew people and houses I was shy of. I skipped past the South Christian Church parsonage, which always smelled of Campbell's Chicken Noodle Soup and where my sister's beautiful friend Cheryl lived. Here was the house of the man who sold a certain kind of corn seed and I thought his name was Todd's Hybrids. I called him Mr. Hybrid when we happened to meet. There was the Farmer's State Bank of Mooreland, where kindly red-haired Joyce Dick worked, who gave me lollipops every time I happened to stroll past the drive-through window even though I never had one single penny to give in return. The bank president, John Taylor, looked exactly like Richard Nixon, and I believed the picture of the President that hung in the post office was actually that of John Taylor, and wondered why our mail was to be in honor of him. Parking lot. Tony's barbershop; the drugstore where all good things waited. The railroad tracks and the grain elevator, then the house where the smart, tough girl Dana lived. I loved her and she was hard as nails. The home of Monk Elliott who charmed me for no particular reason. House after house, all heading out of town, including the big black and white one with the wraparound porch where the two unmarried sisters sat every day as if waiting for their chauffeur, one of them, Peggy, wearing lipstick so bright red it could give a person a headache just to see it. I passed my elementary school, then Astor Main's Funeral Home, and there was Orville's house, right at the town limits. Another half a block beyond was nothing but fields.

I went into the glassed-in porch, which had a very particular smell of potting soil (no potting soil to be seen), then rang the doorbell. Olive appeared, her finger to her lips to indicate Orville was napping or doing whatever Orville did, which was nobody knew what. I crept in like a cat and followed Olive to the kitchen where she proceeded to strip me completely naked and put all my clothes in the washing machine, as she did every time I entered the house. I just held out my arms and legs and let her do it. She ran a bath and scrubbed me so hard I lost the top two layers of my skin, even the gray ring around my neck my sister swore was permanent and marked me as a future juvenile delinquent. Olive's fingernails were cut down short but she dug them into my head, shampooing me with some devilish concoction of tar and lye, which would leave my hair so huge and unmanageable I was surely the first child to wear a Quaker-fro, although I did it without pride or any power to my people. I sat in a big towel on the edge of the tub until my clothes were dry and then I was allowed to come back downstairs and have a cup of Constant Comment so hot I burned my lip, and play Chinese checkers with Olive who beat me every time. I never could remember what color my marbles were or what the object was, so I just moved around hither and yon and Olive let me but she also let me lose.

We didn't say on that afternoon or any other that maybe it was unusual how she had to wash my clothes and give me a bath; Rose's mother did it, too, and she never said anything. Melinda did it year in and year out. Olive didn't mention that I had two grandmothers who were my real grandmothers and I had never once been asked to spend the night with them. A big thing, a gigantic winged thing, hovered where that conversation might have been, and only my sister would speak of it, how we loved my Mom Mary and Donita with all our hearts and souls, but she and my aunt and uncles kept to themselves and loved my cousins and took them places. They went to every school function and came and went from one another's homes, but there was something about us that kept us out and made us other. Mom Mary was good to us when we were there but it was my cousins she saw every day, and my uncle Kenny's wife Aunt Donna loved me but it was the rest of the family that clung together like a unit while Bobby's children, my father's children, watched from a distance and took it in. My sister would say with her teeth closed tight that she wouldn't stand outside the door like a war orphan, begging for admittance, but I didn't know what a war orphan was (although I was compared to one often enough, given my sense of fashion) and I'd never begged for a thing in my life. So I was fine. I was happy enough. Olive's house was silent but for the ticking of a clock, just like in our Quaker Meeting House, and the clicking of her pale blue marbles as she jumped, jumped, jumped over my little mess of red ones, trying in her way to teach me something I simply couldn't get around to learning.

Orville's great-niece and nephews were coming for a visit; that was part of the reason I'd been invited. They were coming from another state, the children of a niece or nephew who had never visited Mooreland before (and like many others, would never return). The children were around my age but strange and talkative; they were dressed as if for church and they seemed to take everything for granted. Orville's porch meant nothing to them, nor the skreaky leather chair or rugs with the birds of paradise. I followed them around unsure of what to do. They asked me questions that made no sense and they wouldn't settle down and play anything good and they wouldn't go outside. I was prepared to take them to the part of the railroad tracks where hoboes camped, or to the gravel pit where we could each risk drowning. If all else failed there was the teeter-totter filled with splinters that would take up a good part of the afternoon.

Instead, they wanted to open the china case in the parlor and take out Orville's collection of glass animals. Such a thing would not have crossed my mind in 879 years, but as soon as the doors were opened and the chattery niece had removed a delicate swan with a red bill and dots of black glass for eyes, my hand reached out as if I'd lost my scant bit of mind. I held it in the palm of my hand and it weighed nothing; it was impossible and beautiful.

"Look at this one," the niece said, taking out a sheep with tiny black hooves.

"I want the horse," a nephew said, his clumsy hand reaching in for what looked to be an underfed quarter horse, brown with a black mane. In reaching for the horse, he knocked over a family of ducks and a polar bear, and in that tinkling moment, Olive came around the corner where I stood, the palm of my hand flat out and the swan resting there as if on a placid lake.

"What are you doing?" she hissed at all of us, in a voice I'd never heard before.

"We wanted to look at Uncle Orville's animals," the niece said blandly, and without a glance at Olive.

"Put them back immediately," Olive said, growing, it seemed, even angrier.

The children casually put the animals back in no order, leaving the ducks on their sides. Olive snatched the swan from my hand and put it back, then grabbed me hard around my upper arm. "How dare you," she whispered in my ear, her eyes so narrow now they were difficult to see.

I couldn't swallow—I was barely breathing—but I managed to say, "They did it, they opened the cabinet."

Olive squeezed my arm even harder and said, "You are supposed to be better than them. You are *better* than them and I *trusted* you." She let go of my arm and I felt the loosening of the pressure like a bullet in my chest. For a moment I thought I might faint, but instead ran out of the room and up the steps and into Olive's room, where nothing was out of place and there was no sound or dust or confusion. I lay facedown on her bed and cried so hard my eyes swelled shut and my nose stuffed up and I might as well have just gotten pneumonia and died like girls sometimes did in the gothic comic books I kept tucked under my bed at home. I fell asleep that way, and stayed asleep until the niece and nephews were long gone.

Olive called me down for tea and toast. I sat in the bright yellow kitchen with the high ceilings and listened with Olive to Lawrence Welk on the radio as she ironed Orville's white shirts. They were piled in a basket and there were about a million of them. I don't know where he wore them as I don't believe he worked or if he did it was in a secret place. Olive sprinkled starch on the shirts, sprayed them with water, lowered the old iron that weighed as much as a Buick. The steam rose up and made mayhem of her pincurls, and sometimes she took a handkerchief from her pocket and wiped her brow. Everything Lawrence Welk said and did was plain stupid, but I ate my toast and drank my tea and let my legs swing under the table. Olive's kitchen was the cleanest place on God's acre, and I was clean and my clothes were clean, and mostly Olive and I sat in silence.

When it was time for bed she lent me a pink nightgown that was so big I could have fit in just the sleeve but I took it gratefully. I slipped out of my clothes and folded them in front of the closet door, knowing I'd be wearing them again without a washing and it was hard to say how long. Olive changed on the other side of the room into her own, peach-colored nightgown. We had changed in the same room before, but on this night I accidentally turned too soon and saw her standing there, her girdle removed, her huge gray bra lying on the dresser. She was in just her underpants and was about to slip the nightgown over her head.

I quick snuck under the covers and pretended to be so sleepy I was about to die. My heart was yapping around in my chest hard enough I was sure Olive could hear it, and my stomach was doing an extra weird thing that caused it to sink in on itself in spasms. My feet were freezing and I cursed myself (curses, curses, I said) for having an eye like a camera. I had just added something to the photo album of Things I Wished I'd Never Seen. This one could be cross-referenced under Not Sure What It Was.

Olive's body had been covered with stretch marks and varicose veins, like a map you turn over and can never make sense of. Dotted all around the silvery stripes and the bright blue raised veins were more and more moles, thousands of them. Her breasts were large and hung to her waist, and everything was sinking in folds—a thick ribbon of skin over the elastic of her underpants; pockets above her knees. The skin that wasn't blue with veins or black with moles was as white as the belly of a deer, and then there were those bright red hands, so chapped she no longer had fingerprints.

"Did you say your prayers?" Olive asked, climbing in bed beside me.

"Jesus loves me, God is love, good night," I said, repeating the words my mother made me say before bed every evening.

"God bless *you,*" Olive said, turning over and settling in to sleep.

But I didn't answer. I let my hands rest on my hip bones, which were so pronounced my dad swore he could hang coffee cups from them. My skin was honey-colored in the late summer and taut as a drum. I traced the line of my neck, my sternum, my elbows. I was swimming in the pink nightgown; there was nothing to me and never had been. But even though it was Olive who could see the future, not me, I shook and blinked in the dark silent room, and I just wanted to keep it, I wanted to keep who I was, for the first time in my life.

"Sweetheart," Olive whispered.

I buried my head in my pillow, thought *Dear God I just fell asleep and she's getting me up for church, will there be no end to my punishment.*

"Orville says there's something on television we should see."

I got out of bed and let Olive wrap me in a big blue robe. I held up the hem as we walked quietly down the steps, over the Turkish runner, into the living room where Orville sat in his starched white pajamas and dark paisley robe. He didn't say anything, but nodded at the television.

I sat beside Olive and tried to discern what I was seeing. The Farmer's State Bank president, John Taylor, was speaking to the American public and he was in a sorry state. No, no—it was actually Richard Nixon. I remembered now, because it was Nixon with the jowls and John Taylor who was handsome. Nixon was saying he no longer felt he had the political support to lead the nation and would be resigning that very night. Olive and Orville were motionless, but I was most taken with the blue band crawling across the bottom of the screen, the issuance of a tornado warning for parts of Henry County. A tornado had been spotted . . . somewhere . . . I never understood the parts about north/northeast, or six miles west of 375 North, what the heck did any of that mean anyway. My palms began to sweat, and I turned to Olive and said, "I want to go home, I want to call my dad." She shushed me, seemingly unaware of the possibility of a tornado. Nothing scared me more. Nothing except rats, being kidnapped, or being thrown into black water. Also yellow mustard. But tornadoes were way high on the list of things that terrified me, and since I couldn't get Olive's attention I got up and ran to the big plate glass window in the parlor where I could see the sky.

Behind me Olive and Orville kept their vigil and Richard Nixon got kicked around good, but for the last time. I watched the black sky, trying desperately to hear anything, or the absence of anything, the silence preceding the soul-rumble, the freight train music of a tornado. I stood silent and strained as a dog, watching the sky, waiting for the real disaster to strike. The night was black—nothing like the sickly green that means the end of an entire town—and then there it was, miles above the town and white as the ghost of Jesus who had once appeared in our living room window. A ghost tornado, spinning like a child's toy through the atmosphere, an innocent phenomenon, all things considered. I watched it pass over Astor Main's, and the cornfield next door, then ran outside and watched it spin its way down the Wilbur Wright Road toward the Luellen farms. It would not touch down. It would harm no one. It spared us, and on the following Sunday morning I sat next to Olive at church, rubbing her ruined fingertips with my own, which were smooth as glass, young as lambs.

Late Summer

Dad somehow came by a side of beef not approved by the meat-men of the FDA, with the problem that we would have to package it. The hide was gone, most of the bones were gone, but other than that it was like a cow suit and we had to turn it into frozen packages of civilized dinners.

It was determined we'd hold the festivities at Melinda's house (because Melinda's house was clean, for one thing), and Dad showed up there with a refrigerated truck and a stack of butcher paper and tape. He hung strips of flypaper from the ceiling, because the man would not *tolerate* flies. The gigantic red meat-thing came inside in four pieces, and while Dad and Rick made the various cuts, Mom, Melinda, and I wrapped and labeled. There was a long moment right there at the beginning where I thought I might not be able to do it, might not be able to pick up the quivering liver and center it on the butcher paper, allowing my hands and clothes to become covered in blood. I saw the look on Melinda's face, too, and surely Mother was remembering the time Dad had come home with a raccoon for dinner, which he'd skinned and she'd put in the oven to bake, except that naked and pinky and lying in a pan it looked exactly like a human baby and Mom became a bit agitated, which is to say she became hysterical and swore she would need electric shocks to recover.

But there was something else in us that saw weeks and weeks of dinner, and so we just set to it, and before I realized it had happened I was picking up freshly cut meat and wrapping it with quickness and efficiency, and when I looked down at my largemouth bass T-shirt it was completely red with blood and I didn't care. The shirt was too small for me anyway; I just couldn't let it go.

Ididn't think about it much—but at the end of the day, after the hundreds of pounds of meat had been divided between Rick and Melinda and us, as Dad and I loaded our take into the truck to head for home, I knew, dried blood up to my elbows and in my hair, that it's possible when necessary to get used to *anything*.

The new bike my dad and I built to replace my old one (with the purple sparkly banana seat) weighed about seven hundred pounds, but when I got it going it flew, rendered nearly gravity-free by its momentum. I wanted to ride farther and farther out of town, where the flat streets of Mooreland gave way to some hills. The new bike was far too heavy to jump off the loading dock of the Mooreland post office; it was too bulky to ride along the low walls at the edges of neighbors' yards. What it was built for was speed and long distances, so I embarked on a campaign for freedom. Requesting freedom from my dad was rather like waiting for Jesus to return to Planet Earth: you could hope all you wanted, but the answer was still no.

I was tall and knew Mooreland better than people who'd been

alive three times as long, and Dad still had a little panic about me crossing Broad Street to get to Rose's house. When I was in the bathtub he still called out "Zip?" every seven minutes to make sure I hadn't drowned. Before anyone could touch me as an infant, he enforced hand-washing with rubbing alcohol, including by my own human mother.

We went round and round. I cajoled, and stressed my deep innate sense of personal responsibility, which we both knew to be nonexistent. He shook his head and said it was too dangerous. It was too dangerous because people in rural Indiana (and probably in rural Texas and rural Minnesota) drive country roads as if they are both immortal and participating in a stock car event. It seemed that once a year someone flew up and over a blind hill doing ninety, either in the completely wrong lane or dead in the middle, which is where they ended up. Men especially did this, and farm boys in trucks. It wasn't because they thought they owned the road, as the saying went, it was because they did own the road, and after the fifty-second time you've stuck your hand in a jammed thresher and *still* not lost an arm, what's the Wilbur Wright Road to you?

I won because Dad had other things on his mind, and because I was relentless. He gave in, telling me I could ride as far south as the crossroads at Messick, but then I had to turn around and come back, AND I had to ride with a gigantic flag poking up out of my back fender, a flag six feet tall and colored blaze orange.

"Is that to keep me from getting shot by hunters?" I asked as he installed the thingy the flag slipped into. "Because you know there's not a lot of hunting out in that tomato field, Bobby."

"Stop calling me Bobby."

"Not a lot of deer just hanging around in the wide open four months before hunting season. In the tomatoes."

"Do you understand what orange shows up against?" he asked, giving me a hard eyebrow. "Nature. You ride with the flag on the bike or you stay home and swing from your toes, it's your choice."

"Fine," I said, stomping halfway to the front door. I stomped back. "But I just want you to know I think that flag is ugly on my bike and also it doesn't seem so *aerodynamically sound*."

"Huh," Dad said, tightening a bolt. "You hear that on a commercial?"

I nodded. "The Porsche 911, you know that one with the tunnels?" I sat down on the sidewalk beside him and recounted the entire speedy plot of the advertisement.

The idea was that I could be in a little dip or cresting a hill and an oncoming car would see the flag long before they saw me. I got it. I went out the first day and worked my way up to speed, which near about tore my hamstrings, and by the time I got to the house my sister coveted with all her heart I was pretty much airborne. I was riding on the correct side of the road, flag whistling and flapping and slowing me down, when a car came up over a hill in *entirely the wrong lane* and had to swerve to miss me. A local woman with such beautiful straight blond hair that she refused to roll down her windows passed by, tooted, waved. I had to climb off my bike, sit down in the gravel of the shoulder and hang my head between my knees to keep from hyperventilating. I would never, ever tell Dad about this. I turned around and went home, and the next day went a little farther.

There are horrible tortures in this world, like going to church and that moment your sister notices you have never once in your entire life washed behind your ears. Dinner is routinely late and homework is a given. There are mean boys who talk about underwear, and mean girls, but the only one I knew (Dana) I really liked. There is the torture of the dead baby pig pile at your best friend's house, a pile which is frozen in the winter but in the summer must be faced squarely. Your hamster, Skippy, drowns in your potty chair and your sister and brother WILL NEVER LET YOU FORGET, even though Skippy was a biter, and indeed was found with his mouth wide open and his teeth as long and dangerous as those of a saber-toothed rodent. There is the cruelty of being made to wear shoes; there is the fact of an unheated house in the wintertime; there is a critical lack of plumbing for months at a time.

But no torture I knew as a child compared with canning season, which seems to have been devised by Satan to reproduce the environs of Hell long before we get there. Imagine a kitchen at the height of summer, pans boiling and pressure cookers steaming, Ball jars being sterilized (and not by something *cold*), Dad running the operation like a band director with a grudge and a twitching baton. We put up apple butter, we put up snap beans. We boiled corn on the cob then sliced it off in strips with a sharp knife. There were bread-and-butter pickles, chowchow, yellow squash. But nothing matched the sheer, violent hatefulness of canning tomatoes.

They had to be picked, for one thing, then destemmed, boiled, dumped into the sink, and slipped from their skins while still at a temperature of 8,000 degrees Fahrenheit. The larva part, once denuded, was dropped quickly into jars, plop plop plop, until the jar was full, at which time Dad got the job of the paraffin and the lid, which seemed to me to perhaps be the least of the evils, but of course he was in charge. And if I complained, he'd tell me to stand in front of the fan, which was blowing the whole shebang around like the broiling wind in Death Valley.

On the night before the first tomato canning day I told Dad I was going to get up early because I was going to ride all the way to the end, to the limit. I would stop at the crossroads, have a moment, then turn around and come home. Maybe I'd do it a second time, if I was feeling sprightly.

Dad said no, absolutely not, we were getting an early start. This was a man who went fishing at three in the morning, and each year when Blue River's band marched in the State Fair parade, we left at five A.M. in order to get a good parking spot. He was routinely *up for the day* at four, news blaring by six. So I knew when he said early he meant it, and if I was going to sneak out of the house it might mean doing so in the dead of night, never having slept.

I lay in bed on my daisy sheets, which had been on the bed as long as I could remember, in front of the box fan with the little mouse skeleton still in the bottom. I'd long since stopped staring at it. I tried not to sleep. I imagined Dracula running down the streets of Old London, running right at me, and that got my heart going for a while. I remembered the dream I'd had that a troll was eating my hair, and the time Melinda's clown doll had talked to me from a wicker chair. Those things—terrifying at the time—had worn down, had become just What Happened. The clown doll talked, that's just how it was. The troll was chewing on my hair but when I woke up it was PeeDink, my retarded cat.

So what was really scary? The day my sister got married and left home; that one still stung. The love I felt for my nephew, Josh, and how it felt when I thought he might have stopped breathing. Tornadoes, nuclear bombs, being stranded on a mountaintop in a blizzard, any event that caused me to have to slice off the fatty part of other people's bottoms and eat them because I was starving to death. Mannequins, obviously, and my father's temper—the time he went after Melinda with a belt because he'd gotten her a pair of shoes that didn't fit her and she said so. And something about my mom. Something about my family. I lay on my back in the sweltering night, wide awake and sick with fear, and that line of thought sure worked. That one worked like magic.

Dad got up and went out to his little shed. I turned off the fan and could hear him out there with his beeswax and his traps, his tools and chains, whistling and drinking a cup of coffee. I slipped out of bed, still in yesterday's clothes, and made my way down the creaky steps by sliding on the banister. No one barked, no one saw me. I managed to keep the screen door from slamming, and I wheeled my bike off the porch so quietly I knew I had special powers I would eventually need to investigate.

At the edge of town I pulled the blaze flag out of its slot and left it in front of Astor Main's funeral home. The flag was a prime irritant. I took off, the fields around me just beginning to glow with dawn, a scent in the air and a density of light that *almost* made me understand why Dad got up so ridiculously early. I went up the first hill, past Melinda's Covet Thy Neighbor's House, and sailing down; the tree lines ended and the fields opened up before me, thousands of acres. And I had an image, the way I sometimes thought about being sick just before I got sick, of a time out at Julie's when a fox had streaked across the road in front of us. I remembered the fox and just like *that,* something crashed out of a ravine on the left side of the road and galloped across to the right, maybe a couple hundred feet from me—just close enough for me to see the shape but not the face. I stopped my bike and watched the thing lumber across the field and disappear into a clump of trees.

My breathing was skittery and my right leg shook. I had thought at first it had been a cow, but it wasn't, and it wasn't a horse or a stag. I stared at the fields, replaying the image. I knew exactly what I'd seen. I turned around and headed home.

Dad was waiting on the front porch, his arms crossed, a cigarette burning near his chest. "I'd suggest you get off that bicycle," he said, full of menace.

"Now, listen," I began.

"No, you listen. If I tell you you're not riding your bike of a morning because we're canning tomatoes, what does that mean?"

"I have to tell—"

"WHAT DOES THAT MEAN?"

I leaned my bike against a tree and walked up into the yard. "It means I can't ride my bike."

"Correct. And why can't you?" He never took his eyes off me, which made me have to keep looking down at the scrubby yard.

"Because you said so."

"Get in the house and help your mother." He drew a last time on his Lucky, flipped it nearly halfway across the street.

I walked inside, letting the screen door slam. The inside of the house was already so hot I could feel my lungs shriveling up like prunes. *Some* people, who were more civilized than my dad, built a little canning shed *outside,* so they could do it in the *open air,* rather than in an old kitchen with exactly one window that could be raised exactly three inches.

I opened the screen door again and stuck my head out, knowing I was risking life and limb by disobeying him twice. "That's just fine then, I won't tell you how I got halfway to the crossroads and a MOOSE ran across the road in front of me, I won't bother telling you about that." I quick pulled my head back in and closed the door, then ran into the kitchen where Mom was in her apron boiling tomatoes, her hair undone and frizzed around her face. She, of course, had never known I'd been gone. "Good morning, sweetheart," she said, with the vaguest of glances.

I held one side of the pot as we poured the tomatoes into the big colander. Ball jars were lined up on a towel beside us, as if we were in a science lab. Oh, I was suffering all right. Dad walked in, cool as a bread-and-butter pickle. He looked at the tomatoes on the stove, the bushels on the floor. He crossed his left arm over his chest, studied the nails on his right hand.

"A moose, you say." He didn't look at me and I didn't look at him.

"That's what I said. A moose. Ran right across from just past the Thornburgs', across the road and into a tree clump."

"Hasn't been a moose seen in these parts in"—Dad thought about it a moment—"ever. As far as I can tell."

I dropped my oven mitt and put my hands on my hip. "Do you think I don't know that? I know we don't have mooses. That's the whole point, we don't have mooses and yet I sure as heck-fire saw one."

"Don't yell," Mom said, handing my mitt back to me.

"A moose," Dad said, his head tilted to the left in a way I particularly didn't like.

"That's RIGHT. A MOOSE. Run across the ROAD."

Dad nodded as if it all made sense to him. He walked into the den, which was separated from the kitchen by a "breakfast bar" at which no breakfast was ever eaten, and picked up the green telephone. He paused a moment, checking for a number in the back of the thin phone book, then dialed.

"Hello," I heard him say, in his molasses voice. "Is this WCTW? This is Bob Jarvis calling from Mooreland, Indiana. I'm fine, thank you. I'm just wondering if you or your listeners have gotten any calls about a moose running wild out near the Messick Road?" His lips moved around squirrelly the way they did when he was trying to keep a poker face against laughing. "Oh no, I'm quite serious. My daughter here—" He put his hand over the phone and asked, "Do you want me to tell them your name?"

"No, I do not want you to tell them my name! Hang up from that radio station!"

"My daughter," he continued, "was out riding her bike early this morning when she wasn't supposed to, and a moose just crashed across the road right in front of her." He listened a moment. "Nope, not a deer. Not a cow. She says it was a moose and she's sticking to it." He listened, nodded. "You do that. You put the word out and see if you get any calls. I sure appreciate it."

He hung up, strolled into the kitchen with his victory walk. "Don't worry," he said, "we'll get to the bottom of this."

I was so mad I slipped on the rubber gloves and took up the worst of the tomato jobs: squeezing the boiling blobs out of their skins. I was none too gentle, either. I slammed around a little while, then said, "You could have at least asked them to play 'One Tin Soldier.' If you were gonna make a gigantic fuss you could have at least requested my favorite song."

Mom and Dad worked beside each other silently. She filled the jars; he sealed them, then wrote the date on the brass lids with a permanent marker. His beautiful handwriting. We'd dated the butcher paper on the side of beef, too, before we put it in the chest freezer. We thought we were doing it for one reason, but it turned out we were doing it for another. Those are the sorts of things you only know later, of course. No one called about the moose. No one else ever saw it.

Antrobus:

What? Oh, that's the storm signal. One of those black disks means bad weather; two means storm; three means hurricane; and four means the end of the world.

As they watch it a second black disk rolls into place.

Mrs. Antrobus:

Goodness! I'm going this very minute to buy you all some raincoats.

Gladys:

Putting her cheek against her father's shoulder.

Mama, don't go yet. I like sitting this way. And the ocean coming in and coming in. Papa, don't you like it?

—Thornton Wilder,
The Skin of Our Teeth, Act II

Valediction

For her first day at college my mom wore a voluminous purple shirt with black poodles dancing about, made of polyester, and black polyester pants with a forgiving elastic waistline. She had made the poodle suit herself. She also wore Indian moccasins, because they were the only shoes she had that still fit.

By the time she came home that first day I was hanging around on the front porch, sometimes making the porch swing smack against the house, sometimes spinning around and around in the yard until I fell down. I checked for earthworms but it was a dry September day. I hopped up and down on one foot, chipped some paint off a porch post, tried to get my old imaginary friends, Picky and Bogey, who lived in the house siding, to talk to me again. But they were long gone and I could just imagine what sort of idiot I looked like, standing there with my nose pressed against the gritty vinyl.

Mom drove up in Danny's car, parking it back a ways, leaving room directly in front of the house, the place with the big hole always filled with water, for Dad. She made her way out of the car with unusual weariness, pausing periodically to look around as if she wasn't quite sure where she was. I ignored her, some. I studied her a *little,* but not so she could tell.

She trudged up the sidewalk and stairs, her worn Army surplus backpack heavy on her shoulders. "Hello," she said to me, almost as an afterthought.

"Hey," I said, studying Saffer's store.

As soon as the screen door closed behind her I opened it sneaky and slipped in. Mom headed directly for the den, where she dropped her backpack in a pile of knitting and flopped down on the couch. She sat staring forward, not blinking or speaking.

I dove onto the other couch, arms out like Superman. I landed hard, with a whoomph, and felt a shiver of worry that perhaps my most recent long-lost hamster, Merle, was still somewhere in the sofa where he'd disappeared a few weeks ago. Each day I stuffed crackers or popcorn down between the cushions, just in case, but he'd yet to make an appearance. He was a bit stupid really, as hamsters go. He'd been given to me by a girl down the street who didn't like rodents, and the very first time I took him out of his cage he sank his gigantic curved teeth into my thumb so hard I saw spots. Then I got so mad I grabbed him by the throat to try to make him let go, and his little beady eyes popped out some and the top teeth came free but the ones at the bottom were like the size of elephant tusks and I had to actually pull them out of my own thumb flesh, which was something I tried not to remember when falling asleep at night. I dropped him, naturally, and he skittered down between the couch cushions, and even though I took the thing apart, wearing thick leather gloves, he was never seen again. Dad told me later that once when he was napping on that very sofa, he had felt a *scritch scritch scritch* against his blue jeans. He ignored it. He felt it again: little tiny fingernails frantically scratching *tickatickaticka* against his butt, and consciousness swept over him and he was first horizontal and then he was vertical and standing in another room.

Mom still had not moved or spoken, so I broke the silence.

"Well?" I said, throwing my arms out at her in frustration.

"Well?" She asked, looking at me.

"Well, didja LEARN anything today?"

She looked back at the blank spot on the wall, considered it a moment. "I don't know. Ask me later."

This was no good. I could see what was happening, so I went upstairs and got my Scooby-Doo coloring book and Ray Bradbury's *Twice 22,* a book I'd read so many times it should have been called *Twelve 22,* and came and sat down at the end of Mom's couch, very casual-like, as if she and I just happened to be sitting in the same place even though it was still light outside and I had oh plenty to be doing. There was a hill, for instance, over by the railroad tracks that someone had seen fit to mow for the first time in my life and it was wicked steep for Mooreland. All things being equal. For weeks I'd been riding my bike down it with no hands, causing the bike to shake and very often spin out of control in the soft dirt at the bottom. It was heaven.

Fine, though, fine, I'd just sit in the dim clammy den with Mom in her poodle suit until she picked up the phone and called someone, and then I'd color so quietly she'd forget I was there and pretty soon I'd know what this was all about, this thing she was doing called college.

Soon enough I heard her dialing the green telephone. She was calling Carol, which was good, because she'd tell Carol everything.

Her first class of the day had been American Literature 240, a survey class, which meant nothing to me as I had seen surveyors a thousand times and the thought of them with their instruments trained on a big fat anthology made about as much sense as a house made of hair. Mom sat in the back of the classroom, embarrassed to be among the thin, lovely nineteen-year-olds who rightly deserved to be there. The Professor came in exactly on the hour. He wore a blue suit, a dark tie, and a watch on a chain, which he took out of his pocket and placed on the podium in front of him. There was a decided tremor among the students as he introduced himself: Dr. Satterwhite. He explained that he would not be taking attendance, as there was no need to familiarize himself with people who would, in a matter of days, simply be dropping the class out of fear and laziness anyway. He said, "At least half of you will vanish during drop/add," a term Mom wrote down in her spiral notebook. Drop/add. Like the instructions in a recipe.

Dr. Satterwhite, according to Mom, looked either presidential or like a member of the John Birch Society. I didn't know what the John Birch Society was, but there was a hand-painted sign not so far out in the boondocks past Mount Summit that advertised the club with the message GET U.S. OUT OF THE U.N.! He looked like one of those, but wasn't.

He launched into a lecture without benefit of a book or a note. He lectured for exactly forty-five minutes, during which time Mom took frantic notes in her precise, feminine handwriting. He then led them through the most terrifying syllabus (not the sort of vehicle my sister would put me in, apparently, but a schedule of reading) Mom could imagine. Many students folded it, preparing to leave it in the trash can as they made their way to drop/add. At the end of the hour Dr. Satterwhite snapped his watch closed and asked, "In valediction of today's lesson, does anyone have anything to add?"

No one spoke. "Carol," Mom said into the phone, both laughing and beginning to cry, "I burst into tears."

When the other students had fled the room he asked Mom in

his brisk, military tone, "Madam, may I ask what's the matter with you?"

Mom said, "I live in Mooreland, and I've never heard anyone say 'in valediction' of anything before. I think you're wonderful!"

Dr. Satterwhite flushed, cleared his throat, and left the room abruptly.

Mom called Mom Mary and told her about her next adventure, a psychology class that was held in a big room with 250 students. Mom didn't like it, because the textbook had been expensive and one of the studies they read about described how psychologists had spent $90,000 trying to determine whether babies preferred to be rocked back and forth or side to side. Mom Mary said something and my mom laughed her big laugh, leaning her head back against the couch. When she hung up I said, "What did Mom Mary have to say?"

"She said"—Mom prepared for her perfect imitation of my grandmother—"'Laws, I coulda told them that for fifteen dollars. Everbody knows it ain't natural to rock side to side; front to back is the way rockers is built.'"

I nodded. Mom Mary may have only gotten through the third grade, but you couldn't put much past her.

Mom also had a class that day with Dr. Reiss, a thin woman who wore a watch too big for her so it spun around on her wrist, making her look even smaller. Dr. Reiss taught Speech 210, and her Ph.D. was in Interpersonal Communications, a phrase that set my teeth on edge but I didn't say so. I could tell from the way Mom talked to Jodelle from church that Speech was maybe the place she was really going to shine, even though shining was all she'd done so far. She mentioned other classes she might take, like After Dinner Speaking, which was not something done very often in our house so it was hard to picture. I could have gotten an A+ in

After Dinner Television Watching, but of course I wasn't the college student.

Mom told Jodelle a little about Dr. Satterwhite, and as she spoke she got out the dreaded syllabus. "Our first assignment," Mom said, "is to write a paper on *Of Plymouth Plantation,* and listen to this: he said it has to be coherent and brilliant and *perfect.*" Mom's eyes filled with tears again. It was possible that she was going to cry all through her years of higher education.

Mom wrote her paper first in longhand, then typed it on the old Smith Corona on which she'd written her scary stories, including "Away Game," a story that bothered me so much I knew I would never recover from it. When she got the paper back, Dr. Satterwhite had written, "Concise, well-written, you type splendidly. A."

Dad came in late, the evening of Mom's first day of school. Mom was surrounded by books and sillybuses, her glasses a little crooked. I was watching television and PeeDink was dozing on my chest, drooling. I heard Dad take off his holster, which made enormous leather noises, and hang it on the back of one of the chairs in the living room. He ran a small comb through his hair. He took his cigarettes and lighter out of his pocket and walked through the curtain that divided the two rooms.

"Zip," he said, sitting down in his brown chair, pulling his purple ashtray onto the arm.

"Hey, Daddy."

"Delonda," he said, staring straight at the television.

"Hello, dear," she said, turning the page of a handout. "How was your day?"

"Just fine." Dad flicked the wheel of his lighter, lit his Lucky Strike, snapped the lighter closed.

In the Mood

Oh I hated school, it was *mean* to make me go, my fingers got all crampy around a pencil and my sister said I had the handwriting of a psycho murderer. I didn't understand one thing about math, not one, or science either; Go ahead! I would say to my teachers. Make me draw and color another cell! You might as well make me draw and color a picture of your dead aunt Ethel for all it means to me! And then the *leaf collections,* everybody has to have a leaf collection, it's so very very important to collect leaves for some reason, and if I'm not studying leaves why not make me write over and over that the primary export of Gambia is the cocoa bean or whatever, because *that matters.*

We would get to school, on the days my dad made me go to school, and there would be Rose with every single thing perfectly done, including her leaf collection (for which she had to make a trip to the Richmond Arboretum) and her math and spelling and little stories and cells—she never got one single thing wrong nor did she ever skip anything and she was *left-handed*. It was an epic puzzle to me. I could barely make it through the day, I felt like I was being poked with hot sticks, I felt like there were spiders crawling in my clothes. On many an occasion I had to sit on my hands to keep from jumping up and screaming like a hyena. Why was it like this, I would say to Melinda, why?

"Rose is much smarter than you, for one thing," she answered, stirring Cream of Wheat in a little pan on her stove.

"Well, that's for sure. Rose is smarter than anyone except for Ronnie Lewis." Our class always had the Super Smart Girl category as separate from the Super Smart Boy category. "But how does she *get through the day*?"

"She's probably interested in school. There's a concept."

I crossed my arms, kicked the chair legs. "I'm not interested. I *hate* it."

"I know, so did I."

"So did Danny," I said, remembering my brother's struggles.

"Yep," Melinda said, reaching for a bowl. "We're just defective."

"Oooh, now there's something that interests me, being a detective. Wouldn't I be good at that?"

Melinda thought about it. "We could start our own agency," she said, "I would be the brains and you could do all the gross stuff."

I sighed. She had just named my dream life.

When Mom was registering for classes her first quarter at Ball State, the dean of the Honors College, Dr. Warren Vanderhill, took a look at her SAT scores and told her she should take the Humanities Sequence, a series of three classes over three quarters. You chose a professor and stayed with him or her for the whole year. Dr. Vanderhill recommended Dr. John Mood. "He'll be perfect for you," Dr. Vanderhill said, with a shine in his eye Mom didn't quite understand.

The first class Mom had with Dr. John Mood, on her second day at Ball State, she came home looking as if she had just spent the day being chased by a wild-eyed cow. It was evening time when she wandered in and I was sitting on the couch with my "homework" on my lap and on top of it the Superman coloring book I was steadily making my way through.

"Hey," I said, scooting down and turning my body just slightly, so she couldn't see what I was doing. Not that she would have cared. I don't believe Mom ever asked me one single time if I did my homework, and she sure wasn't suggesting we toodle over to the Richmond Arboretum.

Mom let her backpack fall to the floor, where the dogs began to sniff it; she dropped herself into her hollowed-out place in the corner of the couch. "Ohhh," she said, sighing and closing her eyes. "Where's your father?" she asked, without looking at me.

"Gone."

"Did your sister feed you?"

"Yes, listen, we've started this game where we see who can eat the rawest steak. She thaws them out and then puts them in a pan and flips them over. After about a minute she says, 'Think you can eat it like this?' and I say, 'You bet I can,' and I do, so she has to. That was last week. Tonight she barely cooked it at all, there was just some little brown streaks on the outside, she said to a pretend waiter who had pretend asked us how we wanted our meat prepared, 'Just make it *suffer a little.*' "

"That's nice." Mom still hadn't moved. Even her hands were limp. We both jumped when the phone rang, although I don't know why, as it rang about 700 times a day.

She said hello and then turned her body slightly away from me, as if she didn't want me to hear what she had to say. However, it was indisputably the case that one of the reasons I would be a good detective was that I had incredible powers of both observation and hearing, but could pretend to be uninterested in my surroundings. Mostly I *was* uninterested in my surroundings, so I'd had lots of practice.

"I did," I heard her say, "I had my first class with him today.

Carol, he said that ninety percent," and here she lowered her voice even more, "of farm boys have their first sexual experience with an animal."

My ears lifted up on my head like little Martian antennae. *What???* I knew some very rudimentary things about what my formerly pious mother was so blithely referring to as "sexual experience," and they were not pretty. They were bizarre and wrong and no one actually did them. But adding the word "animal" opened a whole new can of worms.

"I know!" Mom said, her face bright red. "An English class. Dr. Mood," she said, opening her satchel to look for a notebook. "Yes, that's his real name."

Mom had classes with Dr. Mood Tuesday through Thursday, and suddenly I couldn't be anywhere else when she got home. I didn't dare ask questions outright; I just hovered around and waited for her to start talking about him. Here were the things I had learned by either listening or hiding my blue tape recorder behind a pillow on the couch.

1. Dr. Mood was the world's great expert on someone called Raining Maria Rilkuh. This sounded to me like a real live Injun, although I doubted seriously that Tonto would write poetry, nor would a real Indian have a woman's middle name. Curiously, Raining Rilkuh's poems were all in German, and Dr. Mood could speak it and translate it, and had even translated a book of Raining's poems called *Rilkuh: Love and Other Difficulties.* German Indians? I would have to ask Rose.

2. He wore clothes of wild colors, including pants with flowers embroidered up the side. He wore jewelry, a large necklace of something my mom called Onk. With his *sandals* he wore electric-blue socks. This was unspeakably curious. He had long black

hair and long fingernails, and he used said fingernails to tuck said hair behind his ears.

3. Dr. Mood could have been a stand-in for the Devil himself. Mom showed me a picture of him that had been in the paper and I could only whistle and back away. In addition to his long hair he had a beard like a goat; he was thin and black-eyed, and it appeared he was leading a group of students into some rabble-rousing. Behind him there were students all much, much younger than Mother and when I asked Mom what Dr. Mood was doing she said he was reading poems out loud. They were by someone named Allen Ginsberg and who knew a crowd would turn up to hear poems. Probably *after* the reading there was mischief.

4. Before he took up with Raining Rilkuh and became a professor, he had been an evangelical minister. He was an *ordained minister* who had abandoned God for the shadow world of college. He was no longer even a little bit of a Christian, something I secretly loved in a person. I was always looking around for nonbelievers, just to see how they got by without being put in prison. For a while, my dream was to find an atheist midget and then light out for a ghost town in the Wild West with him, but when I mentioned this to Julie she said you didn't really want to put a midget on a horse.

5. Dr. Mood was not an actual medical doctor but Mom called him Dr. anyway.

6. He never actually taught anything. He declaimed some things, and then he read aloud the naughty parts of books. I never once captured Mother on tape describing any of these naughty parts, or even what the books were, a failure as a detective, I admit.

7. Dr. Mood rode a motorcycle to work and rather than park it, he simply drove it straight into the building where he taught his classes and parked it outside the classroom door.

8. Each day he carried an empty tuna fish can into class with him, which he would gradually fill up with ashes and cigarette butts. Fortunately my mom was accustomed to living with my dad, so chain-smoking was fine with her.

9. One day a young man asked Dr. Mood if the papers they turned in had to be in plastic folders. Even *I* could have guessed the answer to that one. Dr. Mood was like *me,* he was not the type to stomach such trivialities. He said, lighting a cigarette, "I don't care if you turn it in on toilet paper, as long as it's good." My eyes lit up like Christmas when I heard this. Schoolwork on toilet paper—now there was a piece of brilliance if ever I'd heard one. The first paper Mom wrote for him she typed up in her normal way but she let me make a cover for it using paper towels. I wrote the title and drew a nature scene. When she got it back, she let me see what he'd written: "*A.* Close reading, great ideas. Cool flowers."

I went right on hating school as much as any vegetable left in vinegar, but Lord I loved college. I didn't want the semesters to ever end. Such scandalous things happened there. The Bible was taught in a *mythology* class; Mom was forced to read books by a group of people called the Existentialists, including an entire book about nothing but vomiting. She read poems by *homosexuals,* and once that concept made its way into my brain a whole lot of things became clear to me about some people I knew whose names I wouldn't mention even to Rose.

Once in the car with Mom, when she'd forgotten something at the library and took me with her to find it, I was thiiiiis close to asking her was it the same for *homosexual* farm boys as the others.

Ninety percent? Closer to fifty? But I kept my mouth closed. If she knew half of what I'd overheard she'd have sent me, those dear evenings, into the living room to freeze to death.

Every day with Dr. Mood was a surprise, I gathered, and not only because of the naughty parts but because, as Mom put it, he had a friendly relationship with a variety of chemicals. A lot of professors were part-time chemists, it seemed, including one man who was consistently declared "a genius" but spent his evenings in working-class bars getting his teeth knocked out. Said genius's teeth were missing the weekend he hosted a poet on campus named W. H. Auden. In fact, as I heard later, Genius managed to get Auden in a bar fight, too. I loved these men and wanted to go to college with Mom instead of elementary school with Rose but Mom would have no part of it. And that one time I'd been in the big library with her, a student had joined us in the elevator and called me a pygmy so it was probably for the best.

It was at the end of her first semester with him that Dr. Mood shocked Mom hardest. He came to class with a handout, the first, last, and only time he would do something so traditional.

It was an outline of the Book of Mark—interestingly enough, the only book of the Bible I either liked or trusted. The rest seemed like a bunch of hooey. He began with an outline of Healings, detailing the Exorcisms, Cleansings, and Restorations, citing chapter and verse for each. They added up, he believed, to a Restoration of the Reader.

Part two was Bread Imagery, and Dr. Mood argued that citations of food (bread, fish, etc.) gradually build to present Jesus as the Bread of Life, preparing the way for the Last Supper. (Although he pointed out that the textual reference to the Last Supper was potentially "spurious," a word that got in me and wouldn't let go. I had no idea what it meant, but it seemed to turn Jesus into a cowboy and there was not one thing better on this earth than that.)

The third section was Numbers in Mark: five sacred loaves of bread, four disciples called, four healings, etc. Dr. Mood knew every single place a number was mentioned in Mark and they seemed to add up to something. Well, they added *up*—to twelve disciples, and *down,* to one loaf of bread (Jesus). Every time I snuck this handout from Mom's Bible I studied hard on the numbers and would have made better sense of it if I'd had even a nodding relationship with math.

The last part was my favorite, because I thought only I had noticed it. Dr. Mood called it Secrecy. There was Implicit Secrecy and Explicit Secrecy, two words I had to actually look up in the dictionary. I hated dictionaries but this was worth it. Because all my life I'd been burning my butt up in church, three times a week sitting there in agony, and we'd read from Mark and I'd see it as if written in neon: *Tell no one I was here.* Now why, I wondered, was it right to say, *Jesus said Blah and so that's what we must do,* and *Jesus said Whatever and so that's what we must do,* but we could just go ahead and ignore the fact that the real betrayal of him was by the multitudes who couldn't keep their stupid mouths shut. Dr. Mood cited all the places Jesus asked, "Do you understand?" "Do you not understand?" "Do you not yet understand?" and "They did not understand," and it seemed to me that there was something gigantic going on and it was near to me and also very far away.

On the day Dr. Mood gave his first, last, and only handout, Mother sat through his lecture enthralled and enraged. When she got home she was still all nervous and indignant, the way she'd been when she discovered that down at the drugstore, on the newsstand, someone had placed *Philosophy in the Bedroom* by the Marquis de Sade. This at a time when the postmaster refused to deliver her *Time* magazine because he said it was Communist.

That evening I scooched up as close as I could to her on the couch. She ignored me when the phone rang. I heard her say, "I went up to him in the hall before he got on his motorcycle and I shook my finger right in his face. I said, 'I came here to *learn* something, you have no idea what this is costing me, and all this semester you have grandstanded and entertained and all the while you could *really teach.* How dare you keep this from me, how dare you not teach me everything you could while you had the time?' I was even shaking the handout in his face."

Carol must have asked what his answer was.

Mom looked down at her lap, twisted the phone cord. "He stared at me for a good long minute and then said, 'Fat women always did turn me on.'"

At the end of that year he disappeared. He took his rose pants, his Onk, his motorcycle and tuna can and headed west. There were lots of rumors, some believable, some not. The most persistent was that he had taken a job driving an ice cream truck around a town with Santa in the title. That made perfect sense to me. I could just imagine him, his black eyes, his Lucifer face, riding around and around to that sinister music. He understood more about Jesus than anyone I'd ever heard of, and he knew what I knew: that Jesus wasn't the thin blond angel boy of *Superstar,* not like I used to think of him. He was an outlaw, he would rather die than give in. Jesus would have put the smack-down on the Richmond Arboretum, just like he did with the fig tree. John Mood, I thought, must have been the same in his way. Whatever the college world had asked of him, Dr. Mood had said no thanks, and he'd spread his arms and flown away. He changed my mother permanently, he changed me, and all he left behind was a book of *Other Difficulties* and a single two-page outline, which Mom kept tucked in her Bible and which she and I both took out periodically and studied, like evidence.

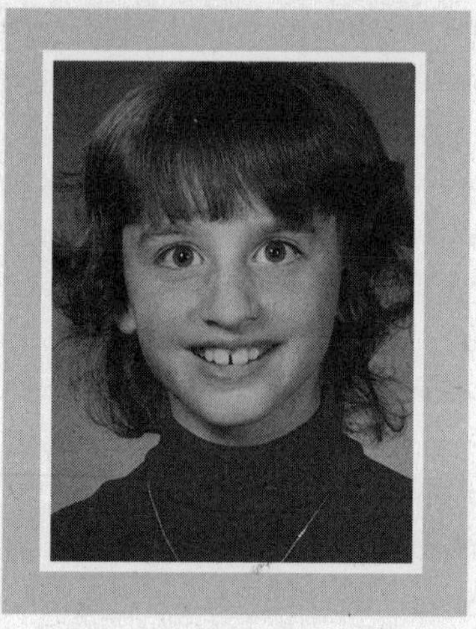

Fall

At the end of the fourth-grade school year, my first ever boyfriend (from kindergarten), walked up to me in the hallway and asked, not cruelly but with genuine curiosity, "Do you even *own* a different pair of pants?" I looked down and realized I'd been wearing the same blue polyester pants Mom Mary had given me for Christmas the entire school year. I didn't know how to answer him. Maybe I had another pair of pants, but if I did I didn't know where they were or what I'd do with them if I found them.

There'd been some decline in the laundry area from *that* plateau since Mother started college, and as a family we hadn't had a lot further to fall. I missed the days at the Laundromat in New Castle, which smelled of Tide and Downy and had fluffy balls of lint floating in the air. A woman worked there, a manager, I guess, who carried a big apron full of quarters and always looked like she'd heard a joke she didn't dare repeat. Outside she smoked cigarette after cigarette with my dad when he went with us, but inside the air was linty and pure, and it was possible to climb in the rolling laundry baskets with the IV poles and create great trouble. Plus you could buy individual boxes of detergent and fabric softener, even bleach, and there was nothing that made me grind my teeth with pleasure more than a real thing shrunken down small. The first time my dad showed me a toothache kit from a box of equipment from the Korean War and I saw the tiny cotton balls (the size of very small ball bearings), I nearly swooned. "Let me hold one of those," I said, almost mad at him. He gave it to me with a tiny pair of tweezers. I let it float in my palm a moment and then made him take it back. Miniaturization was a gift from God, no doubt about it, and there it was, right in a vending machine in the place we used to do our laundry in New Castle, Indiana.

My sister had scrounged up a red polyester shirt for the next school year, and a pair of plaid pants that followed the basic law of my physical deformity. They were long enough, which meant the waist was gigantically too big. I wore them folded over and pinned, just at my belly button. The shirt, the plaid pants, a used pair of shoes. It was a typical year, except for my missing mother.

Miss Slocum, our fifth-grade teacher, belonged to one of the many religions that gave women bun-head and made them wear dresses every day. She was pale and spoke through what appeared to be someone else's nose. That year she read aloud to us every day, starting with *Where the Red Fern Grows,* and I cried so hard at the end I had to go to the principal's office and apologize. He was quite kind about it, given that I'd been in his office for far worse infractions on multiple occasions. Miss Slocum also made us write our own poems and read them aloud to the class, which was for me as torturous and exquisite as a miniature cotton ball. I worked and worked on my poem, which was called "If I Could," and it was in four stanzas. The poem concerned what I would do if I could be four different things—a bird, a lion, an antelope, or a cloud. I wasn't dreamy about it; I was quite, quite practical. I practiced reading it aloud many times, and when the day came to perform it I finally got something right and Miss Slocum liked it and gave me an A, perhaps the only A I ever got in thirteen years of public school. Other kids read their poems and some were I'm sorry just obviously stupid, and then a boy most of the girls had a crush on, a tall jock-ish boy called Tommy, stood up and read aloud a John Denver song, "The Eagle and the Hawk." My chest flushed red and then my face. I turned and looked at Rose, but she'd yet to catch up to the sublimity of John Denver, although in time I would force enough of him on her that she would beg for mercy and demand we return to Paul Simon. Tommy read the whole thing, two perfect stanzas, no chorus, no bridge. It was John at his finest, I thought. *"I am the Hawk and there's blood on my feathers."* Miss Slocum sat perfectly gullible and smiling, because of course the Nazarenes or whoever would not have been studying on John Denver so she just thought Tommy was a genius.

I made fists and popped my jaw muscles like my brother always did and waited for the bell to ring. We were barely out the door to the playground when I turned to Julie and said, spitting mad, "He stole that poem, he didn't write it. He stole it from John Denver, it's one of John's best songs and I can stand right here and tell you the whole thing, every word. And I'll tell you what that makes Mr. Basketball, Julie Ann, it makes him a common thief and a liar."

Julie kept walking.

"I'm going over there, right up to his face, and tell him I know what he did even if no one else does. And then I'm going to Miss Slocum and Mr. Davis and I'm going to tell them what he did, too, because I don't know exactly *what* kind of crime this is, but it is A. Crime. For. Certain."

Julie walked.

"Aren't you going to say something?"

She shook her head. "Nope."

"Are you gonna go with me in case he gets mean?"

Julie stopped, shoved me slightly. "Let it go, Jarvis. Just stop talking."

I stomped over mad as a hen and played tetherball with her even though I should have made her play with a boy named Jeff who was short and tough. Instead Julie beat the crap out of me nine times in a row which I think she thought would make me forget about Tommy but it didn't. I didn't say anything to him or to Miss Slocum, but that evening I rode my bike down to Rose's and while we listened to Dr. Demento on the radio I told her what Tommy had done and Rose got a look on her face like she'd just stepped in something foul. "What a pig," she said, and all that evening, of my two best friends, I loved her most of all.

It was autumn and I'd finally grown into a sweatshirt my sister had passed down to me; it was blue, with our school's name and logo, the Viking head in profile, in red. I loved that sweatshirt and thanked the elements for every day that was cold enough to wear it. In addition there was the roller-skates craze. I think it began with a pretty, new girl called Christina, who lived behind Rose and could sign her name in the shape of a swan. She was an exotically colored person and mysterious. Once she had skates we all had to have them. Mine arrived in much the same way I got my saddle oxfords: I don't know how. The skates were likewise used—bunged up on the plastic wheels and gray at the top and on the sides of the white boots.

Rose and I took to practicing not on the toothy, dangerous sidewalks, but on the paved parking lot next to the North Christian Church. We skated forward and back, forward and back, nothing too fancy. I wanted to skate faster, but there wasn't a single hill in Mooreland that wasn't covered with either gravel or railroad tracks, so I made do with the new church asphalt.

Christina started showing up, and Dana, and even Julie got in on the skate business. Pretty soon she and Dana were better than everyone else, to the point they probably should have just moved out of Mooreland and joined the Olympics. It was Dana who had the idea to form a whip, with me at the front because I was the tallest, pulling the others behind me. By this time the other girls were wearing light jackets, and Rose hung on to my sweatshirt, Christina to Rose's corduroy jacket, then Julie, with Dana at the rear. We started out and the people at the back whipped back and forth and it was really quite hysterical until some force of either momentum or karma caused a domino at the back to fall, and that girl fell on the next, and she on the next, one two three four five girls. I fell forward and tried to catch myself with my arms out straight and my wrists curved outward and in turn each girl fell on top of me.

There was a grinding *pop,* as if a tooth had been extracted from the gum of a giant. Everyone was on top of me and then gradually clambering off, laughing, and I couldn't move at all, but somehow I'd made it to my back. There was the sky. None of this was like me. It was very *un*like me to lie so perfectly still. It was very unlike Julie to freeze as she did, looking down at me, or for Rose to run off saying, I'm getting my mom. I turned my head and looked at my right arm and what I saw was my shoulder touching the ground and the backs of my fingers touching the ground and everything else like a horseshoe pointing toward the asphalt. My arm was in a heap. My *right* arm, which was for all intents and purposes my only arm. Without it I would have to become Catholic and take lessons in Being Good from Rose. I looked back up at the sky and couldn't think. Rose said, "There's my mom" as her station wagon drove up beside me, and two things happened at once: I thought, *Please don't touch me,* and just as I thought it my dad rode up on his bicycle. It was an autumn afternoon. My father was riding a bicycle. He rode directly to the spot I had just fallen, and he arrived at the exact moment that if Joyce had tried to lift me, she would have left my arm behind.

"Hey, Zip," he said, leaning over me.

"Hey, Daddy."

"Girls, every one of you give me your jackets, get them off right now." He piled the jackets on top of me. "You're in a little bit of shock there, sport," he said, never taking his eyes off mine. "Joyce, if you'd go call an ambulance, and also bring back some blankets."

My whip of friends disappeared, although I knew they were there somewhere, on the periphery. I could only see my dad, and the sky.

"Can you tell me what happened here?"

"No," I said, not moving my head.

"Do you know what day it is?"

"I never know what day it is."

"It's Tuesday," Rose said, helpfully.

Joyce came running around the corner with a blanket, and in the distance I could hear a siren, or maybe someone was crying. Dad tucked the blanket around me and I started to look again at the miraculous problem, my arm in a U-shape, but he took ahold of my chin and said, "Can you hear that siren?"

I nodded.

"Why don't you listen to that, and try to concentrate on staying warm."

"I'm not cold," I said, and realized I was shaking.

The young EMTs paused only a moment, shaking their heads and whistling to let me know they were impressed. They radioed the emergency room to say they were on their way, and slipped an oxygen mask over my face, and an air cast over my arm—I wasn't allowed to watch, but there was a moment when everything went black and I felt my dad pinch my cheek, just enough to wake me up. The air cast was gradually inflated and placed on a splint, and I was loaded into the ambulance.

Every time the siren wailed as we sped down Highway 36 I jumped, but Dad made me keep looking at him and talking to him.

"You aren't going to cry, are you?" Dad asked, making a stern face.

I shook my head.

"Because you didn't cry with the rock in your knee, did you."

I had not.

"And you didn't cry with the sixty-six splinters in your butt."

No, I hadn't.

"You can cry if you're sad, but you're the toughest person I know and this is nothing to cry about."

An EMT moved between us, taped my fingers together. "You're a fighter, huh?" he asked me, touching me so gently I wasn't sure it was happening.

"You bet she's a fighter." Dad touched his breast pocket, checking for his cigarettes and lighter. "She can catch or throw anything, I've never seen anyone like her. She pulled out her own baby teeth with a string around a doorknob. She's fallen off her bicycle more times than any living person. I haven't seen the tumble yet that could make this one cry."

I had no idea who he was talking about. It was some girl he liked, that was for sure, but it couldn't be me, because that other girl had bounced off the pavement time and again; I had gone down and stayed. I was broken.

I was well known in the emergency room, but this fussing wasn't like that other fussing. This time there was no waiting, no flirting with my dad by the nurses, no small talk. There were shots, a falling twilight. I was awakened in a private room, dark but for a single light above my bed, by a very large man dressed in scrubs and with what appeared to be a flashlight on his head. My own doctor was there, Dr. Heilman, and Dad had found Mother and gotten her there, and I was being introduced to this enormous man, an orthopedic surgeon from Indianapolis who had apparently been interrupted at home to come tend me.

"You've heard of me, surely," he said, waggling his flashlight.

"Nope."

"I'm Dr. Linceski, I'm known the world 'round. I was at home with my maps and my exotic fish when I got your call. I assume you broke your arm on purpose."

"Nope."

"You didn't do this just to meet me?"

"I *still* don't know who you are."

"Well, that's appropriate. We've only just met." He looked at my parents and Dr. Heilman, raised his eyebrows as if to acknowledge that the odds were against me, given the rascal fringe surrounding me. "From what I heard you were cracking the whip, huh? and a bunch of girls fell on you? It's all a barrel of monkeys, isn't it, with you crazy types, until SOMEBODY has a double compound fracture that EXTRUDES through the skin with portions of bone SHATTERED by the compatriots who landed on you. Do you know what I mean?"

"Not a word."

"Good. All I'm trying to say is heckuva job there, heckuva break. It's going to take all of my foreign medical training to make it right. Now look," he said, as an orderly wheeled in a bed. "We're taking you to the O.R. right now, why waste time is my motto."

I was transferred to the other bed and Dr. Linceski talked and talked. My parents were silent and stricken-looking. They both bent down and kissed my forehead as I was wheeled through the double doors into the shocking lights of the operating room. It happened too fast for me to be afraid.

"And here," Dr. Linceski said, "is my anesthesiologist, Dr. Wang. That is his real name, Dr. Wang, I kid you not. He's going to make sure you stay asleep."

Dr. Wang was round, moonfaced, wearing a little hat. He appeared to be Chinese and was wearing flip-flop slippers, not booties. He had a flyswatter in his hand. "Hello," he said, in a Chinese way, bowing a little and waving at me.

"Is that a flyswatter?" I asked, because when you're about to be made unconscious by Dr. Wang, it's best to know.

"Yes, is fly in room."

Dr. Linceski whistled, scrubbed his arms as if trying to remove a tattoo. He talked to Dr. Wang, who pursued the fly and didn't answer. I heard a swat somewhere behind me, then the spraying of antiseptic and the eek-eek sound of a squeegee.

"Awwwright, then." Dr. Wang was suddenly above me. "We place this mask over your face and you breathe very deep. Then you count to ten backward for me. You do that?" He injected something into my IV, still watching my face. He patted my good arm and said, "We take good care, nothing will happen to you."

I nodded and said ten, and everything went black.

The next day my arm was suspended above me and when Dr. Linceski came in he drew a circle around a place on the cast where I had bled through it in the night. He drew the circle in yellow. The bloodstain was vaguely the shape of Ohio.

"That," he said, "is where the bones protruded and where we had to add a bit of synthetic bone to hold it all together. Guess who made that synthetic bone?"

I shook my head.

"Phillips 66."

"The *gas* station?"

"Yep. I'd keep that a secret if I were you." He tapped on my fingertips. "Can you feel this?"

I couldn't, but I said I did.

"You're lying, but that's okay. I'd lie, too, if I was going to have a scar this big."

"I'm going to have a scar as big as *Ohio*?"

"No, now *I'm* lying. I actually performed cosmetic surgery on you free of charge, because that's the kind of guy I am. You'll have a scar, all right, but it will shrink and shrink as you get older, until someday you won't be able to see it at all."

"Thank you," I said, queasy and wobbly and still somehow back on the ground outside the church, looking at the sky. "Do you know where my mom and dad are?"

"They're in the cafeteria, where I wish all parents would stay. Do you need something?"

"I just . . ." I was afraid to tell him. "I just wonder where my sweatshirt is."

Dr. Linceski pursed his lips as if he understood me completely. "In shreds, I fear. We had to cut you out of it."

I turned and looked out the window, pressing my teeth together so hard I thought my cheeks might burst.

"It was your favorite, huh."

"It just only got to fit me."

He pulled up a chair, straddled it backward. "You know what? I don't tell people this very often. You almost lost that arm. I had to reconnect nerves and you'll still have nerve damage for the next year. That's the worst break I've ever seen off a football field. You're going to be wearing a cast for three months, and we'll take it off when you come in for a skin graft. Then you'll wear a new cast for three months. Here's what saved you: your dad didn't let anyone pick you up, and you were wearing a sweatshirt that held your arm together until the ambulance got there. So it was a good one, but it's done for now."

I stared at the ceiling and wouldn't answer.

Dr. Linceski stood up, put his chair back against the wall. "I've heard all about you, things stuck up your nose and in your ears, a particular little incident where you ran over your own foot with the bicycle you were on." He patted his pockets. "You overwhelm me with respect. I shall return on the morrow."

When he was almost out the door I said, "You still shouldn't have cut it off."

He shrugged, gave a wave. In the hallway he shouted, "When I am President of these Onion States, I shall make all roller-skating illegal post facto! Pronto!"

Every day during the hospital visiting hours there was this silent painful thing between my parents: my dad didn't want my mom to go to school while I was still hospitalized; I wanted her to go. I wanted it for her, and because I wanted to hear more about her professors and the things they said about the dirty parts of books. Then Melinda would arrive and somehow sweep everything out into the hallway, and either Mom would be there or she wouldn't, but there Dad would be, sitting in the same chair at the foot of the bed, until the nurses asked him to leave. He sat with his arms crossed, his face like a brick.

Melinda made up a slew of occasional jokes that went like this: Q: What do you call a one-armed girl at a flute recital? A: Zippy. Q: What do you call a one-armed girl who can't get her pants all the way fastened? A: Zippy. On and on, oh you are just *tremendously* funny, I'd say to her, narrowing up my eyes and giving her the what-for.

Eventually I was allowed to go home, wearing a cast with a bloodstain circled in yellow and signed by all the nurses, the cast in a light blue sling with padding at the neck. I also had a stuffed autograph dog and my favorite signature on it was Mom Mary's, because she had only finished the third grade and I loved it when she wrote something. I had a bag filled with strange hospital accessories—my own vomit tray (never used), a water pitcher with my room number on it, a bottle of lotion, a container of baby powder, a toothbrush, and a tube of Colgate so small I kept it in the palm of my good hand all the way home.

I was taken down to the front door in a wheelchair that wasn't necessary; I kept saying it, "I don't need a wheelchair," but in truth I was diminished, thinner than when I'd arrived and still shaken. When I closed my eyes I saw Dr. Wang leaning over me, telling me to count to ten backward; I remembered the feeling of blackness so complete I knew death had to be something just like it. I wondered what I had looked like (something that had never crossed my mind before), lying there on the pavement under the blue Indiana sky, or in the emergency room, my lights out as surely as those animals I'd seen alive one minute and gone the next.

It was just him and me, he reminded me, and he got to decide when I went back to school. So for the first week he said, "Let's see if you can ride your bike with one hand." A breeze. The second week became, "Let's see if you can bat left-handed, or pitch," then could I go bowling, could I cast my Shakespeare rod and reel, could I write my name both forward and backward (something he could do with either hand). My blue sling grew grotty but no one thought to wash it.

Some days he disappeared all day and I simply lay on the couch in the den, watching movies and scratching inside my cast with a pencil. Other days he said, "Let's see what's new in the world," so we'd go into New Castle and I'd end up with a milk shake. Every few days Rose or Julie brought my homework assignments to me and I didn't so much as look in the direction of them. The rest of the house grew cold, and then too cold, and I knew that everything I'd left in my bedroom before I fell would remain just as it was until spring—the record albums, the sheet of paper in the typewriter, where I was trying to improve on my first poem.

Mom came home in the evenings and sat in her corner of the couch with her books spread out around her, talking on the phone with one hand and taking notes with another. Heaven knows what the woman would have accomplished had she been born an octopus. When she was home, Dad was gone, and I stayed on the other couch, facing the TV.

In the wall above the television all manner of things had gone wrong; the plaster and lath had disintegrated and there seemed to be nothing between the old gray wallpaper (some of which was coming apart) and the out-of-doors. One day I heard a sound in the wall and climbed up on a footstool. There was a sparrow trapped in a pocket of wallpaper, cheeping away. I couldn't see how it got in or how to get it back out, but I realized that the house must be riddled with avenues for coming and going—the mice in the ceiling, the rats in the laundry room, and now a house sparrow right in the den. It cheeped all that day. I told Dad and he said he'd look into it. I told Mom and she said to tell Dad.

Something happened from lying on my back all that time and it involved my kidneys, which I had not until then known existed. By the time I was supposed to go back into the hospital I was feverish, but well enough to call Melinda and say, "Lindy, you better send Rick down here. A bird has moved in." Even for a person with no standards, the smell coming from my cast was heinous enough to make me slightly proud.

Dr. Linceski said he'd never SEEN such a horror as the inside of my cast; he asked had I been trying to write *Moby Dick* inside there.

I said, "I have no idea what you're talking about."

"Look at all this!" He carried my old cast, cut in half, into my hospital room after my second surgery.

It was horrible: dead skin and dried blood, and about seven

thousand pencil marks. "Well. I couldn't very well scratch with the eraser end, could I?"

"Are you some sort of pygmy?" he asked. "Have you never heard of LEAD POISONING?" He was the second person in my life to call me a pygmy, a fact that would require thought when I reached the point of thinking about things.

"I asked Mom for a knitting needle but she said no."

"What about the possibility of NOT SCRATCHING?"

"Are you always so loud?"

"You had an *open wound* in there. You are *scarred for life.* I cannot get through to you; it's like talking to one of my fish."

I stared at him.

"I shall return in one moon," he said, turning toward the door, rubbing his flashlight up and down on his forehead, like a bear scratching his back against a tree. "And I shall hope you have changed in the meantime."

Antibiotics cleared up my infection and I started to regain feeling in two of my fingers. By the time I got back home, the bird was gone and winter had fully arrived.

By the spring my second cast was removed and what was revealed was an arm the size of a chicken wing, gray-skinned, with a pink puckered scar where my bones had EXTRUDED. Dr. Linceski assured me the arm would become stronger, but it was curved just slightly, and I had grown accustomed to holding it against my side like a kitten. I had missed forty-one days of school that year, with one thing and another, and while the doctor said the arm would return to normal he also said, "You must never throw a bowling ball with it; you must never hit a volleyball or a tetherball; you must never, ever break it again, or even land on it with your hand bent backward." So it seemed as if he meant one thing by normal and I understood another.

Sometimes I caught myself actually carrying my arm around,

resting my right wrist in my left hand as I walked. I carried it up the stairs when the house was once again warm enough to venture into. I passed the piano I hadn't played for six months and touched the keys; the hammers sounded damp, bereft. I walked into my parents' bedroom, where the mountain of dirty clothes still held the winter's chill, and up the stairs to my bedroom. I kicked my way through the debris and opened my window with the left hand, and Dad had been correct—that arm had grown very competent. I sat in the open window and looked out at the backyard of the Hickses and at the buds on the trees, the new green, the new daffodils, everything so new.

Experience It

During Mom's first year at Ball State, having given my brother's car back to him, she rode to and from Muncie with seventeen different people. Sometimes they would remember to pick her up but forget to bring her home, and in the way of things a different someone would arrive and say *Hop in, I was going that way*—though no one is ever *really* going the direction of Mooreland.

Roger was her longest connection, and they rode to and from Muncie with Roger's stereo playing so loudly Mom had to wear earplugs just to survive the onslaught. Even then the music got up in her rib cage and rattled some things loose. Roger dropped out of school after three weeks, and Mom was certain it was because he was stone-deaf and hadn't heard a single lecture in their time together.

Then Mom read in the paper about a Volkswagen Beetle for sale in Mount Summit for $200, which was both good and bad—

good because she could afford $200 out of the National Defense Loan she'd taken out for tuition, and bad because, well, it was a car for $200—so she went to see it. There was also a bit of destiny in the find, she thought, because it had been a Beetle she'd first learned to drive with Big Fat Bonnie.

The seller, a man named Pete, said he'd meet us at the edge of a gravel pit near Mount Summit. Melinda drove us over to see it. We pulled in, and there she sat. I could only whistle and shake my head as proxy for my dad, who was neither there nor did he know we were. But he was there in spirit, certainly, a man who loved a new car, a new truck, a husband and father who had nearly bankrupted us more than once by showing up in an unexpected vehicle more shiny and immaculate than a surgical floor.

The doors of the VW only locked from the outside, so if you wanted to be secure inside you had to roll down the windows, lean out, and lock yourself in with the key. The process had to be reversed to get out. I started to explain that this seemed a wicked bad idea to me, as periodically a person is called to make a swift and dramatic exit from a car, as when one stalls on a train track, or when the Cavalry is charging, or when you go flying off a bridge into dark water. Mom shushed me.

We opened the doors and there was that very particular VW smell, which I guess was the decay of German rubber and efficiency. Also something about the sixties, which had passed away. Mom wedged herself in and put the key in the ignition; the car started, but barely. It sounded like a barnyard animal down and not soon to rise.

"Oh boy," Melinda said.

There was a switch for the windshield wipers and there were windshield wipers but the two had no relationship. "How do you get these to work?" Mom asked Pete.

He rubbed his nose, looked at the ground. "My daughter used a string, I think."

"A string?"

"Yep."

Mom sat and Melinda and I stood in puzzlement.

"Where did she put the string?" Mom asked, finally.

"Awww, you know," Pete said, looking out at the horizon. "She held one end on her side and her boyfriend held the other on his side, and they moved it up and down the windshield, like this." He made a teeter-totter motion with his arms.

I nodded. We'd done that before out on the Newmans' farm. I already knew the implications, but it took a second before they settled on Mom and Lindy.

"So in essence," Mom began, "your left arm is out the window in the rainstorm? And you're steering and shifting gears with your right at the same time?"

"That's about it," he agreed.

"Isn't that . . ." Mom might have said "futile" but chose ". . . dangerous?"

Pete nodded. "She done had one wreck in it, that place I showed you on the front quarter panel. I dinged it out fine." The place on the front quarter panel looked like a piece of aluminum foil used and saved and used and saved by some old woman who remembered World War I.

"Does the heat work?" Melinda asked. She had a Bug of her own and knew that the Germans considered heaters a demand of the weak.

The man scratched his head. "Well, it depends on what you mean by 'work.' The car will eventually get warm because the engine will eventually get warm, if you see what I mean."

Melinda just flat-out laughed. "So it works in the summer really well, huh?"

"Yep," he said. "That's for sure."

"How are the brakes?" Mom asked, pulling up on the emergency brake and discovering it offered no resistance.

Pete teeter-tottered his hand again. "Nyeh. But it don't hardly go faster than thirty miles an hour so it don't hardly make a difference." He scuffed his foot in the dirt, spat. "You'll notice it's got a sunroof. That's an extry."

"Well, yes," Mom said, looking above her. "I see it has a sunroof, but does it close?"

He shrugged. "Almost."

Melinda wandered over and sat down under the lone tree in the dusty lot. "Tell me when this over," she said, "or after someone is killed."

I circled the car, counting rust spots. I kicked a rear tire for good measure.

"I wouldn't do that," Pete said.

"You're *supposed* to kick tires," I said, giving him the eye.

"Yeah, well. I wouldn't, is all."

Melinda called out from the under the tree, where her eyes were closed, "Mom, ask does it come with bicycle pedals, or squirrels on a wheel, something like that."

"Squirrels, Mom," I explained, "like on Fred Flintstone's car."

Mom sighed, put her head down on the wheel. "I'll take it," she said, reaching for the checkbook, an account that had, for the first time in her life, only her name on it.

On the drive back to Mooreland Melinda followed us, certain Mom's new car was going to give out any second and we'd have to push it off Highway 36 into a ditch like a dead deer. Even after we reached our top cruising speed of thirty, Melinda continued to drive very closely and flash her headlights. I'd turn around and wave and Melinda would wave back, her gleeful, evil smile perfectly visible in the sunny day. Sometimes Melinda would honk and even that sounded as if she were enjoying the whole thing very very much.

"Honk back," I said.

"I can't, I'm concentrating."

"Mom, we're coasting straight downhill."

"You honk, then."

I poked around on the steering wheel where a proper horn would be but nothing happened. I pushed on some very rudimentary-looking sticks, things that ought to have been turn signals, but nothing happened. Finally my hand landed on something (we never could find it again), and a terrible little sound emerged, like a boot on the neck of a mallard duck. Melinda must have heard it, because she tooted back and flashed her lights and was in all ways a menace.

We pulled up in front of the house and Mom got out, looking as if she'd run a very cruel obstacle course. When she tried to close the driver's door it swung shut and then open again. She closed it; it opened. She gave up and rested the door against the frame, then put both hands on the roof, like a circuit preacher performing a healing. "I'm naming her Sabrina," she said, her eyes closed.

Melinda nodded. "Optimistic."

Mom had always had Carol Hoopingarner, whom I loved for a thousand different reasons, and then she found a second Carol, Carol Johnson, who lived in New Castle and needed a ride to Ball State every day. They hooked up together and Carol paid Mom $1 a day, which gave Mom just enough to get something, even a small thing, for lunch. Carol was studying psychology and was loud, she said *exactly* what was on her mind, and if it hurt your feelings all the better because probably it was something you were in denial about and needed to hear. I adored her even though she hurt my feelings approximately every time I saw her. I had grown up with the quietest, most polite Quaker women, with only Rose's mother Joyce and Julie's mom Debbie to show me any other way. But Carol J. was in a class all her own, and we had the same birthday. That was two people I shared it with, my cousin Mike Jarvis and now Carol. I secretly believed we formed a little tribunal and would eventually be called upon to make judgments upon the world, something both Carol and I seemed more than prepared to do.

Carol had a deep, husky laugh like a smoker and a husband situation I never could get straight. She said things about my dad I prayed to the sleeping infant Jesus Dad would never hear. She was more than willing to pull the windshield screen on rainy days, and, like many people who arrive unbidden, she was yet another form of salvation for my mother.

It was interesting, I'd hear Mom say at church or to her friends on the phone, how long a person can make a car last relying only on gravity and Good Samaritans. Every day Mom parked Sabrina on a hill in a parking garage, and spent the entire curly route down power-clutching her into ignition. But it was only a matter of time before her luck ran out, and we all knew it.

One evening she came home with an ad she'd found in the Ball State *Daily News* for a corporation called Beetleboards of America. Beetleboards was based in Los Angeles, and they'd had the very bright idea of using Volkswagen Bugs as rolling billboards, marketing the campaign directly at college students. The ad stated that Beetleboards would pay students $20 a month to allow their cars to be repainted with graphics advertising a variety of things, but primarily cigarettes, blue jeans, stereos, and beer. The graphics were matched to the driver; for instance, blue jeans companies preferred clean-cut, athletic young men. It seemed, in fact, that all of the products favored young men of one stripe or another. Mother remained overweight, middle-aged, and missing teeth.

We studied and studied the ad. It seemed a bit hopeless, but Mom couldn't get over the idea of the $20 a month, which would pay for both gas and parking, and the car would get repainted in the process.

It was Carol Johnson who finally convinced her there was no harm in calling. She could just *call,* for heaven's sake, how many other decorated Bugs were there at Ball State? How much money was Beetleboards making off somebody else's behind in Muncie, she asked, using decidedly different language? So Mom nervously called Los Angeles, this at a time when one simply did not make long-distance phone calls, and California was as much a concept, and as far away, as a Bangladeshi prison. Mom spoke to someone, explaining the situation, and he kindly called her back to spare her the bill. She used *the voice,* a voice that would cause her to be a hit in speech classes and in theater classes and in radio—anywhere, in fact, that voices matter. It was unassuming, melodic, and intimate, and gave away nothing of the actual facts of her life. She used the phone in the living room and I paced in the den, eavesdropping but hearing only sounds, no words. I knew what Mr. Beetleboards was going to say: there was no advertisement appropriate to her condition, particularly not in Mooreland, Indiana. And if by chance she got him so far as to be convinced she was a long-haired athletic young man in athletic young blue jeans, and then he saw THE CAR—oh, all was lost.

But somehow none of that happened. The man in California suggested that Mom and Sabrina might be perfect for a new campaign—Miss Clairol, specifically the Herbal Essence Girl, who was a blond cartoon waif with long flowing hair rising up out of a tropical pool. (She was the opposite of the Swamp Girl, in other words.)

Mom drove the car slowly and with painful deliberation all the way to Indianapolis, to a dealership owned by Earl Scheib, where Sabrina was painted the requisite seafoam green. While there it seems she was tinkered with just a bit, just enough to make the ride home feel slightly more luxurious and less like a careening disaster at a two-bit carnival operated by convicts. Then a young man flew all the way from Los Angeles to apply the decals, and when he was done what was sitting in front of our house was something the likes of which Mooreland, Indiana, had never seen.

The Herbal Essence Girl rose up and covered each door panel. Her face was impassive; her hair fell in sheets of silken crème. One of her hands was turned palm up and sitting on it was a bottle of bright green Herbal Essence shampoo, so lifelike you could nearly smell it. The hood and trunk of the car were covered with exotic butterflies, and a banner across the rear window read "Experience It."

The design contained, as Mom was the first to admit, a fair amount of what she called innuendo. The Clairol Girl was naked after all, rising up out of a pool the temperature of a hot bath. It looked that way. Even the butterflies were slightly obscene, flying all over the place, including on the roof where other drivers couldn't see them. It was as if the car had just blossomed out of some wildly lively place—the most un-Quaker, un-Mooreland, un-Hoosier spot on an imaginary map. Mom *adored* it. Dad was *stunned*. The best part—if there could be said to be any one part better than another—was that the deal included a gigantic box of free samples. I don't know what we'd used for shampoo before Miss Clairol came to town; indeed, I have no memory of shampoo before her at all. But afterward there was always a little bottle of bright green Herbal Essence in the bathroom, along with a conditioner, and it did in fact smell like Paradise.

They were quite a pair after that, Mom and Carol Johnson, Herbal Essencing off to Ball State to study psychology and public speaking and English. One morning Dad and I were sitting on the front porch as Mom left to pick up Carol. Sabrina still sputtered, was still fickle at stop signs and climbing hills. Dad watched Mom make the turn onto Broad Street with his arms crossed over his chest.

"Nothing stops her," he said, shaking his head and flipping his cigarette out into the street.

"Nope," I said, unsure how to measure the word. There was a lot he meant to tell me, and I could feel it all in the pit of my stomach like the approach of a flu. Nothing, he meant, as in no money, no driver's license, no teeth, no job, no support, no supplies, no safe car. And *nothing,* he meant, as in himself. Or me. I knew he was right, in a dark sad corner of my bones, and still. Still, I was proud of her. Still, it was a *beautiful* car.

Teeth

Mrs. Schaeffer was a wonderful music teacher and because of her I knew plenty about the world of theater. In the second grade she'd allowed me to sing a solo in class, "Feed the Birds," from *Mary Poppins,* and told me I had a lovely soprano. At Halloween time every year she showed us a filmstrip called *Danse Macabre,* accompanied by a record on her portable turntable; in each scene a corpse or a pumpkin or a tree in a dark cemetery danced to classical music. That was the closest I'd ever come to great art, and I wished we could watch it every day. But Mrs. Schaeffer was right to hold on to it and let us see it only during Halloween.

In the fifth grade we were old enough to start putting on shows for the public, and Mrs. Schaeffer decided we would do not a play, but a medley of songs from the all-time perfect musicals, performed in the gym. The problem was how to avoid giving all the songs to Rose, who not only had the most beautiful singing voice but also knew how to stand just so and look a little ways up and into the distance, her head thrust just slightly forward. Her mother helped her put on lipstick for special occasions, something my own mother would have eaten a toad before doing. Rose was in all ways more prepared for a life onstage, and everyone could see it.

In the end she was given "I'm Gonna Wash That Man Right Outa My Hair," sung with a group of other girls, and "Some Enchanted Evening," from *South Pacific.* Her "Enchanted Evening" was so professional that my sister turned to me in the audience and said, "A shame you have to follow that." Rose had even remembered to enunciate, as Mrs. Schaeffer taught her, "you may meet a strang-ooor." Jock-ish Tommy, who was feet taller than anyone else in the class, got to sing "Old Man River," and shockingly, he had a flat-out bass voice. *Fifth* grade. I sang "Edelweiss" and was part of the chorus for the song "Oklahoma!" which meant I had to do a little two-step I found demeaning and hoped my sister would somehow sleep through. She did not.

Once the theater bug was awakened in us, Rose and I couldn't stop. We stole her mother's two-album soundtrack to *Jesus Christ Superstar* and played it over and over in Rose's room, wearing old diapers on our heads so we would like look the Blessed Virgin Mary. Well, Rose looked like the BVM and I looked like Mary Magdalene, but that was fine because that meant I got the greatest song in the whole play, "I Don't Know How to Love Him." Certainly that had been true of Jesus and me my whole life, so I felt justified in claiming the part. Eventually Rose got tired of singing "Hosanna" and said she wanted to be Mary Magdalene (casting against type, I tried to explain), although her younger sister Maggie was always happy to be Herod. Maggie had a preternaturally deep voice for a third-grader, and pulled off the Herod role with great aplomb. We sang with the record for a long time, then began singing into my blue tape recorder, listening to ourselves critically and trying to imagine how Mrs. Schaeffer would have us say certain words differently. I was convinced that M. Magdalene would say, "He's a mahn, he's just a mahn," sort of like the bald man in the 7-Up commercials who put the lime in the coconut. (No coconut in 7-Up as far as I could tell, but I adored bald men.)

Mom said she had a surprise for me. She was going to take me to Ball State, just the two of us, to see a play.

"I already know a lot about plays," I said.

"I'm sure you do."

"I've been in . . . gosh, *Sound of Music, Oklahoma!,* I had that bit in *Music Man.*"

"This isn't a musical," Mom said, looking for the tickets in the satchel that had replaced her Army surplus backpack. "Here we go. Friday night—a date?"

"A date," I said, looking away. It had been a long time since I'd spent any time with just my mom, and I was thrilled and also horrified and what if the actors were terrible? Would I be able to sit through it? I wished that Rose could go with me, so we could hold hands and criticize.

We took off, Sabrina sputtering and threatening to stall every time Mom touched the brake.

"It's freezing in here," I said, tucking my hands under my armpits.

"It'll warm up."

I waited a minute. Maybe half. "It's freezing in here."

"The heat comes off the engine, so the engine has to get warm first. I keep a blanket in the backseat; spread it over your legs."

"Let's listen to the radio," I reached for the strange, foreign-looking knobs.

"You know the radio doesn't work."

"How about turning on the heat then?"

"It'll warm up."

"What does this button do?" I asked, pointing to a black, rubbery knob that appeared part chewed by rodents.

"I think it's the— I don't know," Mom said, struggling to get the little foreign gearshift into third.

"I know a song about a gearshift called 'Beep Beep (The Little Nash Rambler).' Would you like to hear it?"

Mom nodded. "I know that song."

I took off singing it in the self-important voice of the man in the Cadillac who looks in his rearview mirror and is surprised to find the silly Rambler following him. Mom didn't know the words so well, and got lost, especially when the song sped up to its desperately fast conclusion.

"Whew!" she said, as if I'd worn her out.

"No kidding. It took me years to be able to sing that whole thing. What is this play called again?"

"*The Skin of Our Teeth.* It's by Thornton Wilder."

"*The Skin of Our Teeth*?! Do teeth *have* skin?" It was a gruesome concept.

"Not literally, no."

"Then is it a *stupid* play?"

"Not at all."

"Do you know this man, Thorn Wild?"

"Thornton Wilder." Mom leaned toward the windshield as if she could make the car go faster. "No, he's a famous playwright, he's not from around here. He wrote the play *Our Town.*" Mother had seriously taken up with the drama department. She was all the time reading plays and talking about them and had even *written* one.

"*Our Town,* hmmm," I said, scrubbing frost off the inside of the windshield. "You could write a play called that."

"Not nearly as well, I'm afraid." She scrubbed at the frost on the windshield. "But maybe you could."

I thought about it. "Maybe so. I did write that one good poem." We reached Highway 3 and headed toward Muncie. Mom drove this route every day, it occurred to me. She did things every day that had nothing to do with me. I swallowed, feeling homesick, but I wasn't sure what for. Our house was so cold we'd had to put a rollaway bed right next to the coal stove and that's where I slept at night. And it wasn't as if Dad was there, anyway, sitting in his brown chair with his glass of water and his pint of whiskey. It wasn't as if he was staring in his fixed way at the television, the rifle rack behind him, his brown radio set to the Emergency Channel, his collection of animal teeth in a jar on the table beside him. It wasn't as if I knew where he was. The house was just back there, empty and freezing except for the animals, who slept curled up against each other in little knots, cat indistinguishable from dog. "This play doesn't even have any *music* in it?" I asked, aggrieved.

"Not like you mean, sweetheart." Mom leaned forward, looking out the one square of window Sabrina's defroster had managed to defrost. She kept her eye on the space available to her.

Mom knew exactly how to get to the parking garage, which was possibly my first parking garage. She knew how to walk down Riverside Avenue to Emens Auditorium and up the circular drive into the bright space of the lobby, where hundreds of people were milling around talking, drinking what appeared to be apple cider out of plastic cups. The lobby was bright and loud as if some great excitement had taken over everyone, something bigger than a basketball tournament or the Fair Queen contest at the Mooreland Fair, where the trick was to look as if you didn't care at all. Here people laughed loudly and shouted to discover yet another acquaintance, and there were women dressed in ways I'd never seen before, men in suits of strange colors, men with *ponytails.* Oh dear oh dear, I thought, imagining if Dad could see this what he would say. It would not be Christian (though neither was he) or repeatable. There were some Vietnam veterans out in the far reaches of the county and some of them had ponytails, but I was not to speak to them even though my dad was dead patriotic. *These* ponytailed men were employed—they were ticket holders to the theater—not gun-toting hair triggers hooked on skunkweed. (I was unclear what that last part meant, but it got said often enough.)

Mom had our tickets out and we passed through a series of doors, older men and women in bright red blazers handing us a little book about the play and directing us to our seats. We were led to the left bank of seats, close to the front and near the aisle, where I could see everything very clearly.

Emens Auditorium was so enormous I would have guessed it sat one hundred thousand people. My mom said actually two. Two thousand. And there was something going on everywhere, more people milling around and ushers studying ticket stubs and an orchestra somewhere unseen tuning up. This could not have been more different from the gym in the Mooreland Elementary School, where our musicals had been held. We didn't have actual sets, for one thing; we just dressed in costumes (whatever we could find at home) and came out on stage and sang. The gym was so old everything had faded to a uniform shade of gray. There were enormous metal support poles in the buckled floor that ran up to the ceiling, and they'd been wrapped in thick padding—obviously to prevent traumatic brain injury—and the padding had gone gray and shreddy. The walls above and behind the bleachers were faded to the color of rock. A wooden board still bore Big Dave Newman's scoring record from the late 1950s, when Mooreland had its own basketball team, the Bobcats, before all the county schools incorporated and the Bobcats became ghosts. And Emens Auditorium was very different from the Blue River High School cafetorium where plays were held, called as such because there was a stage at the end of the cafeteria. An economical design. Despite the discrepancy, a jangle was set up inside me, remembering a traumatic moment in my way past.

Years earlier we'd gone, Mom and Dad and me, to the cafetorium to see my sister perform in a play called *Up the Down Staircase.* I was a really stupid little girl, maybe only six years old, and the set looked like the outside of a school building, three stories high. Characters opened the windows and spoke. There was no way to know Lindy was behind one of those windows until the cardboard shutters opened and she spoke her lines, and I was very shocked to see her there and also she was quite convincing and the whole thing upset me. I didn't know what to do or say, so I just kept watching, and then came the worst part: one of Melinda's oldest friends, Debby Shively, who was a real actress—she was such a real actress she was at Ball State right this minute studying acting as I sat in Emens—had the most important part and she got in a fight with her teacher. It was just the two of them in the classroom. The teacher was reading from a letter Debby had written, reading in a mean way, as Debby crossed her arms and looked miserable. The teacher said something like, "'I love you' is a cliché." It wasn't just the way he said it, or the words themselves, but that Debby's eyes very subtly filled with tears, the way they would if you were a bad girl, or maybe a good girl having a very bad day. My stomach flew up into my throat and I thought I was going to burst out crying, too, and I couldn't put it together that this was a *play,* Debby was *acting,* all I saw was my sister's old friend, someone I'd known my whole life, her arms crossed and an expression on her face like loss, or doom.

And then the house lights dimmed. I glanced over at Mom for reassurance and she smiled at me from behind her old cat's-eye glasses, and the Thorn Wild play began. On the black velvet curtain, which seemed to stretch a city block, a grainy newsreel ran with the words NEWS EVENTS OF THE WORLD. There was a picture of a sunrise and an announcer telling us, deep-voiced and authoritative, that the sun had risen that morning and so the world had once again not ended. There was a picture of a glacier, and the announcer said the unexpected summer freeze had pushed some piece of world I didn't recognize the name of to some other piece of world far away. The tone was funny, menacing. I squirmed in my chair, decided to take up nail-biting, one of the only bad habits I'd never been interested in before.

The curtain opened on a domestic scene, but one off-kilter. There were four walls but periodically one would tilt and a maid (or whatever she was) would have to push it back into place. She was worried the man of the house wouldn't make it home, and get this: there was a dinosaur in the house, and a mastodon. Not real, unfortunately, as that would have made for quite a play.

I leaned over to Mom. "When is this happening, this play?"

Mom whispered, "Pretty much right now. In the 1940s, I think."

I sat back. It was mentioned that the husband, Mr. Antrobus, was busy inventing the wheel and also the alphabet and numbers.

"What about those dinosaurs, I'm wondering?"

"Shhhh."

I didn't understand. I didn't understand the Antrobuses, who had been married five thousand years, as they battled the glacier in the first act, the flood in the second (wherein Mr. Antrobus also became President of the Ancient and Honorable Order of Mammals, Subdivision Humans). I didn't understand the third act, after the unnamed war, and the people wandering around in the back with big clocks, quoting, at nine o'clock, someone called Spinoza, at ten o'clock, Plato, and at the end, Aristotle. But I couldn't move. I could hardly breathe. Everyone seemed so giddy, so optimistic, even when in the second act the black circles began to appear, the first for a regular storm, the second for a hurricane, the third for a flood, the fourth for the end of the world. It was as if the world were about to end *all the time,* every time the

Antrobuses turned around, and yet they loaded the animals two by two, and eventually there they were, back in their little house in their little town, 216 Cedar Street, Excelsior, New Jersey. George Antrobus did as he wished: he invented the wheel, the alphabet, the numbers—he even rejoiced in having the hundred after hundred after hundred, as if he'd gone out and made it so, the way my own dad might build a chicken coop. I was dizzy. I wanted it to never end. I loved the dinosaurs.

After the play Mom took me to Arby's Restaurant, where I had never been. It was just a tiny place not far from Ball State, a counter, really, where you ordered food and sat at one of three tables. There were two exquisite things about Arby's: one was that the floor was inlaid with mosaic tiles that formed the face of a longhorn steer, and the other was that they had potato cakes in place of french fries. Also something called a Jamocha Shake, which tasted unlike anything I'd ever had in my life. We sat at our little table with our roast beef sandwiches and potato cakes and I knew I was a brand-new person.

"What did you think of the play?" Mom asked, as if I were a grown-up with an opinion.

I shrugged. "It was all right."

"Did you understand it?"

"Nope."

Mom took a drink of her shake, pushed her glasses up her nose. I had no memory of her ever talking to me in quite this way. "Do you know the word 'catastrophe'?" she asked.

I thought about it. I did, actually, because in school someone had only recently mispronounced it while reading aloud as "cat-a-strofe." "It means . . . it's something like disaster."

"Yes, it's like disaster, only bigger. A catastrophe is something that changes your life forever. Sometimes they happen in the world, like in nature."

"The way there was a glacier and a flood."

"Right. And sometimes it happens at home," Mom said, looking at me intently.

I swallowed my potato cake, stared at the floor. I said, "Like the way the maid is going to steal the husband and the family will be over."

Mom sat back, smiled at me. "You did too understand it."

"Did not. Also it was just silly, those dinosaurs and animals and people speaking different languages and Gladys popping up out of the floor, that was just about retarded."

We finished eating and headed out into the black, cold night.

"I'm freezing to death," I said, as Mom pulled out of the Arby's parking lot.

"It'll warm up."

We had the highway to ourselves and I could think of nothing but the play, the way George Antrobus kept repeating that they had survived the Depression by the skin of their teeth; one more tight squeeze like that and where would they be? I saw Debby Shively's eyes glazed with tears, her arms crossed protectively over her chest. It was a sad and sinking winter night, and yet I'd never seen the stars so hard in the sky, shining as if they could harm us, but would spare us one more night. Mom leaned forward, pressed the Volkswagen home.

One Leper

Mother always said she was a size 7 woman she kept wrapped in fat to prevent bruising. When she started at Ball State she weighed 268 pounds, so the Thin Mom inside was abundantly safe. But by the end of her second full school year, she had lost a hundred pounds, or *an entire other Thin Mom.* She still had long hair she hated and wore in a bun—Dad wouldn't let her cut it—and she was still missing some of her teeth, but there was no denying she had changed.

It wasn't until I stopped and looked back that I saw what she had done: she had taken the CLEP test and leapfrogged over an acre of requirements. She had finagled rides with seventeen different people over her first year. She had found Sabrina and redeemed her with advertising. Her too solid flesh had melted; she had gone to the theater; she had written a play that had been performed as a staged reading; she had taken me to the big campus and made me feel comfortable there, the way birds make their babies fly farther and farther afield, all the while saying, "See? It's just the world, you know the world." What I hadn't noticed, or hadn't recognized, were the course overloads, the punishing summer schedule, the arguments with advisers who told her no. (She handed to me, in those years, one of her greatest gifts: the ability to say with a smile, "Tell me who will say yes, and then direct me to his office.")

She had done all these things and she was going to graduate summa cum laude, which meant Good But Loud, from the Honors College, and she had done it all in twenty-three months. It takes some people more time to hang a curtain.

Two things happened ten days before graduation: one was that she received a letter from the university president, Dr. Pruis. She opened it on an evening Melinda and Rick were visiting with Josh, and Dad just happened to be home.

"What is it?" Melinda asked. In Jarvis Land an official letter was almost always guaranteed to be a threat of garnished wages or Interrupted Service.

Mom scanned the thick paper. "Dr. Pruis says he's proud of me. He's invited me to come in and see him before graduation."

I whistled. Melinda said, "The president?"

Not moving his eyes from the television Dad said, "It's a form letter."

"No, it isn't," Melinda said, in a tone of voice that would have caused Dad to *go straight up and scatter,* as Mom called it, in the days before Melinda was married, in the days before there was a husband-person sitting there making sure it didn't happen. "He probably knows her story, knows she's graduating with honors and is proud of her."

"It's a form letter," Dad said, lighting a cigarette.

"How do *you*—" Melinda began, her voice rising.

"Lin," Mom said, folding the letter and slipping it back in the envelope. "I'll just make an appointment and find out. How about that?"

"Yes, do that." Melinda reached down and picked up Josh's diaper bag.

"Yes, do that," Dad said, still not looking at any of us.

The next morning Mom walked down to the pay phone at the Newmans' Marathon station; our telephone had been disconnected, although Dad claimed to have paid the bill. She used the coins I hadn't already stolen from her purse to buy Mountain Dews and dialed the number on the Ball State letterhead.

"Office of the President," a woman said, in a special Office of the President voice: ground glass in honey.

"May I speak to Dr. Pruis, please?"

"This is his secretary. What is the nature of your business?"

Mom was perhaps nervous. "Ah, is this an animal, vegetable, or mineral question?"

"What is the nature of your business, madam?" The honey cooled, hardened.

"I received a letter from him," Mom said, clearing her throat, "and he wants me to come in and see him."

"Your name?"

"My name?"

"What is your name, ma'am?"

"Oh. Yes. Delonda Jarvis."

"Hold please." The Office of the President left Mother hanging without benefit of music, then returned. "I handle all of his correspondence and I have no record of such a letter."

Then tell me who will say yes. "It's personal."

O. of P. took her time sighing. "You may see him Tuesday at two."

Mother remembered her own elegant voice. "That will be satisfactory. Thank you." She made the slight, distracted sound of a woman squeezing an obligation into a frightfully busy day, then hung up the pay phone, which reeked of axle grease and gasoline.

Back in the house she contemplated her wardrobe, which did not exist. Her three pairs of black polyester pants no longer fit, and her stunning cherry red pantsuit, which she claimed could cause retinal damage in direct sunlight, was big enough for two or three unbruised mothers. She sat down at her Singer sewing machine, the machine on which she had made all of our clothes (except for Dad's, which were store-bought and fashionable), and the dolls Melinda and I had loved to pieces: Samantha Pollyanna, Rebecca Mathilda, and Suzy Sleepyhead, not to mention Gladly, my Cross-Eyed Bear. She took up the sides of the cherry red pants, did her best with the sprung elastic waistband. She would leave the top as it was and belt it. The problem was that the crotch of the pants now hit her in the knees, so she put them on and practiced taking very small steps. I came downstairs just in time for this runway move and Mom asked me how she looked. I studied her a moment and said, "You look like a radioactive potato."

"Hmmm," Mom said, nodding her head. "That's not so bad." She picked out a wig to wear on the special day, too, a style and color she considered "subtle" and which I thought said "Pekingese."

The second thing that happened in those last ten days involved her professor of Interpersonal Communication, Dr. Reiss. After class on Tuesday—the very Tuesday she was to meet President Pruis—Dr. Reiss asked Mother to step into her office for a moment.

"Could we—is this very—" Mom asked, glancing at the clock in the hallway.

"Just a moment, please."

Dr. Reiss was a tiny woman, but she had a long, manly stride, and she reached her office nearly a full minute before Mother did. "Are you all right, Mrs. Jarvis?" she asked, studying Mom's new gait.

"Fine, fine," Mom said, carefree. "I'm simply trying to slow down and enjoy life more."

Professor Reiss offered Mom a chair and sat down facing her. She crossed her arms over her stomach. Mom tried not to look around for a clock. She tried not to glance down at her watch, or have a nervous breakdown.

"You're a very bright woman," Dr. Reiss said, breaking the interminable silence.

"Thank you."

"And I understand you have a perfect four-point GPA."

Mom brushed away something imaginary from her pants leg. Nothing would actually stick to the red fabric; all was repelled. "Yes, that's right."

"A shame, then, that I shall be giving you a C in this class."

So this was it, Mom thought. She had managed to fool an entire university through the force of will alone, and she had come within inches of making a clean escape. But Dr. Reiss could see through her, could see the whole bleak story: the scholarship to Miami University she'd sacrificed at sixteen to marry my father, who she thought was twenty-six years old and a pilot. (He was eighteen and a gambler.) The twenty-four years of poverty and terror and ennui; the sexy, unpredictable man who managed it all, dominated everyone around him, animals even. Her children, who had never before had any reason to be proud of her, and who now saw her in a new way, children she had adored and ignored simultaneously, because she simply *could not get up off the couch,* she could not clean a condemned house with no running water, she could not cook meals with food that didn't exist or wash clothes without a washing machine. Without clothes. She couldn't drive a car she didn't have, without a license she couldn't acquire. She had taken her vows and then they had taken her, and the forces amassed against her were greater than love, greater than obligation. They were elemental, heavy as a dead planet. One chance—that's what she had seen she had—one flying leap that was really composed of eight thousand separate possibilities for falling, and she had taken that chance and come this far and been found out. And in a stupid class full of selfish, self-indulgent, narcissistic, spoiled children who were encouraged by Dr. Reiss to talk talk talk about their feelings, when what they ought to have been doing was shutting up and studying the conversations of their elders and superiors. It was *here*? Here she would be done in?

Mom nodded, sighed. "Have I not gotten an A on every paper? Attended every class?"

"You have," Dr. Reiss agreed. "But this course is called Interpersonal Communication, Mrs. Jarvis, and I have yet to see—or hear—you communicate with our class at all. You have revealed nothing of yourself this quarter."

Mom sat back, stunned. "You must be joking. The students discuss 'warm fuzzies' and 'cold pricklies.' A diagram of their 'feelings' could be used on *Sesame Street*."

"Nonetheless, you seem not to take the goal of communication very seriously."

"Interpersonal communication, you mean."

"It's an important field of study." Dr. Reiss turned her bracelets around and around her small wrist, leaned toward Mother with intensity. "It is through a more feminine approach to dialogue that we will eventually break through the hegemony of the patriarchy, Delonda. No less than that."

"I see." Mom looked at her watch, took a deep breath. "I have noted that you reveal absolutely nothing of yourself in class, Dr. Reiss. You are as closed as a prison guard."

Professor Reiss sat back, blinked five or six times behind her thick glasses. "Write me a final term paper justifying yourself and I will rethink your grade. You are dismissed."

There was no possibility she could get to the Administration Building on time. She ran up the hill, away from the English Building, ran in teeny tiny steps. A girl on a bicycle stopped to watch her.

"Are you all right?" The girl was young, athletic, tall. "Weren't we in a class together?"

Mother was so winded she could barely control her lips. "I have . . . a . . . oh, God." She held her side, tried to catch her breath. "I have an appointment at the Ad Building in five minutes and I don't think I can make it."

The Tall Girl said, "Bummer. Can you ride a bicycle?"

"Of course I can ride a bicycle," Mom said, thinking of mine, which was trusty and dear and even had a bell.

"This is my boyfriend's bike—you can take it if you'll be careful and lock it up. Just leave it in front of the Ad Building and I'll get it later." Tall Girl took out a combination lock on a chain in a plastic tube. A plastic tube. Mom had absolutely no idea what she was seeing. "Are you ready?"

Mom nodded and tried to get on the bike. It turned out Tall Girl had a Tall Boyfriend, and Mom couldn't get her foot over the center bar, particularly with the crotch of her bright red pants nearly down around her ankles. She hiked up the pants, exposing white tube socks she'd borrowed from Rick. A crowd began to gather. Someone yelled, "Jump on it from the back, like a horse!" She tried that and found it to be regrettable.

Finally, a boy with a Gary, Indiana, accent, someone from the Region, said, "Hey, lady, you wanna get on that bike? Give me your foot." She trusted him with her foot because she had grown up in Whiting and so they were practically family. The boy had two friends brace Mom on her right side; he pulled one foot up and over, the other boys pushed, and before she knew it she was on the seat, the tiny little seat of the Very Tall Boyfriend's bicycle.

The Region boys said, "Ready?"

Mom whispered, "Yes."

They pushed her forward, down the hill toward what was called the scramble light, an intersection where students crossed four lanes of traffic in six directions at the same time, in faith believing that (a) they were immortal, and (b) cars would stop for them because they were young and pretty. But Mom's bike kept gaining speed, no matter how furiously she pedaled backward. She had never heard of hand brakes, I had never heard of hand brakes; all civilized bicycles in all the decent nations of the world had back-pedaling brakes and that was all we knew.

As she approached the masses at the scramble light, realizing that she was homicidally brake-free and traveling at roughly fifty miles an hour, Mom did the only thing she could do: she began screaming, "I'm out of control, I'm out of control! Get out of the way! Run!!!"

Innocent children dove to the ground and Mom made it through the light and onto the sidewalk, where some idiot professor was getting out of his car without even bothering to see if there were formerly fat women barreling down the sidewalk screaming. Mom flew toward him, screaming, and he dove into the bushes around the Science Building.

She was slowing just slightly as she approached the front of the Administration Building, enough that she thought she might be able to get off the bike if she just threw herself sideways, which she did. She landed on her elbows and knees, abrading and de-skinning herself in ways with which I was long familiar. Miraculously, the cherry-red knees of her pants did not tear, but they did turn black from grass and blood. Mom's head landed on her bookbag, breaking the little bottle of Avon Timeless cologne she had carried specially that day in order to dab a bit behind her ears before meeting the president. The bag began to leak.

Mom rose slowly, not even pretending she had reserves of dignity. She was bruised and bleeding, her wig was askew, but she took the time to lock up the bicycle, as she had promised. She marched into the Ad Building and up the stairs to the president's office, limping and trying not to whimper.

Secretary to the Office of the President looked Mother up and down and said, rather faintly, "Are you the two o'clock?"

Mother nodded, gasped.

As the secretary led her into his office, President Pruis rose from behind his vast desk and studied Mom with a cautious expression. His suit was so subtle she almost couldn't see it. "Won't you have a seat?" he asked, directing her to a leather armchair the size of Mom's car, but with more power. She sat, still gasping periodically.

President Pruis began to speak, as a politician will do, to fill the silence, the inexplicable appointment. He told her what a wonderful year it had been for the university, how well the basketball team had done, how much money the alumni committee had raised for a new building. His speech had the comforting rhythm one offers to children, old people, and residents of the Epileptic Village. Finally he asked, "Can you talk?"

"Yes," Mother whispered.

"Can you tell me why you wanted to see me?"

"I got your letter."

"What letter would that be?"

Mom took it out of the bookbag; it was dripping with Timeless cologne. Dr. Pruis held it at arm's length, glanced at it, quickly handed it back. She saw it on his face: it was a form letter. He wasn't proud of her. He didn't know and didn't care that she was being graduated summa cum laude from the Honors College after twenty-three months.

She laughed. She let her body go limp and felt her wig slip just slightly more and knew there was absolutely nothing to do but laugh. "It's a form letter," she said, "but that's okay. It's okay. I guess what I really came to say is that there were ten lepers who were healed, but only one came back to thank Jesus for healing him."

Dr. Pruis blanched a bit, as one does when the word "leprosy" pops up in a peculiar conversation.

"I'm saying I want to thank you for all the things Ball State has done for me. I never dreamed I would finally get a college education, and now I have, thanks to you."

He nodded, asked her what her major was, what classes she had taken. He asked about her scholarships and loans, about the people who had been most helpful to her. At last he asked, gesturing to her, well, everything, "What happened to you?"

She told him the story of the giant bicycle, her perilous journey, the professor who dove into the bushes and would probably sue. President Pruis laughed and laughed, he shook his head and pulled a starched handkerchief from his pocket and wiped his eyes. "Ah," he said. "I'm so glad I invited you to visit. May I walk you back to the English Building?"

Mom told Rose's mother Joyce about Interpersonal Communications and how she had nine days until graduation and had decided just to quit. Joyce was not a woman who abided such nonsense in either word or deed, and she said to Mom, just sharply enough, "You could hang from your damn thumbs for nine days, Delonda, to get that degree." Then she made Mom talk through the paper she would write for Dr. Reiss, and as soon as she began to explain it to Joyce, it all became clear, and she dashed home as quickly as her torn knees would carry her and wrote it.

She based her argument on a book called *The Prince,* by someone named Machiavelli, who I believed was also a sculptor and a kind of aftershave. She described a certain kind of man, a Prince, a President, a Potentate, whose greatest gift was his ability to ingratiate himself to his enemies with false intimacy. Once the enemy's weaknesses were exposed, the Prince destroyed him, and thus was power maintained by the amoral and psychologically canny, or so Mother wrote. She quoted W. H. Auden, a poet who had once gotten in a bar fight in Muncie; she quoted Ralph Waldo Emerson, someone I would for years believe to be a character in a cartoon strip. Mom said there were true and false vulnerabilities, and that there was "no name under which the false vulnerability should be courted, no value in achieving it."

On the last day of her college career, Dr. Reiss gave her back the paper; Mom had gotten an A on the assignment and an A in the class. Dr. Reiss suggested they jointly publish it, with her own name as the lead: she was the one with the credentials, after all. But Mom just opened her hands, she made a gesture of emptiness, smiling, and said to her professor, "Just take it. Just take it for yourself, I don't need it."

Silver

In the old building on campus where Mom had an office as a teaching assistant, everything was either green or going green. She was studying to be a Master of English, and she didn't mind that even though she was about to be the equivalent of a black belt in literature, her office carpet was squishy and smelled like an aquarium. I felt comfortable there, as I was a Pisces. Mom took me with her nearly every day after my school year ended, and I would sit on the floor in the cramped-up space, between old chairs and stacks of books, and color my fairy tales and superheroes. Students came and went and Mom always introduced me as if I were a full-sized person. Professors popped in. Once I looked up and a man with white hair and a white beard but a very young face was leaning around the door frame; Mom said, "Dr. Koontz, this is my daughter," and he nodded and said, "Cute kid," then left without telling her what he had come for.

Professors could be that way and no one thought much of it.

The department secretary was named Mickey Danner and she insisted I call her Mickey, not Mrs., and there was this astonishing fact about her: her real first name was *Zilpha* and she was *not* lying. Her husband was called Howard or Howie, and within about five minutes of meeting each other he and I determined that we had the exact same birthday, which made four people so blessed. Mickey was the first old person I ever knew who was beautiful and I didn't know what to make of it. Howard was old, too, but he was craggled and shambling and his nose looked as if it had melted and been reattached at the School for the Blind. He was what old people were supposed to look like. And Mickey was very very smart; Howard was very very normal. I could tell—anyone could tell—that none of those differences mattered, because Howie and Mickey had already been married so long they'd passed the point of being individuals and instead added up into a single, average human with a nose problem.

College had made me sophisticated, but it was still the case that Mickey Danner's sweetness was so deep and true and constant she made me want to cry, and she made me want to be a better person, or at least lie about the wretched person I truly was. I had never before met someone without a bit of darkness in her, and maybe Mickey was the only one who ever lived. When we went out to lunch together—and she would do that, she would invite me out for lunch, just the two of us—she would say, "Now, go wash your hands before we eat, dear," and I would dash into the bathroom and *wash my hands.* If she asked me to look at a catalog and help her pick out new curtains for her guest room I'd take the magazine as if it were sacred and study the curtains as hard as I could, and never once say or even think, "Pick out your own retarded curtains, I've got bigger fish to fry," which is very likely what I would have said to my sister. With Mickey I cursed myself for not knowing more about fabrics. When I told her, "I'm sorry,

I'm not very good at this," she took my hand and said, in her caramelly voice, her old face so beautiful she should have been on a postage stamp, "Oh, I think you're good at everything you try. You just choose what you think is prettiest and I will take your word for it."

After we'd been friends for a number of months, Mickey announced a contest to guess the date of the first snowfall. Each person in the department got to write their prediction on a slip of paper shaped like a candy cane, our names carefully inscribed by her beforehand. There was no distance Mickey would not go. The prize was a Santa Claus statue with a snow globe in his belly. In the globe was a village with little houses and streetlights. It was mesmerizing and best not considered too closely, as it was undeniable that the village was in Santa's *stomach*.

Before I met Mickey I never would have done what I did when she handed me my candy cane guessing paper. Before Mickey I would not have known such a thing was possible. I told her the truth: I shouldn't be allowed to participate, because I was devilishly good at guessing things and it wouldn't be fair to the Professors. They didn't stand a chance with me in the game. I told her about knowing the number of pennies in the big jar at the Mooreland Fair, and how once Lindy and I had been at Grant's department store and she offered me a penny gumball. She turned the handle on the machine and just as she did so, I said, "It's red." We opened the little gate and there was a red gumball. Before we left the store Melinda had cashed in a quarter and I had guessed the gumball color right twenty-three times. And as if that weren't enough, I got to keep the gumballs for having ESP. When we got home we told Mom about it but she wasn't the least surprised; she remembered when everybody in our family had ESP. Around our house it was just ESP all the time.

It wasn't that Mickey didn't *believe me*—she certainly *believed me*. But she thought my natural advantage might be tempered by the fact we were talking about the weather, and not just weather but snow in Indiana, which was so unpredictable I always expected to see it coming up from the ground one day, flying heavenward in a reversal of physical laws, just to keep us Hoosiers on our toes.

I saw Mickey's point, and accepted my candy cane. I thought a moment, licking the end of my pencil, a habit I'd picked up from my dad. Mickey suggested that licking lead wasn't perhaps the wisest thing to do, and I wondered if there was a connection between my pencil history and the fact I had absolutely no notion of left and right. I could hardly tell the words apart. And Melinda and I both said "yellow" when we looked at the color pink. We said yellow when we looked at the *word* pink, and we both suffered from a phenomenon we called Baker Park, after an actual park in New Castle which was a square with streets around it. Every time Melinda and I got near Baker Park we would become completely lost; I don't mean we didn't know which way was right or left, of course we didn't, I mean *we didn't understand that we were still on Planet Earth*.

I wrote "November 13" and put an exclamation point underneath it. Mickey looked at my prediction and said, "That's pretty early for snow. Are you trying to give everyone else a fighting chance?" I shook my head. Mickey Danner had gotten in my life and messed me up but good; I didn't know if I was coming or going, lying or trying not to lie.

"No," I said, and then, "What was the question?"

November 13 was mild, with clear skies. I sat in Mickey's office while Mom was in class. We talked about things and I read to her from my Judy Blume book. She answered the phone and typed; people came and went and the day passed gently. Neither of us mentioned the contest, and then Mom came up the rickety green steps, panting from her walk across campus, and said, "It's snowing!" I jumped up and looked out the window and the flakes were so big they could have had faces—I could have given each one a name.

"Heavens," Mickey said, her hand over her heart. "I guess I owe you this." She handed me the box with the Santa statue and shook my hand. I opened the box, moved aside the tissue he was wrapped in. There was the sleeping village inside Santa. If the gift had come from Dr. Mood, I would have thought it meant something very strange and beyond me (the village is *in* Santa, the village is IN Santa), but as it was from Mickey I thought it was just the sweetest thing, and had no significance at all.

The year she became a Master, Mom lost another twenty pounds, sold Sabrina to a collector, and wrote thirteen short stories so disorienting and bothersome I memorized one entirely and hid copies of the others in the secret red box in my bedroom. The stories formed the book that would be her thesis. They were all about women; each story was told twice, it seemed to me, or maybe I was wrong about that. Maybe the story I had memorized, "Home Remedy," wasn't the same as "Bondage." In the first a hillbilly woman (I imagined she had my Mom Mary's Kentucky accent) named Lovey is talking to her husband, Elzy Ezekiel Rogers. She is just talking, telling him little things, like how her bed had come from an auction in a rainstorm—her father had stayed all day, soaked through, to get it for her. As a child Lovey had shared the bed with her sister, and then it became her marriage bed. She'd never told anyone that the knobs at the top of the four posters came off. *I used to hide secrets in the posts, like a poem I read one time that made me cry. I copied it off and hid it in the left foot post. And whenever I met you that first time at the church sociable I went home and wrote down your name, Elzy Ezekiel Rogers, and I took off the ball and hid the paper in the post on the top left, nearest to my heart.*

But they aren't just talking, this woman with the soft, mountain accent and her husband. He isn't talking at all, because he is tied to the bedposts, bound and gagged. There are things Lovey must make clear to him: they involve a daughter, Carrie Bell, who is fifteen, a beautiful, innocent child. There is a tray by the bed, and on it a rag soaked with ether; a scalpel; catgut thread and a curved needle. These details added up like numbers, but even memorized I wasn't sure to what sum. *Sometimes I think about those first fifteen years and they're light and golden, like fairy children dancing around a maypole. These last fifteen years are like goblins in a circle, one more added each year that passes. Now the light and the dark are even, but before long another year will make sixteen dark and only fifteen light, dancing, dancing, and soon the darkness will win. It scares me to think on it.*

In "Bondage" the husband's name is Buck; he's a truck-driving bully, and the wife, Claire, is a nurse, so it wasn't the same at all, really, except for the sutures, the needle, the handcuffs. And a daughter named Carrie who is injured. She is talked about but never seen; all through the story her bedroom is quiet, her bed made. There is an old stuffed bear on her pillow, and I wondered about that a lot, that bear.

I didn't understand the stories but I couldn't put them down, wouldn't let them go. Lovey's voice was in my head as sure as my own, and the other women, too: the elementary school teacher, Veronica, found dead in her closet, her secrets spilled all over her apartment. The kitchen floor is covered with coffee and sugar, black against white, stains on white walls, and the policeman who is telling the story knows there is only one body but two dead women: Veronica, the woman the world saw, and Ronnie, the self she despised.

"Alma Mater," about a woman in the cabin in the woods, who presides over a small town's harvest festival. It is she who chooses the Harvest King, and the contest is between two cousins, Michael and Malachi. A middle-aged man, a college recruiter, comes to town to beg her to let his university have Michael, who is a genius; in truth he wants them both. The woman is called Mother; she takes the man into her rose-scented parlor and he is lost an entire day. When he comes to his senses he sees the Mother is old, and he is horrified: her face changes with every shift of light, and she tells him Michael is Chosen and there is no undoing it. "You may take Malachi," she says, slipping into the shadows of her own house, pushing the recruiter out into the blinding daylight and locking the door behind him.

"Michael was Chosen," I would say, lying in bed at night, or sitting on the floor in Mickey Danner's office. At a carnival in the springtime, where he wrestled with his cousin, and won.

"You may take Malachi," Mickey would answer, handing me a stack of letters she needed me to fold.

I knew the Wedding stories, the Mothers-in-law Coming to Visit stories, the Left Turn on Maple. And the woman who had come to believe in the undead; she wore a silver cross she clutched throughout an evening spent with an old friend—a cold evening, a cold conversation over chilled wine, and upstairs in her immaculate house the perfectly preserved room of a four-year-old boy, who had been dead for years.

A woman in Mount Summit named Wilhelmina opened a dress shop in the basement of her house. The dresses were of a mysterious origin: some were very expensive and new; some were expensive and on consignment. Most had come from Somewhere and been marked down many times as they traveled to Mount Summit, the way anything passed from hand to hand dims.

Mother loved it there. She loved to go and visit with Wilhelmina, even if she never bought anything. Wilhelmina was tiny, built like a dancer, and she wore scarves and excessive amounts of jewelry. She smoked and gossiped and complimented every woman who came through the door. After leaving the shop empty-handed many times, Mom walked in one afternoon and told Wilhelmina she was ready to try something on. She was about to celebrate her twenty-fifth wedding anniversary and she wanted a new dress.

I didn't want to go to Wilhelmina's. I tried staying in the car, but the interior was black and it was August, and even with every window down I felt all my wickedness melting. I got out of the car and stomped around and that made me hotter. Dresses. My mother was shopping for dresses. Where was ye olde Delonda, I was beginning to wonder, the one who wore Mom Mary's hand-me-downs year after year and never left the house, the person who was somehow *too good* for a place like Wilhelmina's? I sat down under a tree, fanned myself, kicked at some dust to make a point. Never mind the lights being turned off, the lack of plumbing, the cold, humid haze in which Mom slept away the days, year after year, a silent, unmoving, unmovable mountain under blankets and afghans. What need did *she* have for trivialities and costume jewelry? Rising up on Sunday mornings, making do with virtually nothing (and even that nothing had to be pinned together and was so frayed it barely held), she had not seemed embarrassed or concerned. My cheerful, obese, popcorn-eating, science-fiction-reading holy Mother: her eye had been on God. I missed that woman fiercely, but I barely knew why. All I knew is that as long as she was trapped I knew exactly where to find her.

"Honey!" The New Mother, missing 120 pounds of the Old, was standing in the doorway of the dress shop, waving to me. "Come see what I found!"

Even I had to admit the dresses were amazing. They were identical, one black (coffee), the other white (sugar), a finely spun something or other—I knew *nothing* about fabric—that felt as if it were just about to escape your hand. She was wearing the white one, which was fitted but not tight, and made her look like someone who had once had a figure so dangerous she could only hint at it now that she was a grandmother. It was a dress that *concealed,* and in the concealment told a story which seemed to be the one Mom was working on; the fourteenth narrative in her collection of women's faces.

"Look at this," she said, handing me a . . . what was it? Not a belt, but something like that. It was made of the same material, but on each end were three fingerlets of fur. I don't believe "fingerlet" was the technical term. It was fur in three finger-shaped tubes, not long scary fingers, more like little stumps of fur. The belt, or whatever it was, and the fur stumps were so hopelessly glamorous I hoped Mom would buy the dress just so I could steal this part. "You tie it on like this," she said, executing a knot, a little turn in the dressing room mirror. The last of the world as I knew it vanished with a whisper. "Do you think your dad will like it?" she asked, still looking in the mirror.

I once overheard Mom refer to a man as someone who Had Accidents for a Living. I was fairly certain this was my vocation, too, and I wished I could interview the man to figure out how one got paid for what came naturally to me.

My father took some professional falls, too, at his job at Delco Remy. I was always unclear on the details, but I remember the last one, because he never went back to work. There was talk that one of his legs was shorter than the other (or maybe it was longer); it was said that his spine was disintegrating. He told us he would be one hundred percent crippled within the next five years. In the meantime, he was on disability and collecting a pension, and all day every day he got to do whatever he wanted.

My mind wobbled with fear and grief when I considered Dad's future in a wheelchair as a one hundred percent cripple. It would be the worst thing that could happen to him; it would be like putting him in prison. He was meant to *go,* he was built to stand in his garden just before sunrise and study his fruit trees and think his private thoughts, but on his *legs,* not on wheels. A wheelchair would be a mess after rototilling; it would be a disaster in the woods. When I thought too hard about it I'd have to run outside and prop a ladder up against my favorite tree, then climb up and hide in the perfect basket made where the first big limbs parted ways. I could never understand how he always found me, but he did, and I'd pop my head up, then climb down the ladder and never even think about putting it away.

The summer my parents had been married twenty-five years, I had another problem with my dad. It had no name and I couldn't talk about it with anyone, and even thinking about it made me feel like I might throw up or faint. I couldn't tell Mom or Melinda and surely not Rose or Julie. I couldn't write it in the journal I'd started keeping. (The journal had been an assignment at school and I'd hated it like leeches for about five minutes and the next thing I knew I was writing in it all the time and then keeping a different one at home that didn't have anything to do with school. This, too, was private.)

It had happened in June or early July. I'd been upstairs in my room, listening to music and I heard Dad's truck pull up in front of the house. It was late, and I should have been in bed. Mom was asleep on the couch. I quick turned down the music and changed into a nightgown so he'd think I'd been about to go to bed, and then I actually got in bed and rolled around so as to give myself pillow hair. I walked down the steps, casual, yawning. By the time I reached the den he was sitting in his chair as if he'd been there for hours.

"Hey, Daddy," I said, giving him a little wave.

"Zip." Dad nodded, lit a cigarette. "What are you doing up?"

"Oh, nothing. I *was* sleeping but I heard you come in and I just came down to say good night." I stepped over animals and books and a Crockpot that had taken up residence in the middle of the floor of the den; no one could say precisely why and no one would move it. I sat down in Dad's lap and leaned against his chest, as I had done millions upon millions of times before. I breathed in the smell that was the essence of him, a smell that lived in the hollow of his throat, and which when I had been a really little girl I used to try to smell on his pillow when he left for work each day, because I was afraid I wouldn't live until he got home again. The scent was impossible to describe but it never changed and it was intoxicating. Mom could smell it, too; I'd heard her say to Mom Mary that she would have married Dad for that alone.

All those millions of times I'd climbed into his lap. It was routine, so often rehearsed and fully memorized I'd never given it any thought. I was, in some critical way, *a part of Dad's lap,* and I fit inside the curve of his arm like a puzzle piece. There was a hollow place just below his collarbone that had been designed for my head. We were like Howie and Mickey; we were just going about our business, Dad somewhere, me somewhere else, but at the end of the day or when I fell asleep in the car or when I was sick, he picked me up and we were that other person. Just one person.

This time he didn't move, he didn't make the right adjustments or use his arm to pull me up closer and settle me in a position so he could see over my hair. His whole body was stiff; he seemed *angry.*

"Hop up now," he said, his eyes fixed on the television. "You should be in bed." He might as well have hit me. It would have been better if he had hit me. For a moment I just stood by his chair, but he didn't look at me or say anything else, so I stepped back over the Crockpot, the books, the animals. I couldn't see where I was going, but I made it to the doorway without tripping. I was about to cross into the dark living room when he said, "You're a big girl now, too big to sit on my lap." I stopped but didn't turn around. "And listen to me." His voice took on the tone he used when he was about to name a cardinal law, the defiance of which would result in punishment so dire it had no name and had never yet been employed. "*You are not to sit on anyone else's lap, either.* Do you hear me?" I didn't have to look at him to know what his face was doing, the flame of him, his absolute authority. "I *said,* Do you hear me?" I nodded, my back still turned to him, and took off running. I ran past the piano, through the doorway into my parents' bedroom (where they never slept anymore), up the stairs. I nearly flew across the room that had been my sister's and onto my bed, where I lay on my stomach and buried my face in my pillow and hoped I would suffocate, a trick that never worked.

I didn't know what I had done; I could never ask and he wouldn't tell me anyway. But somehow, through a failure of attention—or maybe it had been a series of small crimes added together—I had made him stop loving me. I had lost my father.

Here are the things Melinda was really good at: 1. Having great babies. 2. Undercooking meat. 3. Painting things on walls. 4. Getting impatient and losing her temper and then apologizing for it and maybe buying a present to make up for it. 5. Setting her house on fire. 6. Remembering birthdays and holidays and getting a card for someone and signing it from someone else. The "someone" was usually my mother and the "someone else" was Dad. And she was really excellent at planning things and making unusual decisions and causing good things to appear where they hadn't been before. So when she said there needed to be a party to celebrate Mom and Dad's silver wedding anniversary, everyone knew there would be one and she would make it happen.

Melinda said there should be a photograph taken, a formal portrait that would run in the paper alongside a picture from their wedding. This was a tradition I was highly against, because it was *disturbing.* There were such pictures in the newspaper *every day,* and I didn't understand why other people weren't bothered by them. Oh, here we are when we were young and still had our own hair and both of our arms! And here we are now—the only thing keeping us upright for this picture is the fear we will land on our colostomy bags! (Another thing Melinda was good at: jokes involving colostomy bags. I had no idea what they were for or where one kept them but my *word* they were funny. She could also build a story around the word "tapeworm" like nobody else.) So what if two people had been married sixty-eight years? You'd think the further away you got from having your face *still attached to your head* the more privacy you might crave.

It seemed maybe Dad agreed with me, because he didn't want to go to Olan Mills and have the pictures taken. In fact, he was showing signs of maybe not wishing to have the party at all. For instance, he said to Melinda, when she stopped by to talk to Mom about decorations, "I hope it's her other husband you have in mind for this event, because I'm not coming."

Melinda barely glanced at him. "Yes, you are," she said, showing Mother a sample napkin.

In Mooreland all parties were held in churches, either in the big basement of the North Christian Church, or in our Fellowship Room at Mooreland Friends. That was problem one, right there. Dad didn't like to go in churches; they didn't work for him. The few times I'd seen him at the Friends Meeting, he looked claustrophobic, or as if his tires had been overinflated and he should NOT be driving on them. I couldn't watch it. I didn't like him to go to specials at church, nor weddings, funerals. If it were up to me I'd have kept him away from *anyplace* with pews and hymnals. I think even podiums and a certain kind of light were a bad idea.

Second: he didn't like to be around Church People, particularly the Friends Church People. He didn't say it straight out, but I think he felt judged by them, and with good reason. He knew for a fact that Mom had been praying out loud for his salvation for the past twenty-five years; she prayed *every week,* three times a week, at church and in her prayer cell, for my dad to be saved and join her in a churchgoing life. She prayed for him to become a different sort of man. He *knew* this. He knew that in her out-loud prayers (please see Paul's Letter to the Hebrews) she maybe told some things about him, about our life, that he wouldn't want known. It hardly mattered that she was saying them to God when a bunch of other people were listening, too. And then once in a while he was called upon to go stand among those same people, the righteous and the humble alike, and pretend that everything was even between them all when it was sure not.

He could have had an ally with me on the church question, a powerless one but an ally nonetheless, had it not been for the fact that when it came to churchgoing my dad's Indian name was Speaks Out of Both Sides of Mouth. He made me go with Mom every Sunday. He would not intervene, even if I begged him to explain to her that I was just like him. It didn't matter if she made me go once or eighteen hundred thousand times, I was not going to give in and I was not going to join in and I would not be swayed. But all he ever said was "Do what your mother tells you."

But Dad must have not been entirely clear on the anniversary party, because one step at a time, Melinda was victorious. The photograph at Olan Mills was taken and ran in the paper. Invitations were issued, napkins purchased, the ingredients for the Universal Punch were gathered and waited in the freezer in the church kitchen. I was told I would have to wear a dress, and before I could really get going on the subject Melinda told me she'd already bought it and also here were new tights that weren't too small, so the crotch wouldn't be down holding my knees together. She said Shut up before I'd gotten even one little sound out, so I did.

Mom asked me with great seriousness if I would do the honor of being Guest Book Girl. She asked me this as if there were something marvelous at the other end, and also an enormous amount at stake. Being in plays at Ball State had not been wasted on her; it brought back her sleeping high school acting career, where she had been the star of every show even if she played a minor role, because when she walked onstage everyone else just disappeared and looked silly.

I said I would *certainly* be the Guardian of the Guest Book, even though I knew that the job was the equivalent of being asked to stand next to a pond or a dead tree or a dead person, for that matter. I tried to imagine the responsibility ahead of me, any crises that would require my intervention. The pen could be dropped. That was all I could foresee. I would pick it up if that happened, I told Mother, and we gave one another grave looks and went to get ready.

It was a beautiful Saturday in late August, a day of rare blueness. It was warm but nothing like the usual August day in Indiana, which felt like the inside of a stomach. My dress looked like a piece of yellow Fruit Stripe gum; it had short sleeves and hung straight to the middle of my thighs. It was made of some fabric (I had no idea what) that was both unwrinkleable and unscratchy, a combination I didn't know existed. Altogether it was another little miracle on Melinda's part.

Mom put on the white dress with the fur-fingerlet extra part. Her hair was in a French twist and she put on lipstick from one of the little Avon sample tubes that made me crazy with its shrunkenness. She even clipped on dangly earrings with a pearl at the bottom. Mom didn't "believe" in pierced ears, a vexation in my life I could tell was only going to get worse. I didn't want to wear jewelry but I did want holes in my ears. Mom said piercing anything was savage and a form of ritualistic scarring. Melinda went along with Mom because the thought of actually getting her ears pierced, the process part, made her woozy with horror.

Periodically Mom would say, "Bob? I've laid your suit out, you might want to start getting ready," and there would be no reply. Then she'd say, "Bob, I told Melinda we'd be there at one thirty to help her get set up," and he wouldn't answer from his chair. I had on my new white tights and Lindy had polished my saddle oxfords and I was trying to prevent whatever was inevitable from happening to the tights and also I was keeping an eye on Dad but he didn't give me any eye back. At one point he did call me Barrel of Monkeys and I realized I'd been doing somersaults forward and backward, forward and back, in the doorway to the living room, and my tights were covered with animal hair. *But none had stuck to the dress.* I couldn't wait to tell Melinda she'd discovered the future and that when I grew up I wanted my whole house to be made of it, whatever it was.

Mom and I walked down to the church alone, pretending we hadn't noticed that Dad wasn't with us.

"What a beautiful day for a party!" Mom said, taking a deep breath. "Your sister will be so pleased."

I said, "Want to see me hopscotch all the way there?"

She did, so I did.

Mom, Melinda, Rick, and I set up the tables and covered each with two tablecloths—yellow underneath, lace on top; we set out the centerpieces Melinda had bought: baskets of flowers in shades of yellow and copper and cream. There were taper candles in short brass candlesticks. Rick set up an easel and propped up a large corkboard on which Melinda had made a collage of the last twenty-five years, wedding pictures and birth announcements and family gatherings. It was amazing. Mom stood in front of it a long time.

"And I stood up and realized that no fur had stuck to me," I was saying to Lindy.

"Well, it isn't flame-retardant, so don't get too close to the candles," she answered, straightening the napkins she was arranging in a design.

"You said *retardant.*"

"Don't make me pinch you."

We worked and worked and when everything was ready I couldn't believe what Melinda had made. I had no idea how she imagined such things in the first place, the colors, everything.

Mom and Rick kept looking at their watches; soon I would have to go to the front of the church and take my place by the Guest Book. It was possible he wouldn't come. No one was saying it, no one was even thinking it very loudly. I was thinking it as barely as possible, just as he opened the back door and stepped in. He had skipped the sanctuary, of course.

He was wearing his chocolate brown suit, the one I liked best, with a pink shirt and a champagne-colored tie. I couldn't believe it was possible, but he matched the decorations. His hair was freshly cut, he was so closely shaved his face looked smoother than mine, and he smelled like soap and aftershave, cigarettes and breath mints. Melinda went into the kitchen and brought out two boxes: a corsage for Mother, which Dad pinned on her as if they were going to the prom, and a boutonniere for him. It wasn't until she carried out the cake and put it in the center of the table that Mom understood what Melinda had done, and then I understood it, too, where I'd seen these colors before.

Melinda had re-created our parents' wedding reception from the description in the newspaper and from photographs. She had found their cake top (not a bride and groom but two doves) in a box in the closet and taken it, along with a photograph, to a woman in New Castle who had baked the exact same cake they'd had twenty-five years before. I watched Mom trying to take it in and I waited for her to say something, but at just that moment Aunt Donna came through the door saying, "You know I thought we were going to be late, Kenneth couldn't find the car keys and I was just beside myself and oh honey don't you look pretty," she said to Melinda, "here are Aunt Donna's mints, you don't need to do anything but take the foil off, I've used the silver platter you asked for, Melinda, the one that's in the shape of a leaf, Bobby, come here and let me get a look at you."

I headed toward the waiting Guest Book, but not before I saw that Mom had a handkerchief out and Dad already had that look.

Melinda had asked Jimmy Carnes to take pictures. Jimmy was a great photographer; he had longish blond hair and a blond beard, blue eyes. He drove an Easy Rider sort of motorcycle, was quiet and painfully handsome, shy. Everyone I knew was half in love with him. I was also half in love with his wife, so part of me wanted to marry Jimmy and part of me wanted me to be adopted by him. He stepped into the vestibule where I was standing next to the Guest Book. The camera he had around his neck was so big and impressive this might as well have been a crime scene. I took one look at him and realized I had been wrong in my earlier thinking: I three-quarters wanted to marry him.

"Can I take a picture of you?" he asked.

"I don't much like to have my picture took. Tooken. Taken." Where was my helmet? That's what Melinda would have asked.

"How about just one. I'll make it painless."

Part of the reason Jimmy was such a great photographer was: who on earth could ever turn him down? "Okay," I said. I stood next to the miniature podium on which the Guest Book was displayed, making sure the pen would be in the picture. He didn't lie—he took only one photograph, and when I saw it later I was surprised by how good it was. In a strange twist, the doors behind me were the same color as my hair, so it was impossible to see what was happening on my head. Camouflage was the single solution Melinda and I had overlooked in the search for what to do about my hair, and Jimmy had figured it out right away.

After everyone who was going to arrive had arrived, I wandered back to the Fellowship Room to see how the party was going. It was going boring was how. It was just a bunch of adults milling around with plates and napkins, looking at Melinda's collage of pictures. *Oh my Lord my Lord,* I thought, *I cannot take this for one single second.* Dad was as rigid as a human ironing board, once in a while offering a pretend smile that was *punishing* it was so false. Melinda was busily serving punch and organizing things, and no good could come from being the object of her attention under such circumstances. I walked backward through the doorway I'd just come in, all but invisible, what with my hair matching the woodwork and my dress the same color as the tablecloths. I crept back through the sanctuary and out the front door without a backward glance at the Guest Book.

Our church had a metal handrail on either side of the wide steps; it was a tube, like monkey bars are made of, and at the top of the steps there were about four feet of it across, three or four feet high. Maybe what I'm saying is already clear: either the Friends or God himself had provided me with a little piece of perfect. For years I'd been mastering the handrail, and had worked up some serious moves. My favorite was the simple but impressive Run Across, Hit the Rail at Hip Level, Flip Over, Dismount in Air, Land in the No-Man's-World Beyond the Steps. But I also liked to just flip over and over and over. August was a good time for it, because there were no coats, no zippers, my skin didn't stick to the metal and get peeled off in sad little sheets. The miracle dress fabric was the best I'd found so far—it was frictionless.

I flipped over and over many times. I was almost too tall for this game, which just made it more pleasurable. Each time I reached the upside-down-point my head just *barely* brushed the cement steps. I flipped, then stood up and said, Whoooaaaa, and as soon as I could see straight I started flipping again. I was going for a record number of flips but for some reason could *not* count, when I heard a ruckus in the vestibule and knew right away that something bad was going on in the area of the Guest Book; of course it was, because that's what happens when you think you cannot possibly get caught in your shirking.

I stood up, Whoooaaa, holding the rail for support, just as the big double doors at the front of the church opened and Dad came storming out, my sister right behind him saying, "Please don't, please, Dad, please don't go," in a voice I hadn't heard her use in . . . ever. And that she would use that tone with him? Unimaginable.

Dad was down the stairs and across the street before I really realized what was happening. He walked right past me as if I'd ceased to exist, and he moved down the sidewalk with the speed, the gliding grace he'd always had; nothing at all like a man with one leg either shorter or longer than the other. Lindy stood at the top of the steps in the brown dress Mom had made her, looking as if she was going to cry in some huge, alarming way, the kind of crying that, when she'd done it in the past, made me want to slip out of my body, simply leave it behind like a snakeskin. She hadn't cried that way since she'd grown all the way up and moved away from her blue bedroom at the top of the stairs. I braced myself, but she just turned around and walked back inside, careful to catch the heavy door so it didn't slam shut.

Time was I would have followed him. It was tempting. By now he was tearing off that champagne tie, his head twisted bitterly to one side, and tossing it on the bed. He would take off the jacket, too, but leave on the pants and the pink shirt, with the collar unbuttoned and the sleeves rolled up. He would leave on the oxblood wing tips, and check his pockets for his cigarettes, his lighter, his wallet, gather up the silver on the dresser top. All my life he had looked like a man with money, no matter what. If I were there, in the house, I wouldn't talk and neither would he, and the moment would come when he'd either say, "Get in the truck," and we'd head out together, or he'd say, "'Bye, Zip," and I'd watch him go. Either way, I wouldn't have to face what was waiting at the party.

I thought maybe I'd talk to Mickey Danner. Maybe at lunch one day I'd tell her I had a problem with no name I could think of. I stood in front of the church and imagined the scene, how Mickey's eyes would go wide with concern, the way she would cover my hand with her own and say, "Dear, I'm sure you're mistaken. Everyone knows your father loves you *terribly.*" She would invite me to come spend the night with her and Howie, and sleep in the guest room with the curtains I'd chosen. It was a wonderful, clean, cool room. The floorboards were polished, there was a rug with a sunflower in the center, and Mickey had trained an ivy plant to wind through the bed's brass headboard. Maybe I would tell her. Maybe not.

Sabina:

Oh, oh, oh. Six o'clock and the master not home yet. Pray God nothing serious has happened to him crossing the Hudson River. But I wouldn't be surprised. The whole world's at sixes and sevens, and why the house hasn't fallen down about our ears long ago is a miracle to me.

She comes down to the footlights.

This is where you came in. We have to go on for ages and ages yet.

You go home.

The end of this play isn't written yet.

—THORNTON WILDER,
The Skin of Our Teeth, ACT III

Pink Like Me

Dad couldn't take a paying job and continue to collect his pension and disability, so he had the very smart idea of *volunteering* as a county sheriff's deputy. I can't believe he hadn't thought of it before. The perks for the volunteer were greater than any salary: a car, uniforms, a badge, a nightstick, *a gun*.

At night I used to lie in bed and say the number of his squad car, 33-55, over and over like a chant, trying to make sense of it. I'd picture him wearing the standard-issue shoes with white socks, which my mom said made him look like an overgrown Eagle Scout, and then I'd see the brown pants and shirt tucked in; the badge; the tall, astonishing hat with the silver rope braid. And the black belt: gun, nightstick, blackjack, radio. Someone had given my dad a legally authorized holster with a registered weapon and it had bullets in it. This was not a little belt worn around his calf in which he hid a two-shot Derringer. This was of an entirely different order. I'd say 33-55, 33-55, and I'd see him walking out the door in the uniform, and in short, I was afraid.

Dad took to the cruiser, the uniform, the lingo, as if he'd been born to the job. I knew for a fact that while he might lose his temper and toss a drunk against the side of a building until damage was done to the bricks, he would no way stop and touch a sick animal, and he wouldn't chase anyone on foot because it wasn't dignified, and it seemed to me that more than just a temper was required of a deputy sheriff, but my mom and sister and I kept our worries to ourselves.

Then he started getting partners. He got his first partner and basically we were all living in 1 Adam-12. The partner, Sam, was tall with thinning blond hair and a smile that not in a million years could you trust, and he'd been on "the force" for a long time. He had a way I got used to after a while: he cozied up, and maybe he would hurt you. Sam and Dad made up their routines: Sam was the bad cop and Dad was the good. Or they took turns. One day they arrested a man who had been writing bad checks (who knew this was a crime? And if so, why hadn't Sam arrested Dad?), and as they put the man in the back of the cruiser, he began to stuff something in his mouth and chew frantically. Sam was driving, so Dad reached around and thrust his hand in the Bad Check Man's mouth and pulled out a wad of paper, getting seriously bitten in the process. This caused him to wind up in the emergency room, and when he got home he explained the extreme dangerousness of human saliva, which sounded as toxic as hyena spit. He'd been lucky, he said, that the man was missing most of his front teeth. All in a day's work, my mom said, not looking up from her book.

I had taken to sucking on gravel, which didn't go over well with my sister. I couldn't explain why I wanted to do it, but once a day, when I thought no one was looking, I'd go out and sit by the fence dividing our house from the Newmans' Marathon station, gather up a handful of gravel, and stick it in my mouth. Sometimes I washed it off with the hose, and sometimes I just rubbed it on my shirt. I'd get it in there, move it around. Pea gravel makes a lot of noise in a mouth. It tasted exactly like rock. I'd see how much I could hold in one cheek, then fill the other, too, a game I had played with popcorn, marshmallows, and BBs. I might spit the rocks out one at a time, like watermelon seeds, or if I saw Melinda coming, I'd drop them all at once. This nearly always left a little trail of gravel dirt on my chin, which vexed Lindy no end.

One afternoon I was sitting by the fence, mouth filled with gravel, when a car pulled up I'd never seen before. It stopped right in front of my house. It wasn't just a stranger's car, it was a strange car—long and white and fabulous-looking. The horn honked, and I stood up a little and looked inside. There was my dad, driving.

"Hey, Zip!" he said, happy as could be. "Spit your rocks out and come take a ride with me."

I left my gravel over by the fence and walked toward the passenger door. I didn't even try to hide my whistle, or the shock on my face. This was a long, white Cadillac Coupe de Ville if ever I'd seen one, and it had red leather interior, and there was my dad, sitting down low in the driver's seat, his cigarette arm out the window, wearing his new deputy sheriff aviator sunglasses. I sat down and kept sitting and sitting. I sank into the seat as if it were made of leather-covered Miracle Whip. The car smelled of cigarette smoke and something I'd never met before. I looked around and saw it: a little metal tub of air freshener, like strawberry-scented Vaseline.

"You buy this car?" I asked, as we sped off down Charles Street. The engine made absolutely no noise, and I was thrown back against the seat as if a team of carburetors had spooked. I was trying to imagine the look on my mother's face when she discovered he'd purchased another vehicle, as he periodically did, and always to great surprise and peril.

"Nah, it belongs to my new partner."

I glanced over at him but he was not the sort of deputy who gave anything away. I knew for a dead fact that this was a pimp car, and I couldn't see how Dad was going to get by with it. The sheriff of Henry County, Joe Harris, a man I loved like the Great and Powerful Oz, did not cut anyone a piece of slack. He had once stopped a woman for speeding and noticed on her driver's license that she was supposed to be wearing glasses. He reprimanded her and she said, "I have contacts." He shouted, "I don't care who you know, you get your glasses on!"

"Your new partner?" The car had electric everything, and in the midst of pressing buttons I ended lying completely down in the backseat.

"Yep."

"Where's Sam?" I'd been rather fond of Sam, because he was slick and a liar and always gave me presents.

"Gone undercover. Vice." This was how Dad talked now.

"So who's this guy?"

"Fella named Parchman."

I raised the eyebrow. "Parchman?"

"Parchman Williams. Goes by Willy. Want to use the car phone?" He pointed to the floorboard. Sure enough, there was an old almond-colored phone sitting there. No cords attached to anything.

I picked it up and pushed some numbers.

"Who'd you call?"

"Julie."

"What'd she say?"

"Same as ever."

We drove out onto Highway 36 and sped up. I leaned back against the seat, watched the speedometer climb past 60, 70, 80, 95. The wind rocketed through the open windows and I wanted to laugh out loud but that wasn't really deputy behavior. My hair got all in my face and poked me in my eyes. I'd forgotten I had hair and vowed to do something about it.

"Got any scissors in this car?" I shouted over the wind noise.

"Nope. There's a bowie knife under the seat," he yelled back.

I shook my head. I'd taken knives to my hair before and it was nothing but a bunch of sawing.

We passed a county cruiser and my first thought was, *This is it, we are finally going to jail,* but the cop just flashed his lights and drove on by. Then we came up on a little old man in a Buick driving about forty miles an hour, and Dad slowed down, relaxed even further in the seat. I'd begun to think of old men as Raisins, and their wives as Raisinettes.

"You could pass this Raisin in about two seconds," I said, wishing we were back to driving so fast it felt like space travel.

"Nah," Dad said, tossing his cigarette onto the road. "We're just cruising on a lovely afternoon." He turned off the highway and headed back toward Mooreland.

"I won't tell Mom about the ninety-five miles an hour," I said, sticking one of my bare feet out the window.

"Your mom couldn't care less about where you are or what you're doing," Dad said, just stating the facts. "She's Mrs. College now."

I didn't say anything. We passed the house at the edge of town that set up a hard longing in me, but I couldn't say why. My sister had such a house, too, at the other end of town. I turned and looked away from the house, at a field of beans just shooting up bright green, like a carpet you could walk and walk across. We passed the house where my sister's friend Janet had grown up, and the patch of field with the lucky horse, then turned at the Masonic Lodge on Broad Street and Dad drove extra slow, as if hoping for someone to notice us.

When we pulled up in front of our house I saw that he was right—my mom's little Volkswagen wasn't there, and wouldn't be there.

"You staying?" I asked Dad.

"Nope. Gotta return the car."

It looked to me like a car that more than once had not been returned, but I didn't say so.

Dad winked at me, pointed to the phone on the floor. "Call if you need me," he said, then drove away.

I walked over and sat down, put the rocks in my mouth one by one. There was always the question of who would feed me, and somehow it always got answered. Rose's mom, Julie's mom, my sister. 33-55.

Like every other man I knew, my dad hated all black people and loved Bill Cosby. We had all of Cosby's records and he was one of the few comedians who could make my dad laugh out loud. For a brief time Dad was also for Sammy Davis, Jr., but then he found out that (a) Sammy had only one eye, and (b) he was a Jew. A one-eyed Jewish black man who hung out with Dean Martin was more like a pet to Dad, so he gave Sammy up.

For a little while, a little *tiny* while, no one said that Parchman Williams was black, not even I said it and I'd seen the strawberry-scented Vaseline. Dad would come home in the evenings, or he would not come home, and he'd tell stories about himself and Willy, and Mom would laugh politely. Now as she read she made notes in the margins of her books, something she hadn't done before. And she wrote in spiral notebooks, line after line of her beautiful handwriting, so I assumed she was being punished for something. Mom laughed politely and didn't say anything about how much my dad and every other man in Mooreland hated black people, and I didn't say it, and then one night it was announced that the coming weekend we were going to Willy's house for dinner, and I was going to have to wear shoes.

My dad had gone to the special trouble of picking me up a pair of sandals at Grant's department store. They were just flip-flops, but they were covered with denim, and had a daisy where the two straps met. They confused me. On the one hand they were shoes, my mortal enemy, and on the other, they were covered in denim, my dear dear friend. Then there was the daisy to contend with. I tried pulling it off but it was attached hard. I thought maybe I could ruin the daisy off. I put them on, went outside, and ran the hose over them, then stomped around. I made a mud puddle, stomped around in it, rinsed them off. A terrible thing happened: the flip-flops grew to my feet in a way that reminded me of my old cowboy pajamas, the way I could put them on and they were just cowboy-printed skin. These were shoes, and I loved them. I had to sit down on the swing and try to take the news in. If I could love these shoes, shoes with a flower on top, I was capable of pretty much anything.

That made me think about my hair, so I got on my bike and rode down to Linda's Beauty Shop, still wearing the shoes. I thought I'd just take my chances. If Linda Lee noticed and said something, I'd not only throw them away, I'd maybe cut my feet off. I'd also give her daughter Laurie, one of my best friends, a chance to mock me, though that wasn't really Laurie's way. She was a cousin of the Hickses on her mom's side (everyone but me was a cousin of Hickses, a sad fact), and she was just naturally funny about everything without being mean. I don't know how it happened in that family that most everyone was kind and everyone was just flat-out screaming, falling-down funny, but it was. In my family if you inherited something it was bad hair and a big nose, and if you came from that particular holler in Tennessee, you got everything good, including being pretty.

Laurie was walking around outside with her dog, Pooch. Pooch was a little bit bigger than a Chihuahua, with a tail that curled over his back, and he ruled the town. He went where he wanted, when he wanted. He was like a dog with a pocket full of money and a group of powerful friends. Laurie spent half her time with him and half her time looking for him. She had a way of calling him that was a variation on his name—"Beee-ooo-uuuutch! Beee-ooo-uuuutch!"—that was so funny he'd come home against his will. He walked up to me and smelled my shoes, then wagged his curly tail. I thought to myself, *Hmmmm.* But Pooch and I naturally got along, so maybe he was being courteous.

"I gotta get this hair outta my face, Laurie," I said, scratching Pooch's head.

"You don't hardly have any hair to talk about," she said. I thought about saying, You haven't seen it in a stolen Cadillac going 95 down the highway, but I kept that to myself. Laurie's own hair was silky blond, wavy, and long. But that didn't make me hate her. I didn't hate her even though she owned one of the single most enviable pieces of stuff I'd ever seen in my human life: a fireplace made out of cardboard (with drawn bricks and everything) that got set up at Christmastime. There were cardboard logs and cardboard flames—pretty big ones—that lit up when it was plugged in. When I'd seen it for the first time last Christmas I couldn't tear my eyes away until I was offered a bunch of candy.

"I doubt Mama can cut it today," Laurie said, watching Pooch amble off down the street. "She's got three sets and two perms, and a rinse later in the afternoon." Hair came easy to Laurie, like nothing came easy to me.

I thought about it. I didn't have long before we were going to Parchman Williams's house, and between the hair and the shoes, I didn't want him to get the wrong impression. I only had two other options: my sister, who was likely to stab me in the neck then blame me for it, or Susie's Cut & Curl, on the other side of town. One didn't go to Susie's, even though she was so sweet. She dressed like the Grand Ole Opry and in fact bore a passing resemblance to Loretta Lynn. The more I thought about it, the more she had something of the heartsick miner's daughter to her. But the reason one didn't go there was because of Linda Lee. Linda could be funny, she could slap you in the face if you happened to convince her son to eat dirt, she could be terrible mean, she could give you a good dinner if you needed one, she could comb your hair too hard or just right. But you did not cross her. I knew this as sure as I knew not to steal one of my dad's guns, though I was often and sorely tempted. Also Linda would cut my hair and let somebody else pay later, and I never looked a credit horse in the mouth.

"See ya, then," I said, starting to pedal away.

Laurie waved good-bye, called out "Bee-ooo-uuutch!" and I about had to stop my bike for laughing.

At home I did the worst possible thing, something I did almost every day. I broke into one of my mom's dresser drawers and stole from her collection of John F. Kennedy money pieces. I didn't know how much they were worth, fifty cents, a dollar, something like that, but I knew they added up to a lemon phosphate and a bag of chips if I was starving to death. She collected them not the way my dad collected things—because they were solid silver or pewter or fired raw gunpowder or whatever—but because she had grieved so mightily over Kennedy's death. She had been vacuuming when the news was announced, and she happened to be passing the television and could see that something was going on without being able to hear what it was. She turned off the sweeper, heard the news, and had to sit down on the couch before she fainted. I'd never heard her say that or anything like it before, that she nearly fainted. So I felt guilty some, every day stealing Kennedy's face out of her little plastic bag of Kennedys, but not very much, because money is money. Also the whole thing, the sweeping and the fainting, had happened before I was even born so it didn't count.

I grabbed a few moneys and hopped back on my bike and rode the opposite direction from Linda's Beauty Shop. I felt guilty about that, too, but again, just barely.

"How much of a haircut will this buy me?" I said to Susie as she opened the door of her shop, handing her the Kennedys.

"Sit down, honey," she said, in her thick Kentucky accent. Mooreland was absolutely nothing but hillbillies, but some of our flatbed trucks had arrived later than others. She barely glanced at the change, just put it in a jar on her counter. As Linda did, Susie cut hair in the front room of her house, which had been outfitted with tilty chairs and sinks and hair dryers shaped like UFOs. Susie tipped my chair back and washed my hair, and unlike Linda, she didn't scrub at my scalp with her fingernails until I was certain blood was streaming away with the soap. When she'd toweled off most of the water, she held up pieces of my hair and said, "Whatchoo want me to do here?" with that same tone of hopelessness I'd heard my whole life. On the other hand, she looked in general as if her husband had run off with both her best friend and her coonhound.

"I don't know. Just cut it," I said. "I don't like it getting on me."

Susie sighed, and turned the chair away from the mirror, starting on the back. Tammy Wynette was playing on an eight-track player in the corner. I had that tape, too, and in fact, d-i-v-o-r-c-e was the only word I could spell backward and forward. Susie cut and cut, sighing, and at one point said something about giving me something "modern." That meant completely zero to me. Then she turned the chair around, and I looked in the mirror.

I was speechless. Susie was speechless, though her eyes seemed filled with tears. I kept on saying nothing. Tammy Wynette got her heart broken a thousand times. Finally I swallowed. I looked exactly like a rooster. I said, "What do you call this haircut?"

"A Rooster," Susie said, and wiped the tears off her face.

I rode to my sister's little house, praying she was home. I prayed like this: *Jesus, if you don't make Melinda be home, I'm gonna make those forty days in the desert look like a cakewalk*. I *threatened* the Lord.

She was there all right, and when she opened the door, instead of saying, as she generally did, "What do you want to eat?" she said, "Oh my God, I'll get the hat."

I'd been the one to find the hat at Grant's last winter and it was like stumbling on a pile of rubies. It was just a white yarn bowl, like a white ball cut in half, elastic around the rim, but coming from the crown, where on a normal hat there'd be a puffy ball, there was *a long red yarn braid.* This was a hat that came with its own hair. I don't know why it hadn't been thought of before. In many ways it was better than my wig (which was a "fall," and so held on with a comb) because the cats were less likely to steal it. I couldn't count the number of times I'd seen my wig flying out the door in PeeDink's mouth. Sometimes he just sucked on it and sometimes he tried to kill it. I think it was a combination of a rat and a baby to him. Of course, he had fallen out of many a tree, and so his relationship with a wig was bound to be complicated.

I put the hat on as if it would save my life. Lindy said, "It's awful doggone hot outside for that hat."

"You got another suggestion?"

She studied me a minute. "What happened? Did you try to mow your head?"

"I'll have you know this is a modern haircut, Melinda, called a Rooster."

Melinda covered her mouth. "Did you go to *Susie*?"

I nodded.

"Oh ho ho, oh this is going to be rich," she said, sitting down at the kitchen table. She was filled with glee: a very bad sign.

"Linda don't have to know."

"She *doesn't* have to know, and yes, she does. How many people do you think walk around Mooreland sporting the Rooster? Exactly one little idiot child. And could you tell me . . . are you wearing shoes? Is that a FLOWER?"

I stood up to leave. I swung my head around so my long, bright red braid nearly hit my sister in the face. She just batted it away, and as I slammed the screen door she was still tapping on the table with her fingernails, another of her signs of evil happiness.

On Saturday evening we got in the truck to go to Parchman Williams's house. I sat between my parents and put one denim sandal on either side of the gearshift. I pulled my red braid over my shoulder so I wouldn't sit on it. We drove out of town silent, Mom thinking her thoughts, Dad smoking. I for one was desperately trying to imagine what was about to happen. I figured the best plan would be for me to act like everything in my life was just black, black, black. Here were the black things I knew: *Sanford & Son.* "We was robbed! We was robbed!" Very funny. *Good Times.* Funny + disturbing. The dad in that show, for a reason I couldn't put my finger on, reminded me exactly of my brother. He had the same uprightness and intensity; he flared his nostrils when he was vexed. I mean he *looked* like my brother to me, even, a fact I had not yet told anyone. Maybe I could say that, I could say, "Ah, of course, my brother is black." Black people ate things but I didn't know what. I could say, "This week at the Newmans' I had my favorite breakfast, fried beef brains and scrambled eggs, and then afterward we went out and did black farmwork." Black people wore clothes, but surely not the same ones I wore, and they lived in . . . that was it. They lived in tenements, and *so did I.* Sure, the Sanfords had a junkyard, but we had my dad's shed. And okay, in *Good Times* the elevator never worked, but at our house we often didn't have running water. I started to feel slightly more comfortable. Mom asked did I want to sing, and I said yes, I always said yes to singing. I meant to ask did she happen to know any Negro spirituals, but she chose "Down by the Old Mill Stream," a good choice because it had two parts, and we ended up in a little vaudeville harmony that pleased my dad, although he never said so.

❦

Parchman's house was on I Avenue, a disappointment, as it was not even remotely the ghetto. If New Castle had a ghetto, I wanted to find it. One of the things on my mind as we parked was how I was going to hold this over Rose: My Black People. Although on the one occasion I'd ventured my new treasure, she had announced that her church, St. Anne's, had a black family, and the father wasn't merely black, he was Caribbean and an intellectual. Leave it to Rose to get a black Catholic intellectual before I'd even ridden in the Cadillac.

The Williamses' house was a perfectly normal two-story, with wood shingles and a cement front porch. But right there, right on the porch, something was going on, because it had a railing (unusual among my kind) made of wrought iron with curly-cues. And the outside light wasn't white or even yellow for bugs, but a pinkish shade that made me squint up in suspicion.

We were out of the truck and moving to the door and I felt like everything was too speedy, I wasn't ready. My mom was wearing a dress she'd made and some broken-down shoes, and my dad looked, as always, as if he'd just beat the house in Vegas. We rang the doorbell (a doorbell), and the door was opened and in we stepped.

The house was cool, because there were window air conditioners running in every room. I'd never seen such a thing. In fact, I'd never seen anything like any single part of it.

My dad called him Willy but Mom insisted on calling him Parchman, which he seemed to appreciate, and either way, he was a great, glowing presence, who was suddenly everywhere, shaking hands with my dad as if they'd just met, and telling Mom how lovely it was to finally meet her and how he had heard she was just about the smartest thing to ever grace the planet. He turned to me. "And you, miss? May I take your hat?"

"No thank you," I said, shaking his outstretched hand, *my very first black hand,* "I'll just be keeping it on, but I sure like *Sanford & Son.*"

My mom nearly tipped over with shock, but Parchman said, "Now I do, too; I do, too. I met Redd Foxx once upon a time, I certainly did. We had quite an afternoon." As he led us through the house he told a rambling, quite hazy, and, in Bob Jarvis Land, shady story about spending an afternoon tipping them back with Mr. Foxx, as he put it. Every detail escaped me. I didn't know what a Universal lot was, or why Parchman was on it, or how it happened that he and Mr. Foxx had shared a long afternoon producing "ripostes of such graciousness Bill Shakespeare would have been jealous." I glanced at my mom and saw her mentally recording the phrase.

Everything on the first floor of the house was black and gold. The shag carpet was gold, and as long as the grass in our backyard, which my dad wasn't so interested in cutting. The living room furniture was black leather, and there was an enormous setup against one wall that Parchman called an "entertainment center." There was a large television in it, a stereo, tall speakers, I didn't know what-all. We had an entertainment center at our house, too, which consisted of an old television on a milk crate and a hammer lying nearby. The hammer did seem to solve most problems, including a wobbly picture and volume-control issues. The Williamses' coffee table was glass-topped, and the glass rested on the back of a black panther. On every wall were large paintings of black people doing black things: playing trumpets, dancing in smoky clubs, women flirting around lampposts. And then I saw it: in the corner beside the couch was a wicker basket, and rising out of it was a cobra, obviously made of rubber. I walked toward it and looked inside, and there were a number of rubber snakes, coiled up as if in the noonday sun. A rubber snake was stretched out across the back of the leather couch, and there was another slithering across the entertainment center. But there wasn't a real animal anywhere, I could feel it, and I could tell that there never had been, and wouldn't be. The house was filled with a smell that didn't include animals, but was layered and foreign. There was the strawberry smell as in the Cadillac, and something sweet and smoky (incense, I'd discover later); there was whiskey, and unusual beauty supplies, and a sharp, chemical tang that I realized was acetone. Next to the sofa was a small black table, and on it was a tray covered with bottles of fingernail polish, probably thirty different shades. There was a jar of cotton balls and three different sorts of fingernail polish remover.

What I wanted to do was go from room to room and open every closet door and look in every drawer and smell every single thing, because I was on a different planet, far as I could tell. I was just wandering into the dining room (dark wood paneling, black enameled table and chairs, a family portrait painted *on velvet*), when Parchman's wife emerged from the kitchen.

Rose and I had always been in agreement that my sister was the most beautiful person alive. She looked exactly like the sort of girl who would stay with the squirrels and little birds and sweep up the cabin while the Dwarfs were at work. But since she had gotten married, she'd lost a lot of that shine. I didn't know where it went, or why. There was no one to ask, or even any way to say it out loud. But Libra Williams was of a different order.

She walked toward us with her hand out, a welcoming gesture by a benevolent royal. Her hair was very short and waved against her head, black with gold streaks, just like the living room. I could dream, I could pretend, I could outright lie, but that was not what was happening under my hat. She was tall and thin, broad-shouldered. Her skin was the creamy brown of chocolate milk made exactly right. She was wearing gold hoop earrings, three gold chains around her long neck, gold rings, gold bracelets, and a silky pantsuit in some sort of jungle print. As with Parchman, there was the flurry of activity, the kindness to my mother, the dance around my dad, an offer to me of a Shirley Temple with an actual cherry. Libra called up the stairs for their son, Tyrell, to come downstairs for dinner, and Mom told me to go wash my hands. I stared at her blankly for a moment.

"Go wash your hands before dinner," she said again, this time with her teeth a bit clenched. I considered saying, "Mom, I eat rocks, for heaven's sake," but then it occurred to me I could see the bathroom if I pretended to obey her, so I went.

And lucky me, because here Parchman had outdone himself. The carpet was black, the shag was shaggier, and the walls were papered in shiny gold paper with lion's heads. But the best part was that the sink and toilet were both gold. Not Harvest Wheat. Not some Pale Avocado. Shiny gold, like Libra's jewelry. I was afraid to touch them. It didn't make a lick of sense to me that people peed on jewelry. I decided to go ahead and wash my hands, but the faucet, which was also gold, had a ball on top I couldn't figure out. There was no Hot or Cold. I pushed the ball and nothing happened. I pulled my hand back. I could easily destroy this thing and that would be the end of me and My Black People. I tried turning it, and it moved around freely, but no water came out. Finally, I pushed it up and out came water with a force I can only describe as wealthy. There was no initial spit of rust, no hesitation, no gaps. Before I knew what I was doing, I put my hands under the force, just to feel it, and then because there was a guest soap shaped like a seashell, I used it. I washed my hands, and dried them on a towel embroidered with a white "W," and walked out and held them out to my mom and said, "Ta-da!" She patted my hat and whispered, "Thank you."

Tyrell was nine. He was gangly and never stopped moving. His arms and legs seemed battery-operated. Black people, it turned out, ate exactly what white people ate: meat loaf, mashed potatoes, green beans, dinner rolls. Tyrell and I were given plates with dividers, which I found to be the height of civilization, as food touching made me spitting mad. We were also each given a

Shirley Temple drink, and there was the real cherry, and I couldn't believe how things had turned out. The rubber snakes, the King Midas bathroom, the incredible beauty and kindness of Libra. And free Shirley Temples. I wanted to live with them, and I was willing to change my name to something interesting, like Bocephus.

Tyrell's room was covered with posters of black athletes and musicians, and in a frame above his bed, a photograph of Redd Foxx with Parchman, signed "To Tyrell, Mind Your Daddy." I could hear our parents downstairs, the kind of continuous conversation and laughter that made me want to grow up. I never told anyone this, but I could not imagine a better age than thirty-five. I would someday be grown-up—I thought about it at night, lying awake—and I would drive tractors and own wolves. I would turn up my Glen Campbell records so loudly the wolves would howl, and at dinner we would have milk shakes, and I would erect scarecrows everywhere, I would have an army of scarecrows.

That had been my plan until I saw the home of Parchman Williams. Now I was thinking maybe I would have real snakes and a black panther and an entertainment center.

Tyrell and I ate mostly in silence, and he never said a word about my hat. He seemed to think it was real hair and I understood how maybe the ways of white people were unknown to him, and maybe we all had white heads and yarn braids. When we finished eating we played Rock 'Em Sock 'Em Robots; then we pulled on Stretch Armstrong until Tyrell fell down. He showed me his miniature foosball table and we played that awhile in silence. He was just quiet, which I was used to because of Julie. But his quietness meant I had plenty of time to think, and I was thinking about the scarecrows and maybe adding suits of armor, when I remembered an evening a few summers before when my family had driven to Indianapolis in the Nova we had then to get White Castles. We'd stopped at a gas station and our German shepherd, Kai, was in the backseat of the car, and as a black family walked down the sidewalk he sprang so hard at the window he nearly went through it, barking explosively enough to leave streaks on the glass. It had been terrifying and unexpected; Kai, who was gentle, and read people so well he knew enemies from friends long before we did. Dad seemed to find it funny, but Mom, I remembered now, had turned around, grabbed Kai's collar, shushed him, then said to my dad, in a fierce, angry whisper, "You *make him* do that."

"How did I make him do that?" Dad asked, in his false, innocent tone.

"Because you want him to, because he senses that you hate them."

"Hate who, Delonda?"

Mom looked out the window. "There's a child in the car."

I could hear my parents talking with Parchman and Libra, I could hear the clinking of their plates and glasses. I could not, even for a second, understand what we were doing here, or how we'd gotten here.

"Tyrell, has your dad always been a deputy?" I knew Parchman, like my dad, was a volunteer, so where had all this stuff come from?

Tyrell shook his head no.

"What did he do before?"

He shrugged, said something that sounded like "Own't know."

"Does your mom have a job?"

"She work at the drive-up bank."

I liked this way of speaking. Perhaps I would adopt it for myself. If there was a word or a letter you didn't need, you just left it out. Earlier he'd said, "This my favorite wrestler," and I realized, who needed that "is" in there? I knew what he meant and he got to the point faster.

"Did your dad work in a factory, or like on a farm, or something?"

"A *farm*?" Tyrell tipped back on the floor, held his sides laughing. "That man never cut a blade of grass in his life. A farm."

"Okay, a factory?"

He shook his head. "Naw, no factory. Own't know what he did, 'cept he move money around. All I can tell you. He move money around."

I was about to say something, something about our fathers, or at least my own, when Tyrell said, "You wanna watch TV?" I said yes, so he yelled down the stairs, "Hey Pop! We watch TV in y'all's room?"

Parchman shouted back, "Yes, but you know the rules."

And then Tyrell led me to Parchman and Libra's bedroom, and whatever I'd been on the verge of figuring out, I lost for a good long time.

The room was papered in black and gold foil. I know it was foil because I ran my hands over it. And up against one of those walls was a *round bed* the size of a swimming pool, and in fact it was like a swimming pool in that it was filled with *water,* and it was covered with *fur.* I stood dead still with my hand on the wallpaper, but Tyrell just walked over, flopped down on the bed, which swished around underneath him, and slid open a door in the black, arched headboard. The headboard arched halfway *over the bed* is what I'm saying, this was a bed with a *roof,* and when Tyrell pushed the button a television came on in the roof above him and he lay back on big, tiger-striped fur pillows and watched television. Lying on his back. On a round fur water bed. I walked slowly toward him, slipped off my new sandals, and lay down. In addition to the television there were stereo speakers built into the roof, and it was entirely covered with *mirrors.* So I could see the TV, and I could see myself and Tyrell, there was not one thing I couldn't see on the bed. I lay there perfectly still, thinking, *Rose will never believe me, Melinda will never believe me.* I myself would never have believed me. I tore my eyes away from the mirror and that's when I saw it: directly across from the bed was a large painting, and it was of nothing but a black man and a black woman, and they were naked as jays. I couldn't tell exactly what they were doing, and heaven knew that was for the best, but the fact of their nakedness had put a shock on my heart I thought might finally kill me. I tried to not move, to just take it all in, but every time Tyrell laughed at something on TV the whole bed sloshed around and nearly tossed me out. His arms and legs never did stop moving, which I could for sure see now that I was in a bed surrounded by mirrors. And there was that very strong smell again, that strawberry gelatin air freshener, and hair sprays I couldn't name, and those clothes made for black people and everything was very clean and of course there was the absence of even one real live animal in this house, not a hamster or even a goldfish, only the rubber snakes and the glass panthers and whatnot. I tried to picture Libra in a house with just one little well-behaved snow-white kitten and it was impossible. Not even a black-and-gold-foil kitten. Not with Libra's fingernails and leather sofas and bathrooms made of melted-down gold jewelry.

"Zip?" my dad called up the stairs. "You ready to go?"

I leapt off the bed as if scalded. "'Bye," I said to Tyrell.

"Later," he nodded, still watching TV.

I grabbed my shoes and scooted past the naked painting without looking at it. I didn't look at what was on top of the black dressers, either, but I did notice, for the first time, a photograph on a small side table out in the hallway. It was an Olan Mills picture, taken when Tyrell was probably three years old. There was Libra, the same air of untouchable beauty. She was the sort of woman my mom called fixey. And Tyrell wearing a small, dark green suit and bow tie. He wasn't happy. But no sign of Parchman anywhere. I leaned down and looked at Libra's hands (each fingernail was at least an inch long and in this picture they were scarlet, but tonight they had been a darker red with a gold streak through the center), and there were rings on every finger except the one.

"Zip?"

"Coming," I yelled, heart pounding as if I'd been doing something wrong.

When I got to the bottom of the stairs everyone was still laughing and talking. There was my mom in her mom clothes, her old glasses, her battered shoes. Libra, Parchman, and my dad made a little triangle and Mom wasn't in it. She said to me, "Thank your hosts," as she did every time we went anywhere, which was one of the reasons I hated going anywhere, and it was a stupid rule and made me physically ill, which I'd tried to explain 897 times. Nobody Cares If I Say That, I'd tried to tell her. THE WORLD WILL NOT END IF WE SKIP THAT PART. But somehow, tonight, it was easy. I held out my hand to Libra and she took it. Hers was cool, long, and narrow. She was a very kind woman, it seemed to me, and she deserved to live in this castle. "It was a very nice evening thank you for having me," I said, as had been drilled into me.

She pulled me to her, tapped the top of my hat. "You're welcome. Come back anytime."

Dad leaned over and said something to Parchman, said it in one of his many Dad voices out the corner of his mouth, and Parchman threw his head back and laughed with a great busting-out joy, a way I wasn't used to men laughing. He pounded on Dad's back a couple times between the shoulder blades, then Dad was laughing, too, and we were all moving toward the door, floating, really. We floated to the truck in such goodwill, and I sat between my parents and we drove off down I Avenue.

"What an evening," Dad said, lighting a cigarette.

"It certainly was," Mom agreed.

"Plain nice people, nothing more to be said than that."

"Very nice. How did Parchman get that gold toilet, I wonder?"

Dad laughed again, flicked his ashes out the wing. "He spray-painted it. Tub and sink, too."

Mom laughed, I looked back and forth between them. Dad seemed genuinely happy, which was sure never guaranteed, not one minute of any day, but Mom kept wearing that polite face. I'd seen it a thousand times. I'd seen it when he suggested we get a bigger camper, when he decided we had to move to Alaska, when he explained why he couldn't fix something broken in the house, why some things needed to wait, wait, and some things needed to be done yesterday, like getting a new truck. I saw Parchman throw his head back with laughter; Kai hit the window, teeth bared. *Because you hate them.*

One day the Williamses weren't there and the next they were a constant feature. Here is the music my dad would tolerate in the Before Time: Herb Alpert and the Tijuana Brass. Glen Campbell, but mostly for my sake. Glenn Yarbrough. Lena Horne. Dean Martin or Frank Sinatra. After Willie we might pause the truck radio on Smokey Robinson, who was said to have quite a bit of talent, all of a sudden. Same with a number of Motown artists formerly unknown in Mooreland, Indiana. Dad wouldn't go the distance and listen to some of the things we heard at the Williamses' I thought were especially delicious, particularly Isaac Hayes, who made me have un-Christian feelings. All of my worst crushes were on bald men, beginning with Telly Savalas and staying a long, long time on Yul Brynner. Once I realized there were bald black men in addition to bald tan men I knew the world was opening wide.

I stayed home with my dad while Mom was student teaching in summer school, every day, all day, and Parchman didn't have a day job, either, and then in the evenings he and my dad were partners on a night shift. Except it seemed they only worked when they wanted to, so we spent a lot of evenings at their house, too. They never came to ours.

One afternoon I was lying on one of the leather sofas holding a rubber boa constrictor, reading a comic I'd gotten that day. It was grim. It was the story of a woman who had been sent to an Insane Asylum because she believed a little goat-footed varmint was after her, and her Doctor was a man who wore eyeglasses but it was dark behind them, not like sunglasses, but like there was nothing behind his glasses, and he suggested she take up the flute. And not just any flute, but a flute made of reeds strapped together, each smaller than the last. A Pan flute, he called it. First he caused her to make the flute in a class with other crazy people, then he taught her to play it, then he made her go out into the garden at night, under a full moon, and play it to a fountain, where there was . . . a statue of the very goat-boy she feared. I was just getting to the good part when Parchman strolled in from the kitchen and sat down right on the glass coffee table. He tugged on my red braid.

"Zip," he said, "it's time we had the talk."

I glanced up at him. "What talk."

"The talk about racism. Now here's how I'm going to start it: you've got your chocolate milk, and you've got your white milk."

I raised an eyebrow.

"That's not going to work." He thought a minute. "Okay, okay—listen. Have you ever heard anyone say, 'Some of my best friends are black'?"

I could not abide a lecture, not even from Parchman Williams. "Some of my best friends are white," I said, looking back down at my comic book.

Parchman slapped his knees with his open palms. "Well. That about takes care of that," he said, patting me on the shoulder as he left the room. In the kitchen I heard him say, "You've got your hands full with that one. Lord, Bobby."

I heard the wheel of Dad's lighter, him taking a deep breath. "Yep. She's my pride and joy."

Sometimes when the four of them played cards I hung out in the kitchen instead of playing with Tyrell. I liked him just fine, but I could only spend so much time talking about Kareem Abdul-Jabbar or lying on that fur bed. The sloshy part made me nervous after a while. I would begin to think, *What's really in here?* If there's water and you can't see into it, there is always something in it. Maybe it has teeth, maybe it has tentacles, maybe it just has dumb fins. I didn't like thinking about it.

I remembered being four, five, six. I remembered how I was so quiet I was ghostly, and the way I could hide under tables or behind sofas and no one ever knew I was there. I still had the knack, even though I had gotten too tall to hide. Grown-ups still talked as if I weren't there, and I didn't understand why. When I was thirty-five I would never, ever let children hear anything I said or thought.

Dad had met his match in Parchman Williams, as far as cards went. They had the same gifts: the quick hands, the mask face, the wit that disguised wild-animal competitiveness. They bluffed and distracted, they told funny, cold jokes, and only bad luck—not lack of skill—could defeat either of them. Mom and Libra played like the wives of master gamblers. They were patient and even; good partners who just kept pace and didn't make mistakes.

"Libra told me if I want more children I'll have to have them with my next wife," Parchman said, taking a drink of beer.

"You heard that right," Libra said, tapping the dummy hand with one of her fingernails. "I'm done raising anything except my tax bracket."

Parchman said, "I think I'll make it diamonds. Diamonds for my dear wife."

"His next wife can do a lot of things different," Libra said, and everyone laughed.

"Would you ever remarry?" Parchman asked my mom.

My ears raised up on the sides of my head as if I were a fox listening for the farmer coming up the drive. *Remarry?* This was a word I had never heard spoken in the presence of my parents. It was not a word Rose's parents would ever use, nor Julie's parents, either. It was not in the vocabulary of their friends, the Spillmans. It was a word un-uttered in the Mooreland Friends Church. My mother? Parchman was asking this of my mother, who had given one piece of advice to my sister when she married: *Do not ever allow the word "divorce" to be spoken in your home. If you say it once, you let it in.*

I watched her. I opened and closed my hands, trying to flex out the panic. I watched my father. His face was blank as the night sky. She studied her cards, blinked patiently behind her old glasses. There had not been one moment I felt that Parchman and Libra and Tyrell were any different from us, really. Not a single moment, regardless of the magnificent house and the snakes. And depending on my mother's answer, I would know whether they were.

But she just shook her head. "It's not something I've ever considered," she said, without looking up, and I knew I should let it out, the terrified breath I was holding, but I didn't. I stood there at the edge of the room, watching them play the hand out. With men who played that well, it hardly mattered who won. The game itself was the joy.

Slumber Party, 1977

From kindergarten through fourth grade we had one class at the Mooreland Elementary School; we were all together every year, moving from the first- to the second-grade classroom when the time came. Why this didn't lead to a Kill the Weakest Member of the Herd type of behavior I don't know, but no one ever died or was eaten. That's where the friendships form that go back as far as memory allows: Rose and Julie, Anita and Annette, Kirsten who was beautiful even in kindergarten and never had a bad year. Margaret, Tod, Ronnie, Debby, Tony, Kelly Hicks of the next-door Hickses. I think we would have been happy to stay together through high school and higher education (Rose, Margaret, Ronnie for sure), or light jail time (me), and on out into the world, except that during the summer between fourth and fifth grades the Mount Summit elementary school closed, which I'm thinking must have been a sad thing, and their students moved over and joined us in Mooreland.

Now, I am sorry to say that those Mount Summit kids just weren't like us in some invisible way, and they kept to themselves and we did the same. The plan was to keep permanent divisions between us so there would be no cross-pollination and I was all for that, except it seemed like only four or five minutes had gone by and I was friends with a girl called Jeanne Ann who was a longtime friend of Anita and Annette because of something, church or 4-H, so it was natural to be with Anita and Annette and there was Jeanne Ann and oh, also she was hilarious and I got along with her dandy. Then there was this girl called Kathy, she was tall like me and I loved her, and strangely enough I knew her dad because he knew my dad. Her dad sold camping trailers on a lot next to the Ramrod Gun and Knife shop, which was just about my favorite store in the history of commerce. If I had to say what would be on a particular avenue in heaven I'd say let's start with Ramrod Gun and Knife, and yes, absolutely put camping trailers next to it, it's a natural. There should be a bait shop somewhere, and a store that sells beef jerky and lemon phosphates, and we're good to go.

I'd visited with her dad already so I went ahead and took up with Kathy, and she was a friend of Jeanne Ann's anyway, and then I don't know how it happened but we were all squashed up together, and by the sixth grade it was hard to remember when I didn't know the Mount Summit kids.

Kathy had a slumber party at her house and let me tell you: when the girl in school with *stuff* is also fun and generous and smart? Yes, you want to go to her slumber parties, and swim in her pool and ride around on her motorbike, which was small and orange and the exhaust pipe or the engine or something heated up to 3,000 degrees Fahrenheit after about three minutes of riding, and we were constantly yelling to one another, "Don't let your leg touch anything!" If we wobbled even slightly Kathy would yell,

"For God's sake, don't fall or the engine will melt your flesh!" We tore around the flat acreage behind her house like bandits, then jumped in the pool again. That night we slept in a camper her dad set up in the backyard. A brilliant idea, and it made me long for my own sales lot from which to choose for entertaining. There was mayhem in the trailer; it involved first s'mores and then raspberry jelly, and at some point Anita announced she'd either forgotten or couldn't find her pillow and Jeanne Ann sat up with one in her hands. She held it out to Anita and said, in the Kentucky tilt of her church's minister, "The Lord giveth"—Jeanne Ann pulled the pillow back—"and the Lord taketh away." I'd never laughed that hard before—it was the kind of laughing that weakens you and makes you exhausted, and then starts all over again. We were trying to stay up all night—that would be the goal at every party—and I was the one, always, who never fell asleep. I could have probably stayed awake for two or three days, really. I didn't mention it at the parties, especially in front of Annette, who played every sport ever invented (she possibly made up two or three extras) and so was always tired. She'd come to a slumber party straight from some grueling three hours of running up a straight, sheer cliff, at the top of which she was made to heave boulders at wildlife or whatever, and she'd be tired by dinnertime. I loved her and I always wanted to draw her over to the Other Side, the non–organized sports side of life, where there were no coaches (I'd discovered that coaches never liked me and I returned the disdain) or schedules or whistles blowing. I was already figuring out there is no profit in adding pain to a day, but for some girls, sports—the pressure, the physical toll, the group identity—were a *good* thing. I'd have to practice saying it: for them, the agony, self-chosen and self-perpetuated, is a *good* thing. They sure didn't harass me for lounging around on the front porch all summer, reading books and drinking Mountain Dew, waiting for the moment something would come along and determine the tune of the day. By the time I wandered over to the Coke machine at Newman's Marathon in my pajamas, Julie and Annette had already been training for *something* for hours. I was, too, it turns out: I was training to lie around reading.

Then Jeanne Ann had a slumber party and it was different from Kathy's because she was an only child of Older Parents who were practical and didn't have a pool or a flaming motorbike. She lived in the cleanest, squarest house I've ever been in and it turned out we didn't need the other stuff because have *mercy* it was outrageously fun. Jeanne Ann was in gymnastics and could do strange things, like a backbend and then spider walk across the floor. She was so flexible it was unholy and we all tried to imitate her, to much screaming hilarity and permanent damage to our cartilage. Hours were spent trying to teach me to belch, an impossibility as I'd made clear from the beginning. I didn't have the proper mechanism, I was missing a flap or something. I'd never in my whole life so much as burped. It was shameful but I'd adjusted. Jeanne Ann endeared herself to me forever by getting out a tape recorder as we practiced belching, or as she belched in various eloquent ways and I did what she told me and opened my mouth and nothing came out: a little silence on the tape. She fried bologna and we watched Sammy Terry on television, and the worst came when we realized Annette was asleep and someone, I won't say who, made a little fart very near her ear to try and wake her up. That was it for me. I thought I would have to be hospitalized.

I'd never had a slumber party at my house for the obvious reasons—in fact, I never had anyone over at all. I visited my friends; they didn't visit me. I noticed this, but it was rather like belching—I just didn't have the equipment. My sister decided she would host a slumber party for me at her little house where there was barely room for Melinda, Rick, and Josh, not to mention I was there pretty much all the time. The solution was we would have the slumber party in the backyard, and Melinda would put up a tent for us to sleep in.

We had a great time, it was quite shockingly fun, but I noticed Melinda becoming slightly more frazzled with every hour that passed. She was pregnant with a New Baby and I wasn't even thinking about that as I wanted no part of it. When we trooped in through the back door, past the laundry room, down the hallway that sloped to one side, past the bathroom, and into the kitchen for Kool-Aid, Lindy was fine, she didn't make any threats or anything. She decided to bring the popcorn to us which I understood, but it wasn't as if we were going to pee in the *garden,* we weren't *savages.* In fact we preferred to pee as a group, the opposite of savagery I believe, so we did that. We used up all the toilet paper but that was okay because there was a box of tissues so we used it instead.

I got out the sandwich maker from when we used to go camping. Julie and I built a fire and we took bread, buttered on the outside, and scoops of fruit pie filling (blueberry being the obvious first choice) and closed the cast-iron sandwich shape around it, cut off the crusts. Some of the other girls were amateurs and didn't want to wait for the bread to toast—a disaster in the culinary arts, impatience. What you have without toast is nothing. It's goo. We were all licking our fingers and contemplating our third-degree burns from the boiling fruit filling when Melinda opened the back screen door and stepped out onto the dark step, the light of the laundry room behind her.

"Uh-oh," Jeanne Ann said as I forced myself to stand and face it, whatever it was.

I walked toward my sister slowly. I'd be having a cigarette and a blindfold, please. She was completely still, an awful sign, as Melinda usually went frozen just before she struck. I was reminded of the vipers in Africa I'd read about, the largest and most powerful of all venomous snakes, who could move from a coiled position and strike at fifty-five miles an hour, probably the speed limit for most things. They could shatter the glass of moving safari vehicles. I remembered everything I could about vipers as I walked, step by step, toward the light of the back door, but none of it was good.

"Do you know what you've done?" Melinda asked, in the quiet way that was the way of the viper.

I shook my head.

"You put an entire box of Kleenex into our septic system."

What could I say? I believed her, but it was sort of news to me.

"You've stopped up our *septic system.*" She said this as if we had brought down the walls of the Alamo. "We're going to have to call a plumber."

"I'm sorry."

Melinda closed the door and went back inside without another word. I went back to my friends and reported the damage. No one understood the big problem, but we did understand we couldn't go back in the house or we would get our windshields shattered. But where to pee?

"Let's just pee in the garden!" Jeanne Ann said.

"Yes, let's just pee in the garden!" It was agreed upon and undertaken with such joy that Melinda popped her head out one more time, around two in the morning, and told me if she heard us, if she heard a single sound again, not to mention if we woke up Josh, whose bedroom window faced the yard, she would do unto us things I could not repeat to my friends. I slunk back to the tent and said we were going to have to be quiet, and that was so funny we all had to bury our faces in our sleeping bags, and then someone announced she had to pee.

In the dense darkness at four we decided to walk around town. We walked all over, up and down most of the streets, down to our own dark and silent elementary school, which spooked us. We walked past Edythe's house which everyone found unbearable, the knowing she was in there with her bathtub filled with newspapers and her blackened fingernails, the piano, her long hair. What no one said was what scared me most: what was she like *inside*?

We stopped in front of my own house. I stood there in the street with my friends. "Well, this is weird," I said, so we moved on.

The Mooreland Friends Church, the houses on Jefferson Street—the town was an entirely strange and surreal place at the edge of sleep like this. I couldn't get my mind around it, that behind every door there were people still in bed, they'd been in bed all night, and some of them, like my dad, were just about to open their eyes and have the world remade for them, as it was remade every day. Only we, who had been on watch through the hours, knew that it hadn't come undone in the meantime, things had hummed along fairly much as usual, just waiting.

We got in the tent and climbed in our sleeping bags, chilled. There was some crazy talk and it started to rain. The sound of the rain on the tent was enough, and one by one my friends fell asleep. I was shocked that they could do so, that their bodies could let go in such a way. My body did nothing unless I told it to, and even then sometimes coercion was necessary. I had reached an age where it was impossible for me to fall asleep by accident, it did not and could not happen, and I lay in my sleeping bag and imagined the consequences. It would be I, like my father, who could drive all night while the rest of the car slept. I would be the one pacing a hospital floor or working a strange shift in a factory. I didn't even like coffee; I'd have to figure that one out.

With everyone asleep I imagined Melinda's relief, the silence from the backyard. Melinda had a child, she was pregnant. It remained a shock. I could remember so clearly the night *she'd* had a slumber party and the whole cast was there, all her friends. They'd had a séance in the living room, gathered in a circle on the floor right next to the couch where I was trying to sleep. In the middle of it I'd looked at one of the tall, narrow windows and seen Jesus floating many feet off the ground, in the arms of the trees. I had seen him—I could not be argued out of it. But I hadn't seen him since.

It occurred to me that there might be nothing more hysterical in all the world than if I suddenly began to sing "The Star-Spangled Banner" as the sun rose. I wouldn't sing it loudly, but with reverence, as if I'd been waiting all night and this was my job, to comfort the troops. I opened my mouth but it was *too* funny and I began to laugh in that silent, organ-shaking way. I let some moments pass and tried to get ahold of myself, opened my mouth again. I laughed even harder and had to curl up in a little ball inside my sleeping bag and bite my knees. The third time I skipped directly to crying, tears ran down my face in streams, collected in my ears in little pools. I was on the verge of sobbing, so I buried my face in my pillow and held my breath. I waited for it to pass. My friends were so silent, sleeping sound, that with my eyes closed and pressed against my pillow's dark, I wondered if they were there at all.

Blizzard Baby, 1978

In Indiana, weather was considered a *very* interesting topic of conversation. It was talked about off and on all day, every day. No one simply stuck a hand out the door and made decisions accordingly, oh no. The local television news was consulted, as was the radio, and for good measure it never hurt to call Time & Temperature, in case your hand was lying. Hoosiers have always put stock in meteorologists; if, for instance, Bob Gregory—the best of all weather people—said bundle up you bundled up and if you were slightly overdressed then thank you, Bob, because that's better than freezing into a log person. If Bob said it looked like we were going to get heavy rains and we did, thank you, Bob, and if we didn't, thank you, Bob. Better, always, to be prepared for the emergency that *doesn't* arrive than to be found thumb-twiddling and half starved when rescued from the one that *does.*

❦

My sister was pregnant with the New Baby and I was part excited and part opposed, because there was nothing wrong with the Old One and I just didn't see how the whole thing was going to work out. The world, as far as I could tell, was Josh's world and we were just hanging around getting in the way, which he was sweet about. I knew my role, which was to serve, an assignment that would have earned a spitting from me if anyone had told me ahead of time but thankfully no one did. The summer between my tenth and eleventh birthdays I dreamed all of Mooreland was deserted and I had been left there alone with Josh, who needed an emergency appendectomy. The only car in town was a stick shift and I didn't know how to drive it, as the only truck I'd driven in real life had a gearshift on the column, a kind of transmission not much in demand even then. I woke up in a panicky sweat, called Melinda, and said, "All right. You better take me out and teach me to drive a stick shift." We went out on the Messick Road and she let me grind the gears and murder the clutch 757 times and eventually I figured it out and drove us home. So that was taken care of. What was a second baby going to do to my life and where would we put it? Melinda's house was simply not big enough and anyway I was tired.

I'd managed to avoid thinking about "the baby" as "a baby" until about mid-December, when someone pointed out that Melinda's due date was in early February, and how isn't it the case that January is the month with the average greatest snowfall and the lowest temperatures, ha ha what if Lindy went into labor early at home or in a car during some severe weather, I guess everyone should keep towels and boiling water handy. Ha ha. It was then I realized Melinda was going to have a *baby,* like Josh was a *baby,* and it was a rather bleak Christmas for a few reasons not least of which was I was so nervous I was all but twitching and I believe I developed a holiday facial tic.

❦

Oh she was very pregnant by January 23. The weather had been completely manageable up to then, so she could have gone ahead and gotten the whole thing over with and let me get some rest. The town began to stir; it was pointed out that the last baby born in the town limits had been Bucky Gard who was full-grown, and there formed a little band of supporters for having the New Baby right in town somewhere. I thought they were out of their minds. Oh *really,* I wanted to say. Where did the crazies think it should happen? At the drugstore? On the fairgrounds? Such charges were answered by Jack and Marianne Halstead, who belonged to the Friends Meeting and who knew our family well. In Jack's case I'd say he knew me *too* well, as every time he saw me he turned just slightly as if to avoid being hit by imaginary arrows. I'd say, "Hey, mister," and he'd say, "Don't shoot!" even though I'd had *yet* to shoot him with anything. I loved those people. Jack and Marianne announced they would be delivering the baby, and they carefully devised a plan for getting Melinda from her house to theirs (a straight walk down an alley and across Broad Street) and even hung a sign above their guest-room door: MATERNITY WARD. When I said, "Who's the doctor in this picture?" Jack reminded me that Marianne worked at the hospital and I said okay then.

On January 24 it rained. What's rain? It's nothing is what it is. Somewhere in there, January 23 or 24, just usual weather, nothing to get in a fuss about, there began to be talk about a high-pressure overhead thing meeting an ungrounded low-voltage outlet from Nova Scotia. These two catastrophes would be converging over the Midwest, like a weather system association that chooses Chicago for its convention.

The news of the proposed disaster caused much grumbling and radio tuning and preparedness checking, especially in my house. My father *loved* an emergency; it brought out the best in him in many ways although I have to say I doubt emergencies felt very good to him until they were barely survived. His anxiety was its own sort of storm cloud hovering over the house—the pacing, the listening to the radio and television at the same time, the measuring of provisions. He'd tell me to count the blankets and I'd start to say I'd already counted them but then I'd get very nervous and not know what the number was so I'd go count the blankets. He'd say check those canned goods again and make sure the can opener is where we can see it and I'd think I'd already done that but when I looked at the mental canned goods section it was sure empty. Fuel canisters for the Coleman stove? Check. Gallons of water? Yes, twenty gallons in four five-gallon containers. Blankets? Didn't I already go over the blankets?

Now we got to add, as if I needed to add anything, CALL YOUR SISTER. So we called my sister and asked about her progress as people from Indiana will do, which is to say we asked nothing outright because the whole situation is a bit juicy for a Hoosier. Instead we'd inquire about her *feelings.* How are you feeling, are you feeling anything, like that, right up until Melinda threatened brutal violence against us if we called her again. I'd hang up, pace, check the rain, listen to the radio, watch Dad smoke and pace and listen to the radio.

Early on the twenty-fifth the temperature seemed ominous. The high that day was 36 degrees (balmy) but then the temperature dropped to 19 (still rather warm, all things in balance), and the rain turned to snow. Four inches fell that day, and Dad stepped up our exercises until I began to see blurry shapes at the edges of my vision. And the weather people! This was their Shangri-la! Finally they got to say what they'd always wanted to, which is that we can neither run nor hide, because atmospheric conditions will prevail in the end. We are *nits* compared to the weather, and at last there would be proof.

But even the specter of nationally respected television personalities weeping on the air, even their tooth-gnashing and hair-pulling, didn't cause me to turn the corner into outright terror. That didn't happen until Melinda called to say that Dr. Heilman had said only a Lifeline helicopter could reach her if she went into labor, because it certainly appeared we were about to be stranded and the New Baby was almost forty weeks cooked. Dr. Heilman was the least alarmist man I ever knew, so in essence the Beast had taken over the White House and revealed his tattoo of sixes. And who knew if Henry County Hospital even *had* a helicopter? And what did they do with it when there weren't emergencies? And how could I finagle a ride? I wondered in my more lucid moments. I told my parents I was going to stay with Rick and Melinda, and Dad said absolutely not, he wasn't letting one more of his children out of his sight, if we died we were all going to die together, and had I checked the fuel in the Coleman stove? Lying on my cot by the stove that night, certain I would never sleep on my last night alive, I had a glimmer of an idea. It was the closest I would ever come to a scientific hypothesis: in the same way water seeks its own level (one of my mother's favorite things to say, though no one knew what it meant), *the anxiety level of a home will rise to meet the requirements of the most anxious person in it.* Or at least that was how it worked in my house. Against immense odds, I fell asleep, and it was snowing.

It might have been the simple sound of Dad's lighter, the power of his attention that woke me up, or it might have been because I heard Mom say, "My God." And then, "Snow is general over Ireland."

I sat up. "Are we in Ireland?!?" It was a shocking idea, but feasible.

"No, no," Mom said, continuing to stare out the door that had once led to the back porch and erstwhile laundry room (the porch had been torn off when the house was bathed in vinyl siding and also I'd never known laundry-doing to be accomplished there) and now looked out directly onto the backyard. "It's from the end of a story by Joyce."

She was forever quoting someone, I can't describe how powerfully vexing it was. And here it turned out that Joyce Dick from the bank had started writing stories, too, which meant the whole town was lost. I got up and could feel it, the hum of the low-voltage outlet, general over Mooreland. There was the wind, which first pounded the house like a fist, then backed off, choosing to thread its way through the doors and windowpanes and the walls without insulation. But it was the sound under the wind that I think we could all feel, staring out the small window into the backyard. There was *nothing* in that sound. No one was moving or closing a car door or calling out the back door for the dogs to shut up. There were no dogs, no birds, no grinding buggy noises. I remembered a story by Jack London, something Dad loved; at the end a man is dying, freezing to death with his dog. That was all I recalled of it. When I'd read it the first time I cared only about the fate of the dog—people seemed rather expendable compared to animals. But now I could imagine the entire scene, the world and all of us in it brought to our knees, and it was thrilling in a way, and I could see how it would take a gigantic will to endure it.

"It never really got dark," Dad said, and I realized he'd been standing right there for a long time. I felt as if I'd seen it with him, the snow falling so hard and fast it carried its own light and illuminated the sky as it covered the ground.

"How's Melinda?" I asked, slightly breathless even though I'd only taken a few steps.

"Phone's out," he answered, not looking at me.

On the twenty-sixth, the temperature dropped to zero with wind gusts reaching fifty-five miles an hour, lowering the windchill to sixty below. By the end of the day seventeen inches of snow had blown into drifts that ranged from ten to twenty feet high, and still it continued snowing. Dad had to move to the window in the kitchen; the back door was completely covered. The radio was never turned off, and the more I listened the worse things got: the announcers were stranded at the station and sounded happily crazed, desperate. There was no topic other than the blizzard and the same things were said again and again until it seemed we'd all been at it for weeks, undertaking this event. A few times Dad said he was going to try to start digging us out, that he would find a way to Melinda's, but even I could see that he wasn't going anywhere. I wondered if we'd hear the helicopter over the wind, but I didn't dare ask for fear Dad would tell me the truth: Melinda couldn't call for the helicopter, and even if she could, no one could fly under such conditions. She couldn't call; they wouldn't come; they couldn't find her anyway.

I lay on my cot near the stove, in my sleeping bag, for hours at a time. I couldn't concentrate on anything except the sad facts. It wasn't just Melinda and the baby—everyone I loved, everyone in the world to me, was buried as we were. Mom Mary and Donita, my brother and his wife and daughters, my aunts and uncles and cousins, Rose and her family, Julie and hers, and the animals at their farm—I couldn't think straight when I considered the possibilities. Why hadn't Dad and I called them all, why hadn't I gone to Rose's and counted her blankets and checked her water supply? I could have comforted myself with the memory of the many freezers Rose's family kept filled with everything from venison to last summer's vegetables, along with bread and milk. Instead I concluded she was probably living on Velveeta cheese and those peculiar sandwiches she made with butter and sugar. That poor girl, I hated those sandwiches. And she was also most likely being made to read *Jane Eyre* again, just to escape her siblings. My eyes filled with tears and I ducked down inside my sleeping bag so Dad wouldn't see.

❦

On the twenty-seventh, the temperature stayed between zero and eighteen degrees, with a windchill still in double-digit negatives. The average wind speed for the day was twenty miles an hour, and twenty inches of snow had fallen.

On the twenty-eighth, when I woke up, it was three degrees and snowing. The phone was still out.

By the twenty-ninth of January, thirty-five inches of snow had fallen on South Bend, forty on some other parts of northern Indiana. In Chicago, snowfall totaled 74.5 inches for the year, setting the record for the city's history. At our house we saw the sky for the first time in days, and by the time I got up Dad was pacing and waiting.

"We're going to your sister's," he said, stubbing out his cigarette.

I rubbed my eyes, thought about it. "You've got a plan, I hope."

He nodded. "First we're going to dig, and as soon as we can open the door we're going to walk."

Well, there it was. I would die like Jack London, or Dad would, and eventually one of us would have to eat the other. Snow was drifted up against every window on the ground floor, and from the upstairs it appeared the specifics of the world had simply been erased—the cars were gone, the fruit trees in the garden were completely consumed, Dad's little toolshed was just a roof floating on a white sea.

"I made us snowshoes," Dad said, and pointed to the floor. He had cut the bottoms out of four clothes baskets, poked holes in a shoe shape in the middle, and lashed our boots to them with the long strands of leather I bought every year when we went to Friendship, Indiana, to watch the muzzle loaders and the people dressed up as cowboys and Indians. I always imagined something very crafty for those leather strips, something involving beads and perhaps feathers. I also talked my way into a deer hide and some rabbit fur most years, and my ultimate dream was to marry the leather, the beads, the feathers, and the fur in a grand design, after which I would truly understand Mother Earth and Father . . . something. Julie would know.

"Nice work with the leather," I said.

"Thanks."

"I probably ought to take my deer hide."

"Probably should."

We worked our way out, starting by digging around the door. In some places it seemed the snow went on forever, and in others we'd dig through to open air—the drifts undulated like dunes. By the time we actually strapped on the snowshoes and stepped out, I saw doom, even with the progress we'd made. We tested our shoes and for the most part they worked. The plastic was very stiff and held up even under Dad's weight. They worked except for my left one, for which Dad had used a sort of flimsy basket. When I stepped on it too hard, the ends curled up and down that leg went, and I'd not only have to work my foot out, I'd have to drag up sixty-seven pounds of snow with the plastic spoon I was wearing.

"This is my truck," Dad said, standing on what seemed to be snow. "And I think the car is right there."

I couldn't really take in what I was seeing, so I just followed behind him, mostly on my right foot. There was a lot to say but I kept quiet. The town continued to be silent and unmoving in a way that caused a winged feeling in my stomach; even through my hat, my hood, and the deer hide wrapped around my head I could hear Dad's breathing as plainly as my own. If he hadn't been leading the way I would have gotten lost, or at least confused. I had thought the trees would serve as markers but they didn't. Weighed down with snow, its trunk buried, every tree looked the same, and the sunlight, weak as it was, was blinding.

"There's Reed and Mary's house," Dad said.

I squinted. "Oh. You're right."

We trudged onward, and at some point Dad knew to turn on Jefferson Street. After that, it was a long, cold walk for him and a long, gamey hop for me.

I proceeded by looking down, but Dad looked in all directions. He paused in front of Max and Adeline's house, but went on. He paused a few times, but kept walking. After what seemed to be days and days, just at the point I was going to start begging him for beef jerky and to just *let me sleep,* like in the movies, he said, "There's smoke," pointing at the roof of Lindy's house.

I was quite certain he meant Melinda had burned the house down, but in fact there was just a ribbon of smoke curling out of the chimney. We stared at it a moment, both thinking that if the worst had happened Rick wouldn't blithely be heating the living room. Surely not. We took a few more steps and I saw something, Dad saw something. It was a little Rick-shaped thing with a shovel, working like a mole, as we had. Dad called out and Rick looked up, yelled back that Melinda was fine, no baby yet. We broke the skin of that storm and set the world moving again. In New Castle, snowplows were already warming up, and all over the county men with big trucks were searching for door handles and some ground to stand on, most of them carrying flasks they would sip from throughout the day. I understood—it was a hard business. We would eventually help Rick, who had a terrible toothache, and we'd make our way inside where I would strip off my coat and deer fur and laundry baskets and swoop up Josh as if I'd just returned from ten years at sea. But first we stood there, on the top of a car or a well house or a chicken coop, and looked around.

"My, my," Dad said. "It's really something, isn't it."

"It's beautiful," I agreed. "It's the most beautiful thing I've ever seen."

Two days later, Rick had four wisdom teeth removed and Melinda went into labor. Only forty-eight hours to exhume the town and the cars, to get to the highway and all the way to New Castle. It wasn't much time, but we took it. And if there was ever anything in the world for which I would feel permanently grateful, something I'd be thanking the universe for to the end of my days, it was that sliver of time. With every step toward civilization we made I said, *Thank you, universe.*

I could hear Rick and Melinda talking in the bedroom as Melinda gathered her bags and her book for the hospital.

"No, I don't think she's too young," Lindy said, and Rick said okay.

I was standing in the living room in front of the Franklin stove, in the very exact spot where I'd been standing the August before, twirling my baton, when my soap opera was interrupted to announce the death of Elvis Presley, causing me to sit down unexpectedly on my butt and also to be hit by my falling baton.

"And we don't have anyone else. Dad and Mom are driving ahead of us to the hospital," Melinda said, and Rick agreed. He made a noise of agreement, that is, because his face had swollen up from the surgery that morning so badly, and in two such distinct spots, that he looked like a neurotic chipmunk, one who hadn't realized winter had already come and done its worst. I was helpless against telling him so, which was unfortunate. Also I had had to bury my face in the pillows on the couch *twice* because I was laughing so hard I feared my lungs had collapsed, not at *Rick* exactly but at *that sad little rodent*.

He made some noises that sounded like, "She's twelve," or at least that's what I heard, because I was twelve.

"That's true," Melinda said, "but we don't have anyone else and we have to go."

They were out the door with instructions and phone numbers and goodbyes, and I don't know what Melinda expected to see on my face but she didn't see it. I watched them creep off down the snow-packed streets behind Dad's truck with the big snow tires, then I snuck into Josh's room and sat on the floor, waiting for him to wake up. When he sat up in his new big-boy bed, talking and rubbing his eyes, I picked him up. He wrapped his arms and legs around me like a junior monkey and we sat in the rocker awhile, rocking. He sighed, waking a bit at a time, then sat up and pointed at the rug on the floor.

"Punt?" he asked. "Ummm, punter?"

Trucks, he meant, and tractors. Would I help him plow the rug in straight even rows with his trucks, his tractors, and his disc? I *absolutely* would. While we were sitting there I said, "Guess what?"

Josh looked up, shrugged.

"We're going to be here alone together for at least three days and two nights. Just you and me."

He stared at me, waiting to hear whether this was good or bad. I raised my arms above my head and said, "Yay!" Josh raised his arms above his head and said, "Yay!" We clapped awhile, plowed the rug. He was two.

I covered his high-chair tray with Cheerios and he sat very still. I knelt down in front of the high chair until he couldn't see me, popped up above, and said, "Pee-boo!" in the voice dogs and children love. Josh jumped, smacked his tray so hard in surprise Cheerios went flying, then laughed so helplessly his nose wrinkled up and he had to put his head down right on the cereal. He raised back up and there were Cheerios stuck to his forehead and chin. "Again?" I asked. He nodded. I did it again, and again, until all the Cheerios were on the floor. Then I got him down and we ate them off the floor, as God intended.

❦

Sometime that day Rick called and said we had a healthy girl. Those were his words, a healthy girl. I thanked him for calling and asked him to give my love to Melinda. What I really meant was "That makes no sense to me. Josh and I are coloring."

After dinner and a raucous bubble bath, a bath during which maybe more bubbles got out of the tub than stayed in, as I was getting Josh ready for bed in his yellow footy pajamas with the bear stitched on, Rick came home. He looked so bad even I couldn't laugh. I asked about Melinda and the baby and he nodded affirmatively, called the baby by name as he lay down on the couch, visibly suffering. Abigail. *Abby,* he said. I zipped up Josh's pajamas but otherwise couldn't move. I thought the word "Abby" and an arrow flew straight into my heart, it *slammed* into my chest, our healthy girl, a baby girl. Abigail. Josh walked over, patted Rick on the chest, said, "Nigh night, Daddy."

Over the next two days, Josh wore his Robin Hood hat and rode his bouncy horse. We lay on the couch like drunkards and watched cartoons and I never said, "That's about enough television, isn't it?" We made art projects that came out very badly. When I said it was nap time he climbed up in his bed and went to sleep. If I thought he might be hungry I asked, then fed him. I kept the fire going in the Franklin stove and never once set the house on fire. After Rick came home at night and went to bed I lay on the couch in the dark. Abby. There was an Abby. I'd had no idea.

When they got home from the hospital, Josh and I were waiting in the kitchen. I'd dressed him in a turtleneck and bib overalls and we held hands as Melinda walked through the door. She seemed tired but otherwise quite cheerful and just like herself, and I really really loved her but I had to stop myself from saying, "Scootch out of the way there, Sister," because Rick was coming through the door carrying Abby. All I could see was the thick white blanket, but I held out my arms and said, "Give her to me, give her to me," and they gave me their newborn. I was the person who had fed a bite of mud pie to Laurie's little brother and made him throw up. I'd helped Rose convince her baby brother Patrick to sit on a box in his bedroom and wait for the bus. I'd helped a girl named Dana write all over her bedroom curtains with an ink pen. But all of that seemed so far away; it was before Josh, before the blizzard, before the moment I lifted the corner of the receiving blanket and saw my perfect, sleeping niece. I smelled her head, her neck. One thing was clear to me all the way in my bones, it was so deep and factual I barely needed to consider it: the more I was trusted, the more trustworthy I became.

"Look, Joshy," I said, kneeling down. "This is your sister."

He leaned over and looked at the little face nestled in the blankets, not getting too close. His blue tennis shoes stayed planted on the floor.

"See her?" I said. He nodded. I lowered the edge of the blanket over Abby's face, lifted it again. "Pee-boo!"

Josh jumped, clapped. He leaned over and took another look.

Gold

If the Mount Summit kids hadn't arrived I never would have had to contemplate how to walk the line between my old life and my new, between my original, steadfast friends and the people suddenly available to me. The originals were doing it, too, and no one made much of a fuss about it. Mom tried to point out to me that the Mount Summit kids had their *own* original friends, people *they'd* started kindergarten with, but there was no percentage in considering such a thing when obviously they had sprung up in fifth grade, fully formed.

Jeanne Ann was new but she didn't seem to be; she was the easiest friend I'd ever had, and at thirteen I loved her fiercely. The fierceness and ease were tied up together, somehow. Julie, by contrast, was family and like family we owned each other permanently but *oh lord* the way that girl ran me ragged. As if the farm weren't enough, she was becoming an athlete of epic proportions and it was a flat punishment for me. There we'd be at school and the girl was like a piece of my own self and not only that but we were and had always been *true* to each other—true in a way everyone could see and I knew it was rare. But in gym class I held my breath and said little prayers to a fluctuating cast of Jesuses that our gym teacher didn't make Julie the student leader because it would mean my certain suffering. And the gym teacher *always* made Julie the student leader because compared to her, Olympic sprinters were fat and lazy. Julie's will was cast iron and if we were assigned fifty sit-ups she saw no reason we shouldn't do seventy-five. Quiet as she was the girl could wrangle sit-ups out of us until our stomach muscles were bleeding and as ruined as old rubber bands. And she tormented me, me specifically! during every manner of grotesque exercise! If we were doing leg-lifts she'd make us hold the most vicious one for hours. The overweight girls would give up first and Julie wouldn't say a word. Then another group would fall and nothing from our leader. But even if the only people left with their legs shaking an inch off the ground were Julie, me, and the three best basketball players on the girls' team, if I lowered my legs she would bark, "Jarvis! Get those legs up!" and I would do it, which was lunatic and I didn't even understand it but there you go.

When we chose an opponent for tennis Julie was the student leader so she got to go first and I tried to hide behind other girls but I was quite tall. I prayed, even letting my lips move a little, *Please Jesus who wanted no one to know You were here, make me invisible as would have been excellent in your own case so that Julie may not see me and choose me as her opponent and then wallop me with tennis balls for the next hour, amen.* But it was no use. I would spend the hour going "Whoa! Ow! Ouch, Julie Ann! You're hitting too hard!" And when things got really desperate I'd try, "I have an idea—ouch! Let's see if we can *mime* playing tennis." In response I'd see a blur, which was Julie's serve traveling 800 miles an hour, and she'd pause just long enough to say, "Seventy-four–love," or however that goes, and then, "No mimes."

Julie had spent our whole lives together trying to make me a better person and many times she came darned close to succeeding. She was both good and good at everything she turned her mind to, which was the opposite of me, there was no sense in denying it even from our earliest times. In track she ran the hardest races and God above she *flew.* She wouldn't tie her hair back and no one made her so it sailed out behind her, part solid, part liquid, like silk caught in the wind and pulled from your hand. One moment it was mahogany, dazzling; the next it was red-wine dark. On the basketball team she was so quick and ferocious she intimidated everyone—taller girls, girls who outweighed her, players who would cheat and hurt someone. And volleyball, and *golf* for the love of Heaven, since when did farm girls master GOLF? Julie was a brilliant painter and she wrote beautiful letters and she always did her homework even in the subjects she didn't like, and most often without a word she tried to take me with her to that land where she lived, a place of grace and power and rightness. She tried to teach me *pride,* the kind you earn, the kind that arrives when brutal effort is transformed into magnificence. Julie was magnificent, I was proud of her with every breath I drew, and freely so. But I didn't need that pride for myself. I was better at giving it away. All those years we'd faced each other, that beloved red-haired girl and I, with our palms wide open—a minor miracle is what it was. If I had anything Julie could share it, I begrudged her nothing. Much more often, maybe all the times that mattered, it was she who had what I needed and it passed from her hands to mine, year after year this was so, and all she asked in return was that *I try just a little harder.* Not as hard as she did, but some. I was *exhausted*.

There was Rose, of course, who was nothing at all like Julie and still we hadn't had it easy. We had to work to keep from breaking each other's noses. We had put up our dukes on more than one occasion and also we'd taken oaths against each other and stomped home in a fit; well, I'm talking about myself here because it was always me having the fit and doing the stomping and it was always me going home from Rose's house not the other way around. I'd march into the den and pointing at the sky I'd say to Mom, "Mark my words! That Rose and I are finished, done, kaput." Maybe Mom would ask what the trouble was this time or maybe she'd skip right ahead to Delonda's Laws of Life, which were repeated so often my sister and I had assigned them numbers. We asked that in the future she simply hold up two fingers if she wanted to remind us not to smoke; one if we'd forgotten there ain't no free lunch. Number four was the one that most often applied to my friendship with Rose: *Is this the hill you're going to die on?* I would shake my head because number five was *There is never the right hill to die on.* Mom was nice about it but left little room for argument. If I clomped down to Melinda's and made my case to her, she was even less sympathetic. She adored Rose and Maggie and Patrick, she'd been their babysitter at a critical time in their development, just like you have to hold puppies close to you for the first six weeks or else they turn to curs. Rose was *not* a cur. If there was a cur in the mix I preferred she not be singled out or called by name. I'd point toward the sky and declare, "Lindy! I am done with Rose as of today," and Melinda would say, not even looking up from her sewing machine or feeding Abby, whatever she was doing, "Lucky Rose. God knows why she ever loved you in the first place."

And that was the holy truth. As soon as I heard it, every time I heard it I turned around and went back to Rose's house and wouldn't you know she acted as if nothing had ever gone wrong and so did I. If beanbags had been involved I just set to cleaning up the beans. I swept up, or Rose did, and then we'd put a Broadway musical on the record player and sing and sing. We'd dream out loud of having straight hair, what it would be like to not break all the family combs, who was to blame for how our hair was anyway.

She was my talking friend, the best girl in the world. We were often mistaken for twins, we loved all the same things, we were absolutely nothing alike. I was an expert on that Rose, I could have testified in court as to her character without fear of perjury. But even though I watched her every move and lived in her house and was raised in no small measure by her parents, something eluded me, I couldn't get it. I couldn't understand how she did it—*it* being everything, life itself. If our teachers said, "This is the assignment and this is when it's due," Rose simply did it and she wasn't angry about it and she did not fuss. Her answers were correct, her handwriting was neat though tragically left-handed. She never got in trouble and the teachers always liked her (how that would feel I'd never know), and it seemed that for Rose school was a set of stairs she truly enjoyed climbing; she was always happy to see what was on the sixth floor and then the seventh.

If it had only been school I could have shrugged it off, having long since adjusted to both my idiocy and my status, and also I was not prone to being haunted by failure. Fortunately. But Rose was also good at going to *church* and being religious—she made it seem effortless—she enjoyed it, she meant it. And she was Catholic! Her church wasn't even in Mooreland, they had to get up and get dressed and wear panty hose (just the females) and then drive all the way to New Castle in all manner of weather and turbulence in order to sit through a Catholic Mass, which what was all *that* about anyway, and she enjoyed it! I went to church with her every chance I got, I studied on her and on the whole thing and it was indescribably weird, at least for a faithless but nonetheless Quaker girl. I couldn't keep up with the choreography of it, the standing and kneeling, I couldn't figure out what I was supposed to be saying at any given time. I could never seem to memorize the Apollo's Creed, as many times as Rose tried to teach it to me. Quakerism had gotten in me, blast it, and so for me for all time church meant a silent, empty room and the hope of an empty mind into which the Spirit might pour. If there was speaking out of that silence, no one, not even God himself, could predict what would be said. I sat in St. Anne's and I loved it, I loved it, who could not love such beauty and drama, what my mother called the Church's *march across Time*? Marching I understood. Mom's longing I understood, the way she never really got over being expelled from the catechism for asking too many questions. She was ten years old. No matter how I loved it, I knew in an instant I couldn't do it, I never would have been able to do it; silence was my familiar, and even if I didn't admit it I knew that the Meeting I was fleeing from had authority over me, silence had authority over me though I swore I wouldn't allow it. But *obedience* was out of the question. Obedience was quite possibly the hill I would die on, which I didn't mention to Mom and assumed Dad already knew. It was his hill, too.

But Rose had been given an astonishing gift, one I envied but did not covet, as that would have been stupid and a complete waste of time. She had the gift of piety, and of radiance. It looked to me as if the assignments, the rules, the order of the Mass, and even the getting up and going were for Rose a sort of freedom. She said, "Tell me what you want and when," and knowing the answer and completing the task were liberties for her, not the death-by-a-thousand-cuts they were for me. She got everything right and she was *still* free.

I know the exact moment I realized it. We were in a World History class and I was seated directly behind her. There was a possibility our teacher was legally insane and so my respect for him was unwavering. That didn't stop me from passing notes to the people all around me, but not to Rose because that wasn't her way. The days when it would have rubbed against me like a cat in a sandpaper suit—the fact of that not being her way—just fell from me, I could feel them falling. I looked at the back of her head, at the thick black hair that would never be straight and I thought, "Oh, she is *dear* to me," and ever after I knew it was true. Never again, never did I imagine my life without Rose in it.

By the time we were thirteen Rose and I had been friends for *nine* years. Nine years is an effort, it requires commitment, and that much history becomes heavy, it has weight. There were all those nosebleeds (Rose was the only person I ever knew with chronic, scary nosebleeds, so I assumed it was a Catholic thing); her strange relationship to "white chocolate," which was, no doubt about it, a left-handed invention. We knew hundreds of songs that only sounded right if we sang them together. I had modified her canopy bed from four posters to three, by jumping out of bed and swinging to the floor. The poster I was swinging on became a gigantic stick in my hand. I had destroyed Rose's *furniture.* I was with her the day she learned that the kindergarten-aged boy of their closest family friends had been killed in an accident so freakish it defied all reason, and I was with her in the days that followed. I knew that on one morning her parents woke up and turned to give each other a kiss hello and at just that moment their cat, Snowball, raised his head between them and they ended up kissing his cat cheeks. That story had caused me to *fall down* laughing. The list was infinite, what I knew about Rose, what she knew about me—if called to testify to her character I could have done so for weeks, months, and Knowledge arrived with Responsibility on its back. *My lord* that can make a person tired.

I was spared that weight with Jeanne Ann. She was a joy to me, she was a new way of being, and like oxygen. Night after night she let me go through every single thing she owned, every item in the room she'd lived in all her life, and ask her about it. Where did this come from? I'd ask, and she'd say, I got that in Florida when we went there on vacation, I was seven, I have pictures of myself feeding seagulls, do you want to see them? I did want to see them. Nothing was off-limits to me, either; she never once asked me not to look at something, not to open a box or a letter or a journal. We did that for hours and then we fried bologna and took it in the living room, where Jeanne Ann practiced gymnastics while we watched horror movies and teenagers dancing on TV. It didn't occur to me that given enough time I'd know her as well as I knew Rose or Julie and that our own history would become a weight we'd either shoulder and carry for life, as Rose and I would, as it would be for Julie and me no matter what. Or else we'd put it down. Who would think of such a thing while watching a movie about a demonic baby called *It's Alive*? What difference did all that make? Jeanne Ann had long, straight, silky blond hair that puddled on the floor like spilled cream as she did backbends. She was painfully funny and pretty and she loved to eat—I'd never met anyone who stayed so close to pleasure. If she wanted a pizza she made one, and her mom kept all the ingredients on hand for the next one. Same with cakes and brownies and cookies. Jeanne Ann cooked and told me stories and I sat at the kitchen table sick from laughing. I was injured from laughing. We ate at all hours of the day and night. We turned on her disco-ball light in the living room and danced like fools and said outrageous things and gave each other nicknames. We wore matching necklaces and divided a wardrobe between us. There was nothing to it; it was as easy as falling off a bridge. At Jeanne Ann's house, or going somewhere in the car with her mom, or walking down to her secret place along the creek bed, I was the happiest I'd ever been, ever ever. We never bickered—there was nothing to bicker about. The trick to such a friendship isn't a trick at all—you just have to have the same goal, and we did: to make the other happy, and to be together. She came out of nowhere, and by that I mean she lived at a crossroads where there were four other houses scattered about and that was it. If she'd told me she didn't have an address I would have believed her but followed her, because who knows where you end up anyway, taking up with someone new? We were thirteen, and lit up like stars.

Law Enforcement

❦

After she became a Master, Mom took her first job teaching English at a high school in Union City, a very fascinating place as anyone from Indiana can tell you. It was either a single town cut in two, or two different towns with the same name that happened to be connected to each other, or. There was probably another way to think about it but I didn't know what that was. As I understood it you could stand in a particular place and straddle an imaginary line (you couldn't see it but it was most assuredly real) and one of your legs would be in Union City, Indiana, and the other would be in Union City, *Ohio.* Indiana and Ohio are two very distinct states no matter what people on television may say. The fact that a single town contains both is not the point. What is the point is that Union City was way bigger than Mooreland—*thousands* (three or four) of people lived there—and they took this madness perfectly in stride EVEN THOUGH Indiana doesn't believe in Daylight Savings Time and Ohio does, and so during half the year one of your legs would be in three o'clock and one would be in four. Oh it was vexing. I became overwhelmed with the desire to find a place directly on the state line and *put my butt on it.* Mom entertained this wish and we looked around until we found a diner we believed would do the trick, and I traced what I believed to be the state line into a booth, and indeed it was rewarding. One buttcheek in Indiana, one in Ohio. Hoosiers, when asked what time it was in Union City, would ask, "Are you on God's time?" meaning ours.

The high school where Mom taught made me not afraid of high school, because unlike when I'd visited Ball State with her when I was much younger and been called a pygmy, in Union City everyone was nice to me and behaved as if I were human. I was especially in love with two of Mom's colleagues, Alwin and Ted.

Alwin looked exactly like a periodic character on *The Beverly Hillbillies,* Mr. Fahrquahr. This moved me. He dressed better than anyone I'd ever met and he did so every day. He wore two-tone shoes, and had a different pair to match all of the colors of his pants. When Mom arrived at work each morning Alwin would glide down the hallway like Fred Astaire, singing, "It's de-light-ful, it's de-lect-able, it's De-lon-da." Her own song. He had been writing one novel for his whole adult life and it was a *thousand pages long*—a fictionalized history of the canal system in Indiana. Mom brought the first volume home and read it more slowly than her usual pace; she alternated reading with sighing and pressing her fingers hard against her temples. I assumed it must be extraordinarily good. We were once invited to Alwin's house for tea, and it was an eye-popper. He lived out in the country in an old house he'd turned into a *mansion.* If there were a museum devoted solely to the great acts of beauty on the Indiana/Ohio line, Alwin's house would be the centerpiece. In just the bathroom—in just one of the bathrooms, for instance, because *there was more than one*—the wall near the ceiling had a niche in it every foot or so, like shadowboxes. For the life of me I couldn't figure out where one found such a wall. And in each niche was a real statue of a man, sometimes just a head, sometimes a whole body, and one of them was flat naked and appeared to be peeling off a section of his own shoulder. How I stared.

Alwin had many things that made me contemplate the Good Life, including a stuffed great horned owl, but it was what he showed us as we were leaving that struck me speechless. Behind the house was a miniature version of the regular house, a skinny version, bricks and metal roof and everything. Looking at it from the outside I saw an answer to prayer, and tried to imagine such a thing in our own yard: a shrunken Mooreland house covered with vinyl siding and with kitchen plumbing that drained right out onto the sidewalk. It would be mine alone. I could do anything I wanted in there and no one would have any say, and I would have my friends over and we would eat popcorn and campfire fruit sandwiches. I would cover every vertical surface with Queen posters because I had recently decided to devote my life to them, and I and my friends would make crazy noises and . . . Alwin opened the door and the replica house was really an outhouse. I smacked my forehead. *Even better.*

Ted was the drama teacher and he made all the plays happen. He was the cleanest-looking person I'd ever met except for Rose, and like her he had the straightest, whitest teeth on Planet Earth. They looked like a shining white tooth bracelet. And he was also like Rose's mom, Joyce, in that he could do anything, including making his own suits—entire suits—and also he was a brilliant cook and he, like Alwin, lived in a fine house. But the best thing about Ted was that when he talked everything got MAGNIFIED and I'd never had that feeling before. In my experience if you asked a grown-up Hoosier a question—and it could be about anything—the answer would be "It was all right," or "It was fine." There was an unspoken rule (which I didn't realize until I saw it broken) against *saying* anything or *describing* anything and most especially about *getting worked up* over anything. But Ted was the opposite. The first time we met he told me he had a wall in his house painted with a scene from *Gone With the Wind*. He said the words and I got a loopy feeling just from hearing them. My whole body remembered the movie, how I sat without moving through hour after hour of it, including the commercials. It had made me heartsick and feverish, the colors and clothes and the lostness of it, the way that world was lost and would never come again. And in all those years in school I had never understood one thing, not a single solitary thing, about the Civil War, but after *Gone With the Wind* I felt like I'd been there. History classes hadn't given me even a smidge of a picture to carry around inside me, not of the people or the houses or anything, just names I forgot as soon as I heard them, and dates, numbers, that added up to nothing and so they too vanished. But once we'd seen the movie on television Rose and I talked about it constantly and she went so far—too far, as she was likely to do—as to get the book and read it, but I wasn't that crazy.

So Ted told me about the wall in his house and my whole stomach area flopped around like a fish, and then he asked if I'd seen *Gone With the Wind* and I was taken aback to be asked a question by an adult stranger and so well trained in not saying anything that I just nodded, as if he'd asked me about *Fat Albert*. (I loved *Fat Albert* but not in the same way.)

Ted grabbed my hands in his and said, "Didn't it slay you? Weren't you happy and sad at the same time? Will you ever forget one single moment of it?"

Yes, yes, and no. I couldn't answer, but that was all right, because he'd moved on to talking about the costumes—who made them and what the cost was, and how expensive it would be if the movie were made today—and the scandal over casting Vivien Leigh. Mom could talk to Ted just fine, her timing was right and everything, but I seemed to be on a slight delay. I wanted to see Ted every day, at Alwin's house if possible, and just listen as he retold the whole world to me, everything I'd already done and seen and everything I would see or do, so I could understand, even in reverse, how amazing and gorgeous and fabulous and insane and wretched and perfect perfect perfect it had all been, and would be.

Mom's commute to Union City was so long she didn't get home until late in the evening and she had to leave every morning while it was still dark. I would have been happy if she'd stayed at that school forever, but her second year as a teacher she got the job she wanted, teaching at our own school, Blue River. She could drive there in fifteen minutes, and we could ride together and I'd never have to take the bus, and all that was good and I was happy for her, but when she left Union City, left Alwin and Ted and her sweet, funny students and came back to Mooreland, back to a town without two time zones, everything went flat and unspoken again. I missed the way things had been, even briefly, and I know she did, too.

By the time Mooreland was hit with a blizzard and Abby was born, Mom was teaching at Blue River and Dad's schedule as a deputy sheriff had grown entirely mysterious. Sometimes he had the car, 33-55, and sometimes he didn't. He worked most days but also most evenings, and who would have ever predicted something as horrible as this: one night at a Blue River home basketball game, *a sacred occasion* the details of which I could describe in a novel of a thousand pages and which would take my whole adult life to write, I looked up from where I was sitting with Julie and whom did I see but my father, in uniform. He was the county sheriff's deputy assigned to patrol the school and the parking lot during the basketball game. I was in a trap and I knew it. Mother taught at the school I attended, which was already going to squash my style something fierce. And here, in my leisure time and at an event where I was supposed to be left ALONE, my dad was walking around carrying a gun.

"Have you *ever*?" I asked Julie, who shook her head no. I closed my eyes and imagined my miniature house with its pies and Queen posters and loud noises, and then remembered that the original had been a toilet. I put my head down on my folded arms and Julie patted me on the back.

❦

If my family could be represented with different-colored blips on a time line, there would be years and years where there were four all huddled up together, although it's best not to dwell too long on that part because it would have been before I was born and it hardly makes any sense anyway. Following that would be just a few years where there were five, and some of that time we were in a pile but for most of them the brother-colored blip was pulling away. Then he was gone. Back to four, but again, only briefly. The sister blip moved away, if not so far. And for some time during the years there were three of us I didn't notice a change because it's difficult to think about what isn't possible. But one day I woke up and it was clear: my mom had a world she had struggled mightily to obtain, and she was *someone* in it. The people, the books, the students (sure enough, at Blue River there were amazing fabulous wonderful smart funny students, too, and Mom had drawn all of them to her like the Pied Piper), these things added up to something good. And my dad had a world, too, and he was important in it. He had friends I barely knew, and it was increasingly hard to figure where he was at any given time (although if a more true and honest history of the man could be written, say by the spirit who presides over time lines and facts and who never gets things wrong or confused, I think that book would include people and adventures *no one* ever knew about but him). They had worlds, but they weren't the same one—not even close. So there would be a little piece of this visual aid, a few inches at most, where I thought there were three of us but I was wrong. At best there was Mom and me together, and sometimes—not nearly so often—Dad and me. But most of the time I was sitting there alone, and didn't realize it. A mercy, that ignorance.

Men become their jobs—this is something probably everyone knew but me. Julie's dad was a farmer, and he was a farmer all the way through. Rose's dad sold insurance, and to name only one way that family got it right, they were insured. But my dad worked in a factory and wasn't a factory worker, and then he was retired more than twenty years before retirement age. As long as I'd known him he had been nothing but himself, an unnameable quantity. My mom and Melinda and I were always trying to label him: we said he was a mountain man. We had a punch line we made up and repeated to each other with resignation: *Well, he's no John Walton.* Even then we must not have understood much, or else there was a category no one had bothered to explain to me. He was a mountain man but not the sort on Walton's Mountain; a husband and father but not like *that.* He wasn't Grizzly Adams or Daniel Boone. He wasn't anyone on television, as a matter of fact, so I don't know how I could have been expected to figure him out.

What I did know, what I'd always known, was that at the Father place in our family there was a bright, knotty contradiction. His rules were ironclad, even if they weren't the same as other Fathers' rules, and his authority was complete. Secrets couldn't be kept from him, although he could demand secrecy from us, and he seemed to see through walls. But he himself was lawless. He wouldn't bend to any man or any code and not *once* did that presiding spirit find my dad on his knees before God. In our house Bob Jarvis was the law and he was also outside it and could do anything he pleased. For the countless millions of things he refrained from, we were grateful. And if he had a God, it sure looked to me like his God was either inside him or *was* him; either way he was an outlaw, which is its own kind of honest. But that uniform changed him.

Dad had found Parchman and his wife and then he found another couple he liked a lot, and he talked about them and Mom listened politely—she was a polite person and so was he—and I ignored the conversation because I didn't know how many more new people I could take in. When we were invited over to this couple's house to play cards one night I said no thanks and spent the night with Jeanne Ann. The next day I came home and asked Mom how it had gone with Dad's new couple friends and she said, "It was fine."

"Did you like them? Were they fun?"

"They were very nice."

"What did you talk about?"

"Honey," Mom asked, putting down her pen, "don't you have something you need to be doing?"

I looked around. "Are you talking to *me*?"

"Homework? Correspondence? Have you thought about cleaning your room?"

I stared at Mother as if looking at her alien replica. Homework and correspondence? I had never cleaned my room one time in my life as was abundantly clear from walking up the stairs, something Mom didn't do, hallelujah. That room was beyond hope or help and I'd thought it wise to surrender. "Actually my only plan was to sit and chat with you."

"Do you remember," Mom asked, turning a page of the paper she was grading, "what I used to say before napping?"

Of course I did, it was number seven. " 'I'll be asleep if you need me, so try not to need me.' "

"Yes, that's it."

We sat a few moments. She finished grading one paper and picked up another.

"Do they have any kids?" I asked, drumming my fingers on my knee.

Mom raised her head, closed her eyes. I had caused her slight pain, which was sometimes necessary for getting her attention. "One," she answered. "A girl. She's a year ahead of you in school, I think. I barely saw her—she's tiny and dark and she moved through the house like a ghost."

"A ghost, you say."

"Yes. What if I gave you money?"

I nodded. "That would work." I took her two dollars and jumped on my bike. It was spring in Indiana and we'd survived the worst blizzard since *Homo sapiens* became farmers. I took the long way to the drugstore, if there could be said to be a long way in Mooreland, just to feel the air. After I got my lemon phosphate and barbecue potato chips, I thought I'd head on over to Melinda's and check on the babies. Then I'd go home and call Jeanne Ann and I'd ask her to tell me everything she'd done since I'd left her house that morning, and she'd probably start by saying something like, "What about peeing? Do you want the peeing in the story?" We talked on the phone for hours that way.

The next morning I went to church with Mom but only because I had to and also to see Josh and Abby. Now that there were two of them, Melinda was even later than in years past; if the pattern continued she would eventually show up in the late afternoon with her perfectly dressed and unbearably sweet children and they would have the sanctuary all to themselves.

As soon as services ended I was up and out the door, a habit I'd picked up from the Catholics. At St. Anne's there was no lollygagging. Those people were efficient, which I appreciated. The sacraments had been received, their business was concluded, and they couldn't see the parking lot soon enough.

I heard Mom call my name from the church doorway, a place where she lollygagged with frightening regularity. Oh, she talked to everyone. She squeezed hands and offered her prayers and nodded sagely when told of an aunt's kidney problems. I couldn't imagine such patience or what was in it for Mother, it just made no sense at all. In order to behave religiously I would have to be drugged and injected with plastic and even then I'd probably end up dragging myself to my car on my mannequin arms before the last Friend was assured of my ongoing concern.

"Whaaaaaaaat, what what what?" I said, walking back up the church steps.

"Wait for me a minute," Mom said, turning back to the little clutch of people who could *never let the thing end*.

"Why why why? Why?"

"Excuse me," she said, and then to me, "I have to run to the school to finish my lesson plans. Go home and change your clothes and you can go with me."

It was tempting. Now that Mom taught at my school I had access to it after hours, when no one was there, not even a janitor. An empty school isn't even the tiniest bit the same as a school with people in it, don't let anyone tell you different. Empty schools are vast and hollow and spooky even in broad daylight; an empty gymnasium is terrifying and best avoided. But the miles of hallway, the floors waxed slick as a skating rink? Mom's wheely chair? Still, it was Sunday and springtime and a school is a school.

"Do I have to?"

"No, your dad said he'd be home today. You can stay with him."

I jumped down the stairs and headed toward the house. I didn't quite believe it, that Dad would be home.

It was Sunday and springtime and beautiful outside so of course I was watching television. I wasn't enjoying it, however, because Dad was pacing like a lion in a cage.

"Do you want me to see what else is on?" I asked.

"Naw no, no." He waved the question away. He disappeared into other rooms, reappeared wearing something slightly different, as if he couldn't get comfortable. Even his hair seemed agitated. He was restless by nature and I'd seen the same look on his face hundreds of times in the past. In the evenings he'd come home from work or from wherever he went when he didn't work anymore and he would seem a little panic-stricken, like how was he going to get through all the coming hours, obligated to be at home with his family but his family was an unreachable and polite woman either reading a book or at school, and a daughter. Me. Eventually he'd give up and sit down in his chair and watch television late into the night.

Sometimes he slept; often he was up at three, four in the morning and he'd go outside to pace. The yard and garden were also cages.

Finally I heard him gather up his keys, his wallet, his gun. He couldn't stay. "I have to run some errands, go get in the squad car," he said, counting the money in his wallet. He always had money.

Errands? "I'm pretty much dandy right where I am, Bob."

"Get in the squad car and don't call me Bob."

"Can I just call Jeanne Ann fir—?"

"*Zip.*" A warning.

"I'm up, I'm going, sheesh. Do I have to wear shoes?"

He glanced at me, the second warning glance, which is only possible if you have a certain sort of eyeball and he certainly did. "Don't push me, now."

"Fine! I'll wear shoes! I'm not pushing!" I rolled off the couch and couldn't find my shoes.

"Don't *tell* me you can't find your shoes."

"All right! I found them! I'm heading out the door!" I carried the shoes instead of putting them on. My brother and sister had done it, too, had stuck an arm through the bars just to see what he would do. Would he slap it, would he tear it off, could they retreat in time? The results had not been favorable for them, my brother and sister, on a few occasions, but it appeared I was in a different category. I knew just how far to go and I stopped before he had something to prove. It never crossed my mind to actually make him angry. That wasn't it. He could be so *oppressive* was the problem, and then he'd gone and had three children who didn't take to being oppressed. Dan and Melinda had gone about it boldly but I had them to learn from, and I was becoming too wide-eyed and quicksilver to catch. Mostly I just stood outside the cage and waved to him, *Hello, hello,* and he watched me with his lion's eyes but let me live, because he remembered me.

"Where are we going?" I asked. I had one bare foot on the dashboard of the squad car, which was brazen but I'd gotten used to cruisers. They'd lost their mystique over time, and this one in particular had come to seem like just a car, except it squawked.

"New Castle," he said, adjusting the dispatcher's radio signal. I could see we were going to New Castle but I didn't say so. And I didn't ask if we could listen to music because I knew what the answer was. Music was in the past and now we listened to the dispatcher speak in a coded monotone. Dad had loved police scanners all my life—there had always been one in the house. He also went through a period of listening to CB radio chatter, which I finally told Mother I would pay good money to have explained to me.

She didn't think about it for even a second. "It's his form of gossip," she said, and went right on knitting.

Dad would have hated that answer if he'd heard it, but for the life of me I couldn't see how she was wrong. The times he'd shushed us in order to hear the address of a fire or a domestic disturbance or a public intoxication were countless. As soon as he heard the road and the crossroad he'd say, "That's a Peckinpaugh," and he was almost always right. He liked to know things, that's all.

Dad popped into the jail and shot the breeze for a while. I stayed in the car and listened to the *music* radio until Joe Harris, the sheriff, came out in civilian clothes and ordered me to step out of the car and put my hands on the hood. I hopped out and hugged him, then slugged him. I loved that man like crazy, he was some kind of perfect. Joe was great big and handsome, bluff and kindhearted and funny. I loved his wife and all his kids, especially his daughter Jamie who was one of Melinda's best friends. I figured there was a lot I didn't know and yet it seemed *possible* Joe was like John Walton, but with a sense of humor.

Joe issued some orders about changing my behavior, told me he was letting me go with a warning, as Dad had. "Don't let this happen again," he said, offering me a handshake.

"You won't catch me next time," I said.

Joe lifted me by my armpits one, two, three times into the air as if I weighed nothing, put me down. "You are some kind of trouble," he said, and headed back into his office. It was a compliment, coming from him.

"Where are we going now?"

"I need to stop and see someone."

Dad wasn't so much the sort to do regular errands. He didn't go to grocery stores or department stores. He wasn't the bank type, really. Before Mom had a driver's license he took us everywhere and that seemed to suit him—he was like the captain of a raggedy little army, and we went where he led us, because he did all the driving. And that got passed along, too, because my brother became the driver in his family and so did my sister and it had already started in me. I could tell I was never going to let anyone else drive, even if I married one of Joe Harris's drop-dead shockingly handsome and masculine sons. Even then I'd hold the keys.

Now Mom was forever attending to something, going to some bank or insurance agent. This was a sentence I was not unaccustomed to hearing: "Honey, do you want to ride with me to the bank?"

Thank goodness I was speedy enough to ask, "Which bank?"

And Mom would say, sort of out of the edge of her mouth and turning away, "The one in Union City."

"The one in Union City! For the love of the sweet little savior! WHY do you still have an account in Union City?!? It is in another STATE, Delonda!"

Sometimes she hesitated; once in a while she fabricated. But the answer was always the same. "I like those people at that bank. They're very kind." She even gave a little ladylike sniff, as if she were dismissing the Help.

I would shake my head, give a click of the tongue to register my disapproval. Banking in another state. It was just the sort of thing Dad wouldn't have tolerated, if he'd still been the only one with keys.

We were at the house of the New Friends. I figured it out just as we pulled up in front. This was either the New Friends' house or it belonged to Different New Friends, because I'd never seen it before and had maybe never even been on this street for visiting.

I looked around—that wasn't quite true. The road we were on was divided by one of the alphabet streets; Parchman lived on I Avenue but this wasn't I. On the opposite side of the avenue, the road curved and vanished into a tangle of giant old trees. The houses over there were probably the most beautiful in town, and they belonged to that particular kind of money which was what my Grandmother Mildred had and what my mom had come from. It went back generations and its source was foggy. I remembered Mom telling me about lounging around with her wealthy cousin during the summer, how they had planned to join the same sorority at IU-Bloomington; the cousin educated Mother in exactly the right china to own, which sterling pattern, everything such people know. But it hadn't turned out that way in Mother's life, married at seventeen to someone she must have thought she knew when in fact she didn't know him at all. There were a few years when Mom couldn't face those cousins at all, and then one day she was obligated to attend a family funeral. She walked in with Dan and Melinda—Dan the age Josh was now, Melinda in her arms. I don't know for sure what Mom was wearing or how she looked but I have a good idea. The cousin looked up and saw her and said, so the whole room could hear, "Why, Delonda, I thought you were dead."

I had been to one of those houses on the other side of the avenue, with Grandmother Mildred. We'd visited one of her old ladies, a church friend or a distant relative and it had been *tiresome.* The houses on this side were much more modest and small and boring-looking, but the street was still pretty. Cherry trees were dropping blossoms on the well-tended lawns. I slipped on my shoes and followed Dad inside.

The house was nothing like it seemed from the outside. The living room was a sea of dark red, thick carpeting, a color out of time. The room was furnished in antiques, unusual ones. I'd lived with my dad long enough to know that all the pieces were fine and valuable. There was a red velvet horsehair sofa with arms that lowered to make it a bed. Beside the sofa a very old teddy bear sat on a tricycle, surrounded by wooden blocks. A tall china cabinet held an entire collection of ruby ware behind its curved glass doors.

Dad asked Mrs. Friend where Mr. Friend was and she said he'd been called into work.

Against the wall sat a *pump organ*. I couldn't imagine how old it was. The keyboard was short, only forty keys, and the tones were controlled by knobs you pulled out or pushed in like a throttle. There was a carved wooden stool with a red velvet seat for the person who could figure out how to play it; just looking at the place a foot would go to depress the bellows made me shake my head.

I was introduced to Mrs. Friend and we shook hands; her nails were the longest I'd ever seen, and painted a glittery white. Mrs. Friend had a daughter a year older than me? It was hard to believe. Who knew mothers could be so . . . not motherly-looking? So young? She was petite (I was many inches taller already), with long black hair. Black eyes. A tan. She wore a finely woven white turtleneck with short sleeves, black pants, black shoes.

"Why don't you come in and have some coffee anyway?" she said, and Dad said okay.

She went into the kitchen and Dad stood in the kitchen doorway, talking to her. I looked around, not touching anything, just wandered from one lovely thing to another. In the dining room area I saw an *ice chest*, the original refrigerator. The outside appeared to be ash wood—I wondered if Dad had *noticed* this—and there were separate doors that opened with metal handles you pulled toward you. I opened the top one and saw that the wood was a frame built around a dense, gray, unusual substance—not quite marble or metal but like a combination of the two. It felt like a very old ice cube tray, the kind designed by Satan's little ice cube tray trolls. One Christmas Eve at Rose's party I'd been trying to crack such an evil thing and couldn't get the metal handle to give at all. I put it down on the counter and held one end while pulling with all my might. It didn't move and it didn't move, and then it slammed backward and pinched a piece of my hand completely off and I still had a scar but who cared, I liked scars.

The top door of the ice chest closed with a smooth click. It was a flawless, amazing thing.

Mrs. Friend came out of the kitchen and gave me a tall glass of Coke filled with ice cubes. I liked both scars and ice cubes very much. I thanked her, and said, "This is beautiful," resting my hand on the glassy smooth ash of the refrigerator.

"Thank you, I think so, too," she said, and told me where they'd found it, what luck it had been. She called her daughter, who was behind a closed door listening to music I could hear through the walls. When the door opened I saw that Ghost Girl had with her two small dogs, one with a lot of hanging-down gray fur that made me nervous, and a dachshund, the only breed of dog that ever bit me. The daughter came out and she was even smaller than her mother, and looked emaciated; she seemed to weigh the equivalent of one of my legs. Even so she was striking. Her hair, too, was long and black, but thicker than Mrs. Friend's, and when she turned her head a certain way it was so black it had a *blue* cast, blacker than Lindy's, even. Her eyes were a nearly solid black, and I wondered if any light could get through them. We went into her room and it would have been clear to even the most incompetent detective that Ghost Girl was insane for Kiss. There was so much Kiss stuff in that room it looked like a checkerboard. And that was the music playing, too. Ghost put my new Queen devotion to shame, and I could see I was going to have to up the amperage, or whatever that phrase was my dad used. And perhaps—this hurt, but might be necessary—I couldn't also give my heart to Steve Martin. I had one record of his, *Let's Get Small,* and my daily music order was *A Night at the Opera,* both sides; *Let's Get Small. A Day at the Races; Let's Get Small.* And the just released *News of the World,* which that unpredictable Julie Newman had gotten me for my birthday even though I hadn't said a word to her about my Queen conversion and never took those records to her house and so she had just reached up into the air and pulled down the best present I'd gotten for a long time. *News of the World,* which was *stunningly* good; *Let's Get Small.* I had the whole record memorized and could quote from it at any spot, a fact which amazed Mother and caused Melinda to threaten me with violence not even invented yet.

"Do you think it's possible to be true to two different things, a band and a comedian," I asked the Ghost Girl, sitting on her bed, "or do I have to pick one?"

She held the nervous little dogs. The gray-haired one shook and I couldn't figure out where its face was and I hoped they stayed over there with her because my instincts had somehow gotten the idea that all shrunken dogs were wormy and I couldn't stop thinking it even though the house I was sitting in was immaculate. Mrs. Friend was not in any way the wormy-dog type. And yet.

"I don't know," GG said, her voice so soft I could barely hear her. She had the accent, too, the Indiana hillbilly twang my mom had told me a writer named Kurt Vonnegut had compared to the sound of a monkey wrench being thrown into a moving engine. He didn't like it, was what I read there. My own inflections tended to be less Indiana and more Kentucky, something I'd picked up from Mom Mary and Dad and I don't know where-all, but I had to pay close attention or I sounded like someone married to her first cousin, both of us the children of first cousins.

"I've only got the one," GG said, and when I realized she was talking she continued, "band."

"Well, you're probably right." Which was true but maybe if I considered the problem while *listening* to Steve Martin that would help me decide.

She didn't talk much and she was very ghosty but I could see that the New Friends' Daughter was as sweet and genuine as a person can be, if that person also happens to be so sad she wants to die and doesn't have one single word to explain why it is so. I'd never met a sadder person in my life, not at a funeral, not even at the nursing home where I sometimes played the piano for my brother while he preached and led hymns. Those nursing home people had been the undisputed champions of sad until I met the Ghost Girl, who, like the old ones, stirred a whole lot of confusion into her sadness. She didn't know how to take even the very next step, it seemed, and I liked her instantly and wished I was smarter and knew something to say. But I didn't know anything. Neither one of us did, but at least I felt fine about it and assumed I'd know more later.

"I should probably see if Dad's ready to go," I said, standing up. "It was nice meeting you."

"You, too," I think she said, but she didn't move from where she sat huddled with the trembling dogs.

They were sitting at a dining room table in a section of the living room that had been separated by a wall that stopped about four feet off the floor and was connected to the ceiling by black poles and widely spaced lattice, all around and through which ivy and some other plant had woven to make a green wall. I looked down where the two parts met to see where the ivy was planted and it turned out to be in the wall itself, which was hollow and filled with dirt. People thought of the most amazing things.

"Sit down, Zip, and let me finish my coffee."

I sat down across from Dad. I told Mrs. Friend that the Ghost Girl was very nice, and she agreed that her daughter was nice. She turned back to Dad and they continued what they'd been talking about when I came out, which turned out to be a long story of Dad's, involving some mayhem he'd gotten into with Parchman and how they'd narrowly escaped it. I was watching Dad talk just as I always had, when something caught my eye—I wasn't sure even then what it was. For all intents and purposes there was nothing to see. He was wearing one of his favorite three-button sport shirts—it was a silky cotton that clung to his broad shoulders and chest—of the palest seafoam green, which showed off his dark skin and the barely discernible green flecks in his dark eyes. (My father's eyes were dark brown, my mother's were an icy green, and it seemed someone was keeping score among their children: Dan's eyes were dark like Dad's, Melinda's were a jewel-like gray/green, and mine—I was unexpected—were an exact cross between the two. Sometimes they were green, sometimes they were brown. It wasn't right.) There was nothing to see and yet I froze and stared at him. He was completely relaxed—the lion in him was nowhere to be seen. And if there was no lion, there was no cage.

He reached the finale, the great line that had been spoken by Parchman but was even funnier coming from Dad, and Mrs. Friend let her head fall back against her chair and she laughed and laughed the way some ladies do; there wasn't anything restrained in it, and right at that second *I knew.* I knew absolutely and without a flicker of doubt, just the way I knew how many pennies had been in that jar and when the first snow would fall. I would not have said I doubted it if a demand was made to me at gunpoint. Dad was laughing, too, so hard his eyes were a little teary and I could see that he was *happy,* as he had been with Parchman and Libra. Happiness was not his daily state. Before that day, at his very best he seemed content, or at brief peace. He was a natural man, after all, and nature was always right there, all around us, and he knew to walk right into it.

There was the one critical thing I knew for certain, but there were a world of things I didn't know at all, and a good thing, too. I didn't know that I would never again see my father's footprints in the snow of our backyard, the ones that traced his path away from the house and back again hours before I woke up. His garden and fruit trees would go untended and die; his little tilty toolshed would rarely be entered again. We turned the wooden handle that held the door closed and left it; as long as it stood the smell never disappeared—his smell of beeswax and traps, of leather and rust and oil in a real oilcan like the kind the Tin Man carried. I didn't know the time would come, and much, much sooner than I would have believed possible, when Mom and I would move the piano over against the wall closest to my parents' bedroom, and night after night—because she couldn't sleep, she thought she'd never sleep again—I'd play the piano for an hour, two hours, and she would listen on the other side of the wall. Nobody knows those things in advance, and certainly no one could have predicted that before that very year was through I would be judged a threat to the state of the new union, because among other things, having me anywhere near was no different than having Delonda Jarvis in the house. I looked like him but I sounded like her, and I would be exiled with a vengeance, still thirteen.

We stood to leave and I told the New Friend it had been a pleasure meeting her, I thanked her for the Coke. Dad and I went out and got in the hot squad car. He was still chuckling as he rolled down the windows and flipped the air conditioner on high; we believed, he and I, in having both kinds of air. Still in the spirit of the visit, he asked if I'd like to go past the Trojan Drive-Thru and get a cherry Coke and I said no for the first time in history and so we headed home. I never said a word on the drive but I don't think he noticed. The dispatcher reported the gossip in short bursts that made me jump.

❦

At home he paced and chain-smoked and drove away again and again, and then the worst thing happened and I got sick and stayed home from school. It was a tough call—do you leave the daughter alone (she's thirteen, after all) when she's sick, particularly if all her life you have been the one who cared for her when the Seven Beautiful Princesses of the Seven Beautiful Kings were no longer Healthy Within Her? Okay, so you're no John Walton but you *are,* or have been to this child, a most excellent good father who is sometimes in a reasonably bad mood. What to do?

He compromised and stayed with me but called her two hundred times. If I walked in the living room he hung up that instant and asked what I was doing. "I'm looking for my book." As soon I walked back in the den he dialed the phone again, and it wasn't as if I could miss it, because for some screwball reason when you dialed the phone in the living room, the dial on the phone in the den ticked the numbers' shadow path. And vice versa. Mom used to say that Mickey Mouse ran our phone company, but it turned out he'd made the phones, too.

After my soap operas were over I went into the living room to read, and Dad hung up as fast as a cat, then moved into the den and dialed.

As soon as Mom got home that afternoon he left on urgent business. His business was always urgent and he was always leaving so Mom didn't notice a thing. She sat down on the couch, sighed with weariness, and took a stack of papers out of her satchel. I waited. I drummed my fingers.

"Mom, Dad is having an affair." Launching things out of thin air is good, I've found. It doesn't lessen the sting but at least it gets things going.

She stared at me a moment, lowered the paper she was grading. "Why would you say such a thing? Why would you say something like that about your father?"

I swallowed. My throat hurt. "Because it's true."

"Why? How do you know it's true?"

"Because I saw it and I know."

"You saw what? What evidence do you have?" Her posture was stiff and she was folding a student's paper in two.

What evidence did I have? I couldn't put it in words, that it had been a red gumball and couldn't possibly have been any other color. "He makes lots of phone calls."

"Your father often talks on the phone. He calls his mother every day."

"He isn't calling Mom Mary."

"Why are you doing this? Have you heard him speaking to someone?"

"No." I kept my eyes on my lap. "But you *could* believe me."

"It would be destructive to believe in something like that if it isn't true."

I tried swallowing again. "Do you want evidence? Is that it?"

Mom kept her eyes on mine. "Not really."

"Well. I'll get it anyway." I pushed my thumbnail into my leg but stopped as soon as it hurt. "I'm staying home from school tomorrow."

There were a million reasons I embarked on that particular campaign and not one of them was known to me. My vision was narrowed to the task at hand, and of course I would have made a fine detective as Melinda had many times pointed out. I took one of my mom's stenographer's pads and a pen and I sat by the phone and listened as he dialed. It really didn't take long; figuring out the digits from the number of clicks was no different from relative pitch in music: if this is a one, that must be a four. But it could have taken much longer and I would have been fine—he dialed it all day long.

As soon as I was certain of the sequence, the rest was public record. I just opened the New Castle phone book. There were the New Friends—listed—and there was the phone number. I stared at it. I looked at the stenographer's pad. I checked the two against each other again and again and they were always exactly the same. The night before I had told Mom something I didn't fully believe myself, and when she didn't believe it either I thought we just might be safe. And then I'd gone and devised the most hare-brained, elementary school trap—something even Trixie Belden hadn't done, that's how stupid it was—and I got it in one.

When Mom arrived home Dad left on urgent business. She came in the den, dropped her satchel, and sat down with a sigh. I was lying on the other couch, watching television with the sound turned down, something only crazy people did as far as I could tell. She asked about my day and I said it had been fine, I told her I was feeling better. I asked about her day and she said it had been busy, then told me a story about how one of her seniors, a cute, muscular boy who drove a hot rod and walked around with his mouth open, had done his demonstration speech that afternoon.

"He walked up to the front of the class without a thing in his hands, it seemed, and announced that he'd really racked his brain trying to figure what was one thing he knew how to do so well he could demonstrate it."

"I'll bet."

"And then he pulled out a box of kitchen matches and said he was going to teach us how he lights matches on the zipper of his fly."

I turned and looked at her. "Seriously?"

"Yes."

"Why wouldn't he just use the side of the box they're in?"

"You'd have to ask him that."

"So what happened?"

"I thought it wasn't maybe the best thing for him to do in a speech class, but not the worst by any means, and I was sitting there trying to figure out a way to stop him without embarrassing him and before I could say anything he'd lit the match and set his pants on fire."

I tipped right over and landed on my pillows. I laughed so hard my throat starting hurting again, so I pulled up my knee and bit it until it distracted me. I took a deep breath, wiped my eyes. "That was a good one," I said.

"Yeah, you should have seen me putting the fire out."

I lay back and stared at the ceiling awhile, at the television some. I watched the clock on Dad's little table. In five minutes I'd hand her the piece of paper I had tucked under a couch cushion. When those five minutes passed, I thought I'd give it five minutes more, and when those were up the phone rang and my heart clattered around in my chest like I'd dropped a box of china plates. What were people *thinking,* just calling like that?

It was Sharon, my mom's best friend at Blue River. I was deeply indebted to Sharon because I was taking her typing class and when she caught me not typing but reading a Stephen King novel she didn't flunk me, as all my other teachers would have done. Instead she made a deal with me: I could read as much Stephen King as I wanted, if I would also type out what I was reading. She was a smart one, because King's novels were so maddeningly interesting I learned to type faster and faster, just so I could read faster. She'd shammed me somehow but I couldn't figure out if it had been for good or ill.

Mom and Sharon talked about some school things and then Mom said, "Oh, it went *so* well. We read the story in class, and then I told them how Hemingway is suffering a real lashing in the academy; women students are complaining and some are refusing to read him at all, saying he's a misogynist and a slaughterer, I don't know what-all. So we talked about those things—the big-game hunting, the bullfights, whether the women characters seem real at all. They said all they had to say and then asked me what I thought, so I told them." I turned on my side and watched her. "I said Hemingway will break your heart. All that fumbling after manhood; the depth and frozenness of those characters. Jake stumbling around impotent and limping, Francis McComber, any of them, really. Those men are *tragic,* ultimately, don't you think? And I also reminded them that he was the same man who wrote *Big Two-Hearted River,* and . . ."

I went back to staring at the ceiling. With every year that passed, more and more of what that woman said made sense to me, which was flat terrifying. She talked on and I half listened, until her voice was just like water flowing past me. She was happy. She sounded happy. I would wait, and tell her tomorrow.

Acknowledgments

I tried to make a list of all the ways my mother assisted me in the writing of this book, but the result was another chapter. Suffice it to say she allowed me access to her journals, she provided me with photographs, and she listened to me read every day's work—the entire book—over the phone. I am more grateful to her than I can ever say.

My sister, Melinda, went to great lengths to get photographs and to get them to me; she also listened to essay after essay, adding details I'd forgotten and correcting my errors. It was an unqualified joy to have her at my side through this process.

I want to thank Dan Jarvis for the very helpful time line and for generally being so supportive. He is one of the good Big Brothers.

Thanks to Pam Jarvis for lending me her favorite picture, and to Debby Shively Parks, Sharon Shively, and Terri McKinsey.

I am, as always, so grateful to my children for their sanity, hilarity, and heartbreaking compassion and tenderness. Thank you, Kat Romerill and Obadiah Kimmel.

I could not have made it through the last few months without Dianne Freund and Joe Galas.

Thank you, Jim and Claudia Svara for an infinite number of kindnesses, and to Kevin Svara, Kerrie Lewis, and Susan and Bob Shircliff.

Amy Scheibe is simply the finest editor and friend imaginable; she is the Platonic *ideal* of Editor, and I hope for her sake she never chooses to do anything else with her life because I can't allow it and will be forced to follow her *pretending* she's still my editor. I will be merciless. Thank you Carolyn Reidy, Dominick

Anfuso, Martha Levin, Carisa Hays, Maris Kreizman, Sybil Pincus, Jolanta Benal (an excellent copy editor), and all the fine people at Free Press.

John Mood is some kind of wonderful. He answered an out-of-the-blue e-mail, sent photographs, and became a friend to my mother and me. Life is quirky and fabulous that way.

For their daily gifts I am grateful to Jody Leonard and Lisa Kelly; Suzanne Finnamore; Don and Meg Kimmel; and of course, as ever and ever, Beth Dalton. All my life I will be indebted to Jim and Judy Pitcher, and to Dave and Debbie Newman. Thanks to Tim Thompson and John MacMullen. And to the Otherwise Most Luscious singer and songwriter in the known world, Dayna Kurtz, and her husband, Jeff Pachman, just tell us where the commune will be and we'll start packing.

Much belated love and gratitude to Jeanne Ann Duncan.

Every day I find a new way to marvel at the wonder of Ben Kimmel.

Tim Sommer, we love you so. Now that my mother has adopted you, I'll expect you to begin spinning me around in the rocking chair.

To my beloved Posse (also known as my *Otters* on less grave occasions), Augusten Burroughs, Christopher Schelling, Robert Rodi, Jeffrey Smith: *con amore furioso.* I hope that translates to "I love you all madly." If it actually pertains to processed fruit pies, it's still true.

I had a dream of sudden riches and when I awakened, there was my husband, John.

And finally to m'dear Leslie Staub: I concur on the subject of Impermanence, but for one point. I will leave the world only if it is a day before you do, so I never have to live in a world without you in it.

About the Author

HAVEN KIMMEL is the author of *Something Rising (Light and Swift), The Solace of Leaving Early, A Girl Named Zippy,* and the children's book *Orville: A Dog Story.* She studied English and creative writing at Ball State University and North Carolina State University and attended seminary at the Earlham School of Religion. She lives in Durham, North Carolina.

SHE GOT UP
OFF THE COUCH

When we last saw Zippy Jarvis, she was completely oblivious to the storm that was brewing in her home. Her mother, Delonda, had literally just gotten up off the couch and disappeared down the road on her bicycle. Zippy's dad was mysteriously absent. And Zippy was lost in her own fabulous world, exploring the fringes of her hometown of Mooreland, Indiana, whether animal, vegetable, or mineral.

In *She Got Up Off the Couch,* Haven Kimmel revisits this quirky, chaotic habitat as she catches up with characters old and new. Zippy's further adventures include witnessing her mother overcome the emotional claustrophobia of her small-town, married-with-children life. Zippy watches as Delonda conquers her depression and learns how to drive a car, even though her mother doesn't have regular access to one once she's learned. Against her husband's wishes, Delonda gets up the courage to apply to the local college and graduates with honors at the age of forty. In many ways, this is Zippy's mother's book. Even as we are entertained by the many stories involving small animals and Zippy's endearing friends, a profound sympathy emerges for the strong mother who found a way not only to save herself, but to set a proud example for her devoted daughter.

Questions for Discussion

1. "Mooreland, Indiana, was paradise for a child . . . small, flat, entirely knowable." Why might Zippy's feelings about her hometown of Mooreland as a child differ from those of her parents and the other adults who live there? How would you characterize the town and population of Mooreland, based on Zippy's adventures?

2. Why does Zippy's mother spend so much time at home, and what finally motivates her to get off the couch? In what ways does Zippy's dad, Bob, discourage his wife from meaningful intellectual or social activity? How does Delonda's decision to enroll in college affect their marriage?

3. "I did not accept Jesus as my personal savior on Tuesday night, or Wednesday, or Thursday, or Friday." What role does religion play in Zippy's life? What do her experiences at church camp and the Mooreland Friends Church reveal about her own feelings about religious faith, and how do those feelings connect to her family's wider attitudes toward religion?

4. When Haven Kimmel writes, "There was no place I was fully safe. My whole life was infested," what does she mean? What does the infestation of mice and rats at Zippy's house represent to her? Is it fair to say Zippy suffered from neglect as a child?

5. How would you describe Zippy's relationship with her father, based on his handling of her record collection, his behavior when she shattered her arm, and their other encounters as father and daughter? What does Zippy's decision to confront her mother with suspicions of her father's extramarital affair reveal about her feelings for him?

6. How does Zippy's older sister, Melinda, help her survive her eccentric childhood? Why does Zippy react so emotionally to Melinda's marriage and the births of her two children? What explains the trust they place in each other, and how does Zippy significantly enlarge that trust during the climactic blizzard of 1978?

7. What does Parchman Williams's unsuccessful effort to have "the talk about racism" suggest about Zippy's upbringing and her parents' respective racial attitudes? How does this talk affect her?

8. How do Delonda and Bob differ in terms of their professional interests and their extracurricular activities? How do you think they managed to stay married for more than twenty-five years? To what extent does the silver anniversary party that Melinda throws them reveal some of the turmoil at work in the state of their union?

9. "Mother's evolution, personal as it was, is also the story of a generation of women who stood up and rocked the foundations of life in America." How do the changes Delonda makes to her life as a middle-aged, married mother of three typify those of other women of her generation? What do these changes mean to Zippy? Does she appreciate her mother's choices?

10. How does Haven Kimmel incorporate humor into her poignant memoir of growing up in Mooreland? Which anecdotes in the memoir did you find especially comical, touching, or memorable? Why?

1. In *She Got Up Off the Couch,* Haven Kimmel describes in detail two friends, Julie and Rose, whose influence stretches into her adulthood. Who are some of the childhood friends who have continued to affect and influence your life? What unique talents and personal characteristics do these friends have? Share your memories and funny anecdotes with the members of your book club. And make sure to bring plenty of embarrassing pictures!

2. Are you interested in seeing what Zippy looks like now? To learn more about Haven Kimmel and to listen to her discuss her work, visit www.havenkimmel.com and click on the links to recent interviews.

3. *She Got Up Off the Couch* is Haven Kimmel's poignant memoir of her childhood. Have you ever considered writing a memoir about *your* life? The Memory Archive, www.memoryarchive.org/en/MemoryArchive, allows visitors to add their fondest memories to an online and constantly growing encyclopedia of personal recollections.

You are the author of several works of fiction. What initially led you to write a memoir?

I was taking a writing class in which we were supposed to begin a book-length project, and I decided to write some essays about Mooreland. Those initial chapters were all about the town and my neighbors; I wasn't in them at all. I wrote about fifty pages, and my professor told me that while he loved them and thought they were very funny, he would enjoy them even more if I was the narrator. So I started over, and each time I finished an essay I read it to my mom and sister, just to amuse them. By the time I completed the first draft of the manuscript I was years away from that writing class, and was writing the stories only for my family. I didn't really ever intend to publish them.

For readers who haven't read *A Girl Named Zippy,* can you explain the origin of your nickname? Does anyone still call you Zippy?

My dad called me Zippy, after a chimp on television who roller-skated. I was a very busy toddler, quite the monkey-girl. Dad was the last person to use that name, and he passed away two years ago.

In your preface, you thank your mother and sister for reading drafts of your book. Were you at all concerned you might be misrepresenting (or misremembering) some aspects of your childhood? Did their comments alter your story in any way?

One of the reasons I read the book to them was in order to make sure I got things right from their point of view. My sister is ten years older than I, so she had a different perspective on events. She also has an amazing memory. If she says it rained on August 10, 1974, I can assume it rained. I also didn't want to write anything that might hurt or offend them. Both Mom and Melinda are brave and generous and would allow me to write anything I want, which is all the more reason to protect them.

How does your mother feel about being the main subject of your book? Did you seek approval from all your family members before writing?

I think Mom is very proud of the book. She's so proud of me I can hardly take her out in public. I have to beg her to put her camera down and to not stand on her chair in restaurants to announce that she's my mother.

I sent the manuscript to all the main characters before I sent it to my editor. My mom and sister, Rose, Julie, and Jeanne Ann all read it and gave their approval. I sent my brother the chapter about him, and he also helped me with details about the blizzard and a timeline of family events.

Now that you're an adult, how do you view your mother's decision to attend college? When reflecting upon your opinions of major issues, which have changed the most since childhood?

I don't really see that event—Mom deciding to attend college—any differently now than I did as a child. I knew even then that it was a shocking act of will, and took enormous courage. I'm sure that watching her do it changed my life; it changed how I perceived my own future. Everything seemed possible for me, if that was possible for her.

Your memoir has been compared to the work of David Sedaris, a writer who mines his family's quirks for their comic potential. Do you think this comparison is accurate?

The comparison is too flattering to me, but I do see the similarities. Our surface subject matter is the same, but more important, we approach the form of the personal essay in a similar way. We both treat each essay as a little book unto itself, with its own metaphorical conceit, and its own characters, conflict, and resolution. Also we're both absurd, and would happily sacrifice our own dignity for a laugh.

You make extensive use of humor in your book. Has humor always come naturally to you? Who is the funniest person you know?

I was a funny child, I think. I was certainly funny looking. It's hard to know for sure, though, because I was surrounded by people who were far, far funnier than I was. My mom is hilarious, and my dad was the single best storyteller I ever knew. But if I had to choose just one person, I'd say my sister is the funniest person in my life. She's a tough act to follow. If I run out of material, I'm just going to start stealing from her. She owes me, anyway, for not revealing how truly evil she was to me when I was a child.

"There was always the question of who would feed me, and somehow it always got answered. Rose's mom, Julie's mom, my sister." It seems that despite your initial fear, you knew you'd always be okay. Is this accurate? Do you still feel the same way?

I was dearly loved as a child, which is a kind of safety in and of itself, and I am dearly loved now. So yes, I remain optimistic. I've tried to repay the kindness of those people who took care of me in Mooreland by making my children feel completely safe. I passed it along to them.

What's your next project? Can readers anticipate another account of Zippy's adventures in Mooreland, Indiana?

I said there would never be a second volume, and it turned out I was wrong. So really I'm not to be trusted with that question.

A gripping, powerful, and compelling new story...

The Used World

A Novel

by Haven Kimmel

Turn the page to read the preface from
Haven Kimmel's upcoming novel,
The Used World

Preface

Claudia Modjeski stood before a full-length mirror in the bedroom she'd inherited from her mother, pointing the gun in her right hand—a Colt .44 Single Action Army with a nickel finish and a walnut grip—at her reflected image. The mirror showed nothing above Claudia's shoulders, because the designation 'full-length' turned out to be as arbitrary as 'one-size.' It may have fit plenty, but it didn't fit her. The .44 was a collector's gun, a cowboy's gun purchased at a weapons show she'd attended with Hazel Hunnicutt last Christmas, without bothering to explain to Hazel (or to herself) why she thought she needed it.

She sat down heavily on the end of her mother's bed. Ludie Modjeski's bed, in Ludie's room. The gun rested in Claudia's slack hand. She had put it away the night before because eliminating the specificity that was Claudia meant erasing all that remained of her mother in this world, what was ambered in Claudia's memory: Christmas, for instance, and the hard candies Ludie used to make each year. There were peppermint ribbons, pink with white stripes. There were spearmint trees and horehound drops covered with sugar crystals. The recipes, the choreography of her mother's steps across the kitchen, an infinity of moments remembered only by her daughter, those too would die.

But tonight she would put the gun back in its case because of the headless cowboy she'd seen in the mirror. Her pajama bottoms had come from the estate of an old man; the top snap had broken, so they were being held closed with a safety pin. The cuffs fell a good two inches above her shins, and when she sat down the washed-thin flannel rode up so vigorously, her revealed legs looked as shocked and naked as refugees from a flash flood. In place of a pajama top, she wore a blue chenille sweater so large that had it been unraveled, there would have been enough yarn to fashion into a yurt. Claudia had looked in her mirror and heard Ludie say, a high, hidden laugh in her voice, *Poor old thing,* and wasn't it the truth, which didn't make living any easier.

She flicked the safety back on, listened to the radiators all through the house click and sigh and generally give up their heat with reluctance. But give up they did, and so did Claudia, at least for one more night, this December 15.

Rebekah Shook lay uneasy in the house of her father, Vernon, in an old part of town, the place farmers moved after the banks had foreclosed and the factories were still hiring. She slept like a foreign traveler in a room too small for the giants of her past: the songs, the language, the native dress. Awake, she rarely understood where she was or what she was doing or if she passed for normal, and in dreams she traversed a featureless, pastel landscape that undulated beneath her feet. She looked for her mother, Ruth, who (like Ludie) was dead and gone and could not be conjured; she searched for her family, the triangle of herself and her parents.

There were tones that never rang clear, distant lights that were never fully lit and never entirely extinguished. She remembered she had taken a lover, but had not seen him in twenty-eight . . . no, thirty-one days. Thirty-one days was either no time at all or quite long indeed, and to try to determine which she woke herself up and began counting, then drifted off again and lost her place. Once she had been thought *dear,* a *treasure,* the little red-haired Holiness girl whose laughter sparkled like light on a lake; now she stood outside the gates of her father's Prophecy, asleep inside his house. Her hair tumbled across her pillow and over the edge of the bed: a flame.

Only Hazel Hunnicutt slept soundly, cats claiming space all around her. The proprietor of Hazel Hunnicutt's Used World Emporium—the station at the end of the line for objects that sometimes appeared tricked into visiting there—often dreamed of the stars, although she never counted them. Her nighttime ephemera included Mercury in retrograde; Saturn in the trine position (a fork in the hand of an old man whose dinner is, in the end, all of us); the Lion, the Virgin, the Scorpion; and figures of the cardinal, the banal, the venal. Hazel was the oldest of the three women by twenty years; she was their patron, and the pause in their conversation. Only she still had a mother (although Hazel would have argued it is mothers who have us); only she could predict the coming weather, having noticed the spill of a white afghan in booth #43 and the billowing of a man's white shirt as he stepped from the front of her store into the heat of the back. White white white. The color of purity and wedding gowns and rooms in the underworld where girls will not eat, but also just whiteness for its own sake. If Hazel were awake she would argue for logic's razor and say that the absence of color is what it is, or what it isn't. But she slept. Her hand twitched slightly, a gesture that would raise the instruments in an orchestra, and her cat Mao could not help but leap at the hand, but he did not bite.

In the Used World Emporium itself nothing lived, nothing moved, but the air was thick with expectancy, nonetheless. It was a cavernous space, filled with the castoffs of countless lives, as much a grave in its way as any ruin. The black eyes of the rocking horses glittered like the eyes of a carp; the ivory keys of an old piano were once the tusks of an African elephant. The racks of period clothing hung motionless, wineskins to be filled with a new vintage. The bottles, the bellows, the genuine, horse-drawn sleigh now bedecked with bells and garlands: These were not stories. They were not ideas. They were just objects, consistent so far from moment to moment, waiting for daybreak like everything else.

It was mid-December in Jonah, Indiana, a place where Fate can be decided by the weather, and a storm was gathering overhead.